Beyond Belief

Robert N. Bellah

BEYOND BELIEF

Essays on Religion in a Post-Traditional World

Harper & Row, Publishers
New York, Hagerstown, San Francisco, London

For Melanie

First Harper & Row paperback edition published in 1976.

LIBRARY OF CONGRESS CATALOG CARD NUMBER: 77-109058

ISBN: 0-06-060775-0

75 76 77 78 79 10 9 8 7 6 5 4 3 2 1

Contents

Acknowledgments

APPRECIATIVE ACKNOWLEDGMENTS are made to the following publishers and journals for permission to reprint copyright material included in this book.

ASIAN CULTURAL STUDIES for article "Values and Social Change in Modern Japan," by Robert Bellah in *Asian Cultural Studies III,* October 1962.

BEACON PRESS for article "Transcendence in Contemporary Piety," by Robert Bellah, from *Transcendence,* edited by Herbert W. Richardson and Donald R. Cutler, copyright © 1969 by Beacon Press.

CAMBRIDGE UNIVERSITY PRESS for article "Meaning and Modernization," by Robert Bellah, from *Religious Studies,* Vol. 4, No. 1, October 1968.

CHRISTIANITY AND CRISIS for article "It Doesn't Go Far Enough," by Robert Bellah, Vol. 23, No. 19, November 11, 1963. Copyright 1963 by Christianity and Crisis, Inc.

DAEDALUS for article "Civil Religion in America," by Robert Bellah, Winter 1967.

HARVARD DIVINITY BULLETIN for article "The Religious Situation in the Far East," by Robert Bellah, Vol. 26, No. 4, 1962.

THE MACMILLAN COMPANY for article "Sociology of Religion," by R. N. Bellah. Reprinted with permission of the Publisher from the *International Encyclopedia of Social Sciences,* David L. Sills, Editor. Vol. XIII, pages 406–413. Copyright © 1968 by Crowell Collier and Macmillan, Inc.

THE PSYCHOANALYTIC REVIEW for article "Father and Son in Christianity and Confucianism," by Robert N. Bellah. Reprinted from *The Psychoanalytic Review,* Vol. 52, No. 2, Summer 1965, through the courtesy of the Editors and the Publisher, National Psychological Association for Psychoanalysis, New York, N.Y.

SEABURY PRESS for article "The Dynamics of Worship," by Robert Bellah, from Myron B. Bloy, Jr.'s (editor) *Multi-Media Worship.* Copyright © 1969 by the Church Society for College Work, Library of Congress catalog card no. 78-92204. Printed in the United States of America. Permission to reprint granted by Seabury Press.

SOCIETY FOR THE SCIENTIFIC STUDY OF RELIGION, INC. for article "Christianity and Symbolic Realism," by Robert Bellah, in the society's *Journal for the Scientific Study of Religion,* Vol. 9, No. 2, Spring 1970. The article appears in this book as Part II of Chapter 15.

THE SOCIETY FOR THE PSYCHOLOGICAL STUDY OF SOCIAL ISSUES for article "Some Reflections on the Protestant Ethic Analogy in Asia," by Robert Bellah, from *Journal of Social Issues,* Vol. XIX, No. 1, January 1963.

THE UNIVERSITY OF CHICAGO PRESS for article "Review of Norman O. Brown's Love's Body," by Robert Bellah, from *History of Religion,* copyright © 1970 by The University of Chicago. All rights reserved.

Preface

RELIGION is still something of a stepchild in the American university. In some major universities there is no department devoted to this aspect of human experience. In others the department is only uncertainly institutionalized and deals with but a fraction of man's religiousness. In a few places excellent programs exist that point the way to what can be done more generally. Like so many others I have come to the field of religion from a particular discipline, in my case, sociology. But I have in recent years become increasingly impatient with the sociology of religion as an isolated perspective. To be genuinely fruitful, it seems to me, the sociology of religion must join other approaches to the actual phenomena of religion. The study of religion seems at the moment to attract a number of mavericks and wanderers in the academy and I am grateful for the opportunities I have had in pursuing it to move outside the established structures and across the usual divisions of the university.

If I have learned much from my colleagues in various fields I have learned even more from my students. It is hard to say what I owe specifically to the students from history, psychology, anthropology, theology, ethics, and comparative religion as well as sociology, who have worked with me. But much of the movement of my thinking has resulted from their unrelenting pressure.

The chapters in this volume were all written independently, though they seem to fit together as aspects of a single process. I am grateful to Donald Cutler for helping me form disparate elements into a whole.

My intellectual indebtednesses are documented at many places in the following chapters and footnotes. But much of my deepest indebtedness is to people who have been close to me and whose names appear casually if at all. They have shaped the context of my experience and thus helped to mold my thinking even when they did not contribute specific ideas.

I will be satisfied if this book makes even a small contribution to the crystallization of religion, broadly understood, as an independent field of reflection and research within the academic community.

R. N. B.

Berkeley, California

Introduction

DAVID RIESMAN has reversed Gilbert Murray's phrase to speak of "the nerve of failure" so perhaps one can transpose another phrase common today and speak of "the faith of loss." "The nerve of failure" and "the faith of loss" point to a situation in which the idols are broken and the gods are dead, but the darkness of negation turns out to be full of rich possibility. Out of the nothingness which has swallowed up all tradition there comes nihilism but also the possibility of a new ecstatic consciousness. The yes and the no, joyfulness and despair, are terribly close together. No one can say whether in this generation we shall have global suicide or New Being. The essays in this book are an effort to define some of the elements of a great religious transformation when the old is no more and the new is not yet, or perhaps better, when the old and the new are so perilously and inextricably intermixed that none of us can be sure what he will be tomorrow.

It might be well in the introduction to anchor what will at times be abstract analysis in the personal experience out of which it comes. The work of every man, even a nuclear physicist, is rooted in his personal myth, in the unique and partly unconscious meanings his work has for him. For many kinds of work it is not necessary or even particularly helpful to know the link between the work and the inner experience, but where the work itself deals with the great collective myths which are dying and being born in our time then it is useful to know something of the private myth of the writer and how it articulates with these pervasive public myths. Within the inevitable limits of self-knowledge I would like to share with the reader the personal experiences out of which this book comes.

The first Bellah to arrive on this continent came in the late seventeenth century to Charleston, South Carolina. He was of Scottish descent, Presbyterian, and had come from Northern Ireland. In successive generations my ancestors—preachers, farmers, tradesmen—moved West, county by county, state by state. My father was born in Texas and grew up in Oklahoma. My mother's family was of English and Scottish descent, and also Presbyterian. She was born in Arkansas where her father was a planter and she met my father at the University of Oklahoma. My father became the editor and publisher of a small-town newspaper in Southwest Oklahoma, where I was born in 1927, but he died before I was three and I grew up with my mother in Los Angeles.

I was raised among the fragments of a once coherent, Southern Protestant culture. My mother's memories of sober Sundays devoted to churchgoing, reading the Bible and *Pilgrim's Progress,* and visiting the cemetery were communicated to me and indeed I seldom missed attending the Presbyterian Sunday School. There the atmosphere was conservative without being fundamentalist. I remember being shocked and a bit outraged when I first heard a public school teacher discuss the theory of evolution in the third grade, for up till then I had only known the Bible story of creation.

When I first read Max Weber's *Protestant Ethic and the Spirit of Capitalism* at Harvard College it spoke to me of an atmosphere I knew well. I remembered an old gentleman speaking to my Sunday School class about "the calling." He told a lugubrious story about a young boy who had a calling from God to be an undertaker, which, the old man said, may not seem pleasant but like all honest callings is necessary and pleasing to God. Although the relatives that I knew were not at all intellectual my mother communicated to me a love of books and writing which had been characteristic of her mother and my father. I grew up with an unself-conscious American patriotism, in which no basic questions about American society ever arose, and with a trace of Southern sentimentalism about the Confederacy and prejudice against Republicans.

But I grew up not in the Bible belt but in Los Angeles in a heterogeneous neighborhood. I was exposed from an early age to people different from my family. Since my father had died when I was small I had no compelling figure with whom to identify, whose views could mold my own. My mother early looked to me for opinions. Thus I had both the necessity and the possibility of forging my own identity and worldview in adolescence out of the fragments of the past and the diversity of the present. In the heterogeneous environment of the Los Angeles public schools the people who were most interesting to me often turned out to be Jews. Among them I found that the culture for which I had learned a formal respect at home was a living reality, especially in the realms of music and literature.

And it was in high school that I met a girl whose refusal to accept sham, whose love of life and whose quest for perfection helped me define my own direction—a girl I later married.

In the atmosphere of the Second World War when I was coming to consciousness I became progressively more liberal, both religiously and politically. With an intensity which has become much more familiar recently I began to test the ideals I had been taught against the realities of life in America and came to doubt the entire structure of religious and political beliefs that I had earlier taken for granted. In my last year in high school I began to read Marxist literature loaned to me by one or two friends.

Harvard was in many ways a liberation for me. Instead of the isolation I felt in high school I felt supported in the intellectual and cultural as well as political ideas I was beginning to develop. The atmosphere was far less radical than it was in the thirties or would be again in the sixties, but there were sizable groups and remarkably intelligent individuals who shared my views. In many ways my Marxism was but a transposition of my Protestantism: idealistic, moral, puritanical. Instead of a mythical apocalypse I looked forward to what I thought was a real one. There would indeed be a new heaven and a new earth at the end of history when man's exploitation of man had finally been overcome. For the moment my religious and political concerns were fused in a single apocalyptic vision. Christianity I no longer took seriously. Marxism fulfilled my needs for personal identity and group belonging. It provided a great escape from the constrictions of provincial American culture—it gave a sweeping view of world history which allowed me to relate critically to my past and present. But even then I had half-conscious doubts that I could at such an early age have found a completely satisfactory worldview that had answers to all questions. My search for alternative visions went on in other realms as well. While Russia never interested me, even repelled me though I tried not to think about it, I was drawn to primitive and exotic cultures. I majored in social anthropology and, long before the hippies, was attracted to the American Indians and other primitive peoples. I was intrigued with what I thought was the wholeness and integrity of those cultures in contrast to the fragmentation I saw around me. I wrote my undergraduate honors thesis on Apache kinship systems. In my last year in college I took a course on East Asian civilization which was the beginning of an abiding interest. The aesthetic intensity of Japanese culture appealed to my parched Protestant soul and even in the midst of my Marxism I began reading about Zen Buddhism. Also as an undergraduate I was first exposed to psychoanalysis and the multiple levels of the inner life which it has revealed. Under the cover of an apparently satisfactory total worldview, multiple apprehensions of reality were growing.

The months after the disaster of the Henry Wallace campaign in 1948 were not easy ones for those in the dwindling American left. In the face of a growing persecution which was being carried out with great publicity by certain congressional and state legistative committees, and of the far more extensive purge which was quietly going on in many institutions of American society, the Marxist left turned upon itself, as the Navaho used to do in time of drought, and began to discover witches in its own midst. It was an ugly picture from any point of view and one that produced great human suffering. I never became a compulsive anti-Communist, a man trapped in a love-hate embrace with that which he has consciously rejected, but for me finally this idol too was broken.

The years of graduate school that followed were a time of spiritual vacuum. I was wrapped up in the time-consuming task of learning Japanese and Chinese and meeting the many requirements of a joint degree in sociology and Far Eastern languages. But it was also in these years that I began a tentative reappropriation of what I had earlier rejected. Talcott Parsons, and through him Max Weber and Emile Durkheim, opened up to me a view of human society and of historical development which was as sweeping as that of Marxism but in its openness and lack of dogmatism more appealing. The last years of Stalin's rule made the somber face of Soviet despotism ever clearer and I began to doubt the likelihood of any earthly utopia. For all its failures I came to believe that American society needed to be reformed rather than abandoned. In other words politically I became a liberal, but it was the chastened liberalism of a man with few illusions.

The religious need, the need for wholeness, which has been strong in me from adolescence, was partly filled in these years through my encounter with the theology of Paul Tillich. Here was the Protestantism of my childhood transmuted through the deepest encounter with the twentieth century. The recognition of despair in Tillich's Christian existentialism corresponded to my mood. His book *The Courage To Be* with its magnificent closing lines made a deep impression on me:

> The courage to take the anxiety of meaninglessness upon oneself is the boundary line up to which the courage to be can go. Beyond it is mere non-being. Within it all forms of courage are re-established in the power of the God above the God of theism. *The courage to be is rooted in the God who appears when God has disappeared in the anxiety of doubt.*[1]

Toward the end of my graduate years the reappropriations I had been making, reappropriations not on the basis of simple affirmations but of doubt and disillusion, were tested by a new series of events. It was perhaps inevitable that I should not escape the McCarthyism which was so pervasive in American universities in those days. First my fellowship was threatened unless I would speak with "complete candor" which meant informing on all those I had ever known politically. There were those who came to my defense and my fellowship was saved for one more year. Then the offer of an instructorship after I had completed my doctoral work was hedged with vaguer but similar conditions. I turned down this proposal and accepted a research fellowship at the Islamic Institute at McGill University, starting in the fall of 1955.

The next two years were in some ways rather grim. I understand how the young men who have gone to Canada rather than Vietnam must feel. I did not know if I could ever come back to the United States or if I would be able to get an academic job even in Canada after my fellowship had ended. I don't want to exaggerate the difficulties. The Islamic Institute was a wonderful place and the work I did there opened up many new opportunities for me later. But for a while it was a kind of personal low ebb. Those were also the years of the Khrushchev revelations of the terror of Stalin's regime and not long after of the drowning in blood of the Hungarian people's uprising. Exiled from my own country there was no other in which I could place hope.

It was in this situation that the new attitude toward Christianity which I had been developing with the help of Paul Tillich came to a kind of fruition. It was then that I understood existentially the Christian doctrine of sin. I saw that the worst is only a hair's breadth away from the best in any man and any society. I saw that unbroken commitment to any individual or any group is bound to be demonic. Nothing human can bear such a weight. The totalism of Communism and the totalism of the "Free World" are equally destructive. And I learned to see the darkness within, that we are all assassins in our hearts. If I am not a murderer it is because of the grace I have received through the love and support of others, not through the lack of murderous impulses within me. The only difference between me and the man on death row is that he somehow received less grace. Feeling all this I could no longer hate, or rather justify hatred. Since I participate in the guilt of every man there is no man I can reject or declare unforgivable. This is what the New Testament taught me in those months contradicting culture Christianity and Marxism, both of which make idolatrous commitments to particular structures and persons and foster a consequent self-righteousness. It was then that I saw that identification with the body of Christ meant identification with all men without exception.

In 1957 I accepted an appointment without conditions and returned to Harvard. The dark clouds of McCarthyism had almost blown away. During most of the decade that followed, the period when the essays in Parts I and II were written, there was room for cautious optimism, not only about America but also about most of the rest of the world. America seemed to be facing up to the scandal of racism and a period of "liberalization" seemed to have set in in Eastern Europe. Nothing in my experience justified any kind of elation but there did seem to be a basis for what I might call a pessimistic optimism which characterizes my writings of those years. My essay on religious evolution, which states the main presuppositions underlying my book, *Tokugawa Religion,* and the earlier essays in this collection, is not a paean to progress for I point out that at every stage the increase in freedom is also an increase in the freedom to choose destruction. But all the same there is a judicious confidence in the Reformation as a model for ideological transformation in the modern world. The papers in Part II are all based on a dialectic of comparison between the great changes in the West which the Reformation heralded and contemporary changes in various parts of the world. The fundamental assumption behind these papers is that modern Western society, especially American society, in spite of all its problems, is *relatively* less problematic than the developing societies with their enormous difficulties in economic growth and political stability. Though my position is far more cautious than that of other American social scientists who have been concerned with the problem of "modernization" it partakes to some extent of the same ethos.

Perhaps my paper on "Civil Religion in America" written late in this period (1966) epitomizes this earlier attitude at the same time that it contains seeds of a new orientation. It is a strong endorsement of core American values, at least in their most self-critical form, but it also, especially in response to the deepening involvement in the Vietnam War, expresses a fundamental doubt about the future.

The essays in Part III reflect a changed situation and a changed reaction on my part. Behind them lies my dismay at the failure of our society to move quickly and efficiently to correct racial injustice, distress at the growing turbulence, much of it meaningless and self-destructive, in the academic community and above all horror at the profoundly immoral and unjustified war in Vietnam. These experiences have led me increasingly in the last few years to feel that the problems of American society, not of the developing societies, are the really most serious ones today. But my thinking has also been influenced by the emergence of a counter-culture in America, a culture of imagination and not of calculation. Even with all its pathological fringes the liberation of the expressive life which we have seen in the hippie movement and more broadly in popular culture in recent years seems to me of great significance. This too seems to be saying that we can take nothing for granted in our culture. There are entirely new possibilities which we must open up.

The move from Harvard to Berkeley in 1967 was an outward expression of an inward change. Harvard is in many ways the finest institution of Protestant culture in this country, confident and self-assured in its own value-commitments in a way most American universities are not. I have seen it at its best and I have seen it at less than its best but in any case after twenty years of close association with it it is an integral part of my life. As against the magisterial certainty of Harvard Berkeley stands in sharpest antithesis: not the calm order of Protestant tradition but the wide-open chaos of the post-Protestant, post-modern era. For all of its inner problems, for all of its tensions with an increasingly unsympathetic environment, Berkeley evinces the intensity, the immediacy, the openness and the precariousness of an emergent social order. For one trying to grapple with and define what that order is it is a good place to be.

Most of the essays in Part III were written in Berkeley. As against the pessimistic optimism of the earlier papers the later ones evince a kind of optimistic pessimism. Perhaps Yeats expresses the mood:

> All things fall and are built again,
> And those that build them again are gay.[2]

In this situation the playful radicalism of Norman O. Brown seems to me healing while the solemn radicalism of Herbert Marcuse seems destructive. I have learned much from the youthful outpouring of recent years but I am no more inclined to idolize this group than any other. They have brought new styles of freedom, new modes of access to the unconscious, but these styles and modes have been remarkably fragile and have easily disintegrated into cultural nihilism or political fanaticism. Behind the mask of the struggle for liberation one often sees the hard face of the authoritarian who will strangle the young rebels of the next generation.

These last papers do not signal a retreat from political responsibility. They do imply, more strongly than ever, the rejection of any kind of political totalism. But they suggest that in the present situation a politics of the imagination, a politics of religion, may be the only sane politics. There is no hope in any of the competing absolutisms. If the forces at war are locked in their own deathlike scenarios perhaps the only responsible politics is to unmask the pretensions of all the contending parties and give witness to the enormous possibilities in human experience, in a word, to waken the actors out of their trance. To this end a human science can perhaps join with a human religion to help create a human politics.

The relation between the personal search for meaning and wholeness which I have sketched above and the work which follows is a close one. Some of the intellectual influences on me have been mentioned above and others can be discovered from the inspection of footnotes in the various chapters. But the work is not the product just of intellectual influences but of the experience of a particular person at a particular place in history. I have discussed my reaction to successive phases of the history of my society but those phases have not dictated my reaction. Others have reacted very differently. One's life and work are an effort to find a form which will reconcile inner needs and outer pressures. The form itself is unique and personal even though both the inner needs and the outer pressures are transpersonal. In my life there has been a long preoccupation with fragmentation and wholeness and it is this which has made religion such an abiding concern.

In the beginning of my life there was a culture and a family which was incomplete, though, in the sense that I yet had no alternatives, total. In attempting to find a form which would be more complete and more satisfying in late adolescence I adopted the totalistic religio-political system of Marxism. Though this ideology played a valuable integrative role at an important transition stage it proved ultimately to be as much of a straitjacket as an uncritical acceptance of established religious and political values had been. After the rejection of Marxism there was no way back even if I had wanted one. A return to the bosom of American society in the middle fifties could only be made by the suicidal sacrifice of my own integrity. For me the search for wholeness from then on had to be made without totalism. A critical stance toward every society, ideology and religion was thenceforth essential. This did not mean that there was no longer any basis for values nor even that various aspects of tradition could not be appropriated. The loss of faith could become the faith of loss. The self-critical, self-revising, nontotalistic aspects of the tradition could be reclaimed. With respect to Christianity this meant Christ crucified, the assertion of faith in spite of the brokenness of every human structure. With respect to America this meant a society dedicated to its own transcendence, to the realization of human values. In neither case was there a total commitment to the existing church or state but rather to that within them which is always questioning their existing reality. Nor did the reassertion in broken form of a commitment to the Christian and American traditions exclude a deep involvement with other traditions and cultures. Wholeness was not to be obtained through exclusion but through a multi-layered inclusion.

In much of my work up until about 1965 there is to be seen an effort to discern a new system which would be an alternative to Marxism but rival it in sweep and comprehensiveness. To some extent this was a modern apology for liberal society and an attempt to show its relevance to the developing areas. I am by no means ready to repudiate this stage of my work, though I am increasingly aware of its limitations. I still believe that some equivalent of Protestant individualism and voluntaristic social organization is a necessary phase for any person or group who would fully participate in the potential freedom of the modern world.

More recently my attention has turned to the problems of post-Protestant man, man who is not only post-traditional—for Protestantism and some of its functional equivalents, among which I would place humanistic Marxism, are already post-traditional—but also in a sense post-modern.

This post-modern phase cannot be seen as simply a continuous projection of the major trends of present relatively modernized societies. Theorists of modernization have been tempted to assume that once a certain degree of individualism, civic culture and industrial development were achieved the future of a society was essentially non-problematic. It is hard in 1970 to make that assumption. In fact we do not know where the most advanced societies are going. The more we understand the recent past the better, but the future is a new project full of contingency. The best guides in a time like this may not be the systematic theorists, the public opinion pollers or the scanners of indices and indicators, but poets and ecstatic aphorists like Norman O. Brown. If modernization has brought far greater knowledge, wealth and power than men have ever had before, then, potentially at least, we are freer than men have ever been and our future is more open to make it what we will. But the same resources which can bring us freedom can also be used for oppression and control. Men are not oppressed by armies and unfair economic systems alone. They are also oppressed by dead ideologies which can be locked into personalities and societies and program them on a course of fatal disaster, often in the name of "realism" and "necessity." Under these conditions we have need more than ever for the dreamers of dreams and the seers of visions. Freedom of the imagination, the ability to live in many realities at once, may be our strongest weapons in the struggle for human liberation. The essays in Part III are concerned with these issues.

The theme of loss, I now realize, is even more pervasive in this story than I had thought when I touched upon it in the beginning of this introduction. It is a story of loss: the lost father, the lost religion, the lost ideology, the lost country. And yet it is not, finally, a story of existential despair. Even Tillich who was so important in expressing my feelings at certain moments was not in his somberest moods wholly convincing. For the deepest truth I have discovered is that if one accepts the loss, if one gives up clinging to what is irretrievably gone, then the nothing which is left is not barren but enormously fruitful. Everything that one has lost comes flooding back again out of the darkness, and one's relation to it is new—free and unclinging. But the richness of the nothing contains far more, it is the all-possible, it is the spring of freedom.[3] In that sense the faith of loss is closer to joy than to despair.

The chapters of this book must stand finally on their own merits, on the cogency of their arguments and the clarity with which they order the empirical data. But the experience out of which they come, which I have tried to discuss in this introduction, is not irrelevant to them and if they succeed it will be not only because they contain convincing arguments but by their capacity to order the common experience. They are attempts to find patterns of meaning in a world where all the great overarching systems of belief, conservative and radical, have lost their viability. These essays are expressions of "belief," in Wallace Stevens' words, "without belief, beyond belief."

NOTES

1 Paul Tillich, *The Courage To Be* (New Haven: Yale Univ. Press, 1952), p. 190. Tillich's collection of sermons, *The Shaking of the Foundations,* was also particularly important to me.

2 From "Lapis Lazuli" in William Butler Yeats, *The Variorum Edition of the Poems* (New York: Macmillan Co., 1968), p. 566.

3 See Chapter 16, "Nothing," in Norman O. Brown, *Love's Body* (New York: Random House, Vintage Books, 1968). Also compare Ienaga Saburō's concept of "the logic of negation" (*hitei no ronri*) mentioned in Chapter 7 below and discussed more thoroughly in my essay "Ienaga Saburō and the Search for Meaning in Modern Japan," in Marius B. Jansen, ed., *Changing Japanese Attitudes Toward Modernization* (Princeton: Princeton Univ. Press, 1965), pp. 369–423. I realize that there are certain parallels between Ienaga's intellectual biography as described in that essay and what I have written in this introduction.

In thinking about the relation of what I have said in this introduction to the scheme presented in Chapter 2 ("Religious Evolution") below it is clear that my own immediate experience has been mainly with stages four and five of that scheme. Nevertheless through scholarly investigation I have participated at every level. This is one of the characteristics of stage five—that within it everything previous may have direct meaning, since through some such mechanism as the faith of loss or the logic of negation one's present commitments are not univocal. Indeed some of the most "primitive" levels of religious experience, the direct participation in myth and symbol, may be especially characteristic of religion in stage five. Auguste Comte claimed to have experienced every stage of his system of religious evolution from fetishism to positivism while in a psychotic state. It may now be possible to do the same thing consciously though perhaps a touch of madness still helps. See particularly Chapters 13, 14 and 15 below.

PART ONE Theoretical Foundations

THE TWO CHAPTERS in Part I constitute between them a preliminary reconnaissance of what I believe are the major theoretical and empirical problems in the study of religion. Many of the highly condensed statements in these chapters are developed at greater length in Parts II and III. There is some value, however, in a relatively concise statement of theoretical issues. It is particularly helpful in allowing a periodic reassessment of one's position. I have included as an Appendix a paper, "The Systematic Study of Religion," which was written in 1955, some ten years before the chapters of Part I. Comparing the Appendix and Part I will allow the reader to observe the gradual development of a conceptual scheme. Naturally further changes have occurred in the last five years. Some of these can be discerned in Part III, most of which is quite recent. Perhaps the major change is an increasing elaboration of the role of symbolism in religious systems. Related to this is the growing awareness that theoretical statements like those in Part I are not just "objectively scientific" but contain within them religious implications as well.

1 The Sociology of Religion

SOCIOLOGISTS have undertaken three main types of religious study. They have studied religion as a central theoretical problem in the understanding of social action. They have studied the relation between religion and other areas of social life, such as economics, politics, and social class. And finally, they have studied religious roles, organizations, and movements. This article is concerned primarily with the theoretical study of religion and secondarily with the relation between religion and the social structure.

Historical Background

The sociological study of religion has grown out of and remains inextricably related to the much broader effort to understand the phenomenon of religion that has been made by scholars in many fields, especially since the eighteenth century in the West and more recently in other parts of the world. Theologians, philosophers, historians, philologists, literary critics, political scientists, anthropologists, and psychologists have all made contributions. In un-

This chapter was written for the International Encyclopedia of the Social Sciences during 1965, while I was at the Center for Advanced Study in the Behavioral Sciences in Stanford, Calif., (Full references for the initial publication of this and succeeding chapters can be found in the Bibliography to this book.) The rubric was given by the encyclopedia but the contents indicate considerable uneasiness with a narrowly disciplinary approach to religion. What I attempted was in fact a condensed statement of a general theory of religion, not one specifically sociological. The immediate theoretical resources came from Karl Deutsch, a political scientist, as well as Talcott Parsons, a sociologist, and I cited a key definition from Clifford Geertz, an anthropologist. Among those I single out as especially promising theoretical innovators are Erik Erikson, a psychologist, and Kenneth Burke, a literary critic interested in symbolism, as well as Philip Slater, a sociologist of small groups.

tangling this immensely complicated story it will be helpful to resort to a simplified schema that focuses on two main lines of intellectual development: the "rationalist" and the "nonrationalist" traditions. (A writer is referred to here as "nonrationalist" not because his thought is considered to be irrational but because he takes the nonrational aspect of human existence as central and irreducible.) Both traditions have roots deep in the history of Western thought and analogues in the thought of some non-Western cultures. The eighteenth century saw a certain crystallization of both traditions, which had important consequences for the nineteenth century and which still affects us in many respects.

The rationalists and nonrationalists. The rationalist tradition, which was closely associated with the rise of secular thought and skepticism in England and France in the seventeenth and eighteenth centuries, later stimulated the nonrationalist tendency as a reaction to it. Of course, the rationalists themselves were partly grappling with the great seventeenth-century antirationalist Blaise Pascal. It was the position of the rationalists that the apparent nonrational could not only be brought within the bounds of rational analysis but also could be eliminated as an influence on human action, though most of them doubted that this would ever be possible for the masses. Thus, they held that the obviously absurd doctrines of established religion had come into existence because of ignorance and the deliberate chicanery of the priests, who were serving their own self-interest as well as that of the secular despots who were often their masters. Behind the absurd historical forms, the deists discerned a natural religion in accordance with the dictates of reason.

Rousseau and Kant were transitional figures. Both believed in a generalized "reasonable" religion in preference to any historical faith, but they grounded their religious convictions on human nature (Rousseau) or on the dictates of ethical experience (Kant) rather than on purely cognitive arguments. The nonrationalist tradition, which subsequently developed mainly in Germany, emphasized the *sui generis* quality of religion. Johann Gottfried Herder held that religion was grounded in specific experience and feeling rather than in reason. In the early nineteenth century Friedrich Schleiermacher undertook the first systematic exposition of this position. He held that religion was to be understood neither as crude philosophy nor as primitive ethics but rather as a reality in its own right; it is grounded neither in knowledge nor in action but in feeling. More specifically, he came to think that religion derives fundamentally from the feeling of absolute dependence. Both Herder and Schleiermacher, rejecting as they did a rationalist understanding of religion, opposed the search for a universal natural religion of self-evident reasonableness. Rather, they insisted on taking seriously the particular forms of culture and religion in all their historical diversity. Herder was, of course, one of the most important forerunners of nineteenth-century historicism, and Schleiermacher was one of the first to develop the tools of cultural interpretation (hermeneutics), which provided the main methodological equipment of the movement in Germany.

While the nonrationalist treatment of religion in Germany was closely related to the development of idealist philosophy there, the rationalist treatment of it was closely related to the rise of positivism in France and utilitarianism in England during the nineteenth century. Historicism cut across these distinctions and came to dominate Anglo-French as well as German thought. In both France and England rationalism in its historicist phase took the form of evolutionism.

Auguste Comte's famous theory of the three stages viewed theology as appropriate in the childhood of man; however, it was to be displaced first by philosophy and then by science as man's rational understanding of the universe gradually increased. Comte interpreted religion in terms that we would now call "functional," stressing the contribution of belief and ritual to social solidarity and the control of personal feelings. While thus recognizing nonrational factors in religion and, indeed, arguing from them that religion is a permanent and inescapable aspect of human existence, he nonetheless stressed cognitive factors almost exclusively in his theory of religious evolution.

In England, Herbert Spencer developed an evolutionary perspective on religion that was even more narrowly cognitive than Comte's, and Sir Edward Tylor also undertook an extensive effort to understand the religious development of mankind in these terms. In treating the development from animism through polytheism to monotheism as a succession of more and more adequate cognitive hypotheses, he remained thoroughly in the rationalist tradition. Sir James Frazer, while formally maintaining the same point of view, embraced a range of material—ritual kingship, human sacrifice, fertility ritual, and the like—that actually demanded a different interpretation. His *Golden Bough*[1] can be viewed as a marvelously intuitive catalogue of central problems that would have to be solved by other means. Finally, in the English tradition, Robert Marett's discussion of mana and preanimism came very near breaking through the preconceptions of the rationalist utilitarian school.[2]

Wilhelm Dilthey, who was a follower of Schleiermacher as well as a neo-Kantian, continued the German nonrationalist tradition by stressing the irreducible nature of the religious *Weltanschauung* and the necessity for an inner understanding (*Verstehen*) of its particular forms. This tradition led directly into the modern sociological study of religion through the work of Ernst Troeltsch and particularly that of Max Weber, who both transcended the tradition in important respects. Postponing a consideration of these men for a moment, we may trace further into the twentieth century the development of the German tradition that was relatively independent of the influence of Weber and Troeltsch. A certain formal culmination was reached in the work of Rudolph Otto. In his important book, *The Idea of the Holy,* he richly developed the basic intuition of Schleiermacher by spelling out the phenomenology of the holy in terms of the numinous—the notion of the *mysterium tremendum et fascinosum.*[3] Here more clearly than ever was the assertion of the *sui generis* nature of religion and its "geometrical location" in a certain kind of immediate experience. That experience, according to Otto, can be phenomenologically understood, but it cannot be explained. This point was made quite explicit in the work of Gerardus van der Leeuw, who shared Otto's essential position: In the preface to *Religion in Essence and Manifestation* van der Leeuw said that he specifically disavowed all "theories." Thus Otto and the later exponents of this tradition—whether they were phenomenologists (such as van der Leeuw and Mircea Eliade) or were specifically interested in the sociology of religion (Joachim Wach and Gustav Mensching)—have given us a rich array of materials without appreciably advancing our theoretical understanding.

Generalizing the argument so far, we may say that while the nonrationalist tradition jealously guarded the specific nature of religion but eschewed any explanation of it, the rationalist tradition provided a number of ways of explaining religion which in the end explained it away. We will argue, following Talcott Parsons' *The*

Structure of Social Action,[5] that around the turn of the twentieth century several men from both traditions broke free of their preconceptions and converged on a more adequate approach to religion (and indeed to social phenomena generally).

However, just as we have noted that the nonrationalist tradition continues to our own day in relatively pure form, so we must point out that the utilitarian rationalist position also continues, not so much as a conscious tradition of scholarship but as a semiconscious preconception of scholars in many fields. This preconception has been strengthened by its gradual fusion with a Marxian understanding of religion as essentially an ideological cover, either for the defense of the social status quo or for protests against it. Here religion is treated as a weapon in the political-economic struggle or as a preliminary stage in a political movement, a stage that may be outgrown with the attainment of political maturity. What is at issue is not the empirical adequacy of such analyses in particular instances, but rather the generalization of them as adequate for the understanding of the phenomenon of religion.

Foundations of an adequate theory. The architects of a more adequate understanding of religion were Durkheim, Weber, and Freud, though others also made important contributions.

Contributions of Weber and Durkheim. Weber maintained the idea of the centrality and irreducibility of nonrational elements in human action as it had developed in the German tradition, but he was not content with a mere phenomenological description of these elements. According to Parsons' analysis, Weber began, at least incipiently, to place these nonrational elements within the context of a general theory of social action. This he did through two of his central concerns. The first was with the problems of *meaning*—of evil, suffering, death, and the like—that are inescapable in human life but insoluble in purely scientific terms. Weber argued that the alternative religious answers to these problems of meaning have had not only profound consequences for the motivation of individuals but also, in the long run, important causal effects on social development. The second of Weber's concerns, which links irrational elements to a more general theory of action, was with what he called *charisma.* Charisma is primarily a quality of the individual that places him above normal expectations and endows him with the authority to utter new commandments. Charisma is a relational concept, that is, it comes into existence only when it is recognized by a group. It links deeper levels of psychic organization, within the charismatic individual and in the members of the group who recognize him, with the social process and particularly with the possibility of radical discontinuities in social development. In both cases Weber was arguing for the importance of religion in social action on the grounds of its closeness to powerful nonrational motivational forces and its capacity to give form and pattern to those forces, including its capacity to create radically new forms and patterns.

The rationalist positivist tradition was decisively broken through from within by Emile Durkheim, when he recognized that religion is a reality *sui generis*. By this he meant that religious representations or symbols are not delusions, nor do they simply stand for some other phenomena, such as natural forces or (contrary to some interpretations of his work) social morphology. Rather, in his social Kantianism, he held that religious representations are constitutive of society. They exist within the minds of individuals so as to inhibit egocentric impulses and to discipline the individual so that he can deal objectively with external reality. These shared representations, with their capacity to direct and control personal motivation, are what make society possible. While his treatment of motivation remained rudimentary, he did point out very clearly the great importance of religious action for stimulating individuals to participate positively in social life[6] and for dealing with tendencies of individuals to withdraw from social life.[7]

Although they started from opposite directions, both Weber and Durkheim seem to have overcome the impasse in which the rationalist and nonrationalist approaches to religion had long been caught: They both placed religion in a theoretical rather than a purely descriptive context, without denying its centrality and irreducibility. However, they lacked any fine-grained structural understanding of the nonrational elements involved, even though they recognized their importance. It was in the work of Freud that a structural understanding of the relevant emotional and motivational elements was to be found for the first time.

Freud's work on religious symbolism. Freud's early work on the stages of psychosexual development was applied to religion in *Totem and Taboo*,[8] where the Oedipus complex, with its mixture of dependence, love, and hostility, was seen as the core problem of religious symbolism, which he treated as largely projective. Freud's later ego psychology, heralded in the important essays "Group Psychology and the Analysis of the Ego"[9] and "The Ego and the Id,"[10] provided the basis for a much more active understanding of religious symbolism, which could now be treated not merely as reflecting psychic conflict but as actually affecting the outcome of psychic conflict and redirecting psychic forces. This point of view was applied to religion in the somewhat idiosyncratic but extraordinarily fruitful *Moses and Monotheism*.[11] "The Future of an Illusion"[12] represents a reversion to the early projective theory of religion and is neither the final statement of Freud's position nor even typical of his own late thinking.

By the early 1920s, then, the elements of a more adequate theory of religion had come into existence. However, at just this point the primary preoccupation with religion displayed by most of the great social scientists of the late nineteenth and early twentieth centuries disappeared. Other issues occupied the center of attention. Even today a theoretical concern with religion is only gradually reviving as a central issue in social science.

A Theory of Religion

Only in the last few years has a new model of human action developed that will allow us to utilize the insights of Weber, Durkheim, and Freud without falling back into the old controversies about idealism and materialism, rationalism and irrationalism, and humanism and science. This is the cybernetic model.[13] Parsons' action theory is the chief link between earlier social science and cybernetic theory and has itself in recent years been increasingly restated in cybernetic terms. This model, whose basic terms are "energy" and "information," seems likely to integrate the range of behavioral research that stretches from the work of biologists such as Nikolaas Tinbergen and J. P. Scott on animal behavior to that of philosophers such as Ernst Cassirer and Susanne K. Langer on symbolic forms.

The cybernetic model. An action system may be defined as the symbolically controlled, systematically organized behavior of one or more biological organisms. The energy of such a system is supplied by the organism and is organized through genetically controlled organic structures that are not directly open to symbolic influence.

Thus the basic motivation of the action system—its drives and needs—is partially determined by organic structure, although it is subject, through learning processes, to a considerable degree of symbolic control. The precise boundary, or, perhaps better, the area of overlap, between what is genetically and what is symbolically controlled is by no means clear, and important research on the problem is continuing. For present purposes it is only necessary to note the relatively broad plasticity for symbolic learning that is usually recognized, at least in the human species.

Information in such a system consists largely of symbolic messages that indicate something about either the internal state or the external situation of the action system. These messages are understood or interpreted by matching them with previously learned symbolic patterns, which make up the memory of the system. New situations can be understood through a recombination of previously learned elements so that a new symbolic pattern is created. Thus, the set of symbolic patterns existing in a system will be partially determined by the nature of the external world with which that system has had to deal and by the nature of the laws governing the cognitive processes of the brain. Within these limits there is a wide range of freedom, within which alternative symbolic patterns may operate with equal or nearly equal effectiveness, as is best illustrated perhaps in the phenomenon of language.

The cybernetic model thus conceives of a human action system as autonomous, purposive, and capable of a wide range of external adaptations and internal rearrangements within the very broad constraints inherent in the nature of energy and information. It is precisely the stress on autonomy, learning capacity, decision, and control the gives the cybernetic model the ability, lacking in previous mechanistic and organic models, to assimilate the contributions of the humanistic disciplines—the *Geisteswissenschaften*—without abandoning an essentially scientific approach.

The openness of an action system is always relative to its particular structure. We have noted that energy is structured by genetic information from the organism and by symbolic information from the culture. Energy and information are further structured by two systems that can be seen as integrating organic motivation and symbols: personality and society. These are symbolically patterned motivational systems; the first centers on individual organisms, the other on groups. Any particular personality or social system will be determined in large part at any given moment by its history, for its learning capacity will be largely a product of the structures it has built up over time. However, if a system has managed to develop a broad and flexible capacity for rapid learning, and if it has a reserve of uncommitted resources, its reaction to any given internal or external situation will be open to a wide variety of alternative choices; in other words, it will have a high degree of freedom.

The role of religion in action systems. Religion emerges in action systems with respect to two main problems. In order to function effectively, it is essential that a person or group have a relatively condensed, and therefore highly general, definition of its environment and itself. Such a definition of the system and the world to which it is related (in more than a transient sense) is a conception of identity. Such a conception is particularly necessary in situations of stress and disturbance because it can provide the most general set of instructions as to how the system is to maintain itself and repair any damage sustained.

In addition to the identity problem, there is the problem of dealing with inputs of motivation from within the system that are not under the immediate control of conscious decision processes. We have already noted that such motivation is partly under the control of genetic rather than symbolic processes. In addition, as Freud discovered, there are important symbolically organized systems of motivation that are partially blocked or screened off from consciousness through the mechanism of repression; this happens partly as a result of the pattern of child raising. Though these unconscious motivational forces exist in individuals, they are to a large degree shared in groups, because human biology and child-raising patterns are, broadly speaking, similar. The emotions can be seen as signaling devices by which the conscious decision process (the ego, in Freud's terms) becomes aware of the existence of important inputs of motivation from unconscious levels of the system.

The problems of identity and of unconscious motivation are closely related, for it is just those situations of threat, uncertainty, and breakdown, which raise the identity issue, that also rouse deep unconscious feelings of anxiety, hope, and fear. An identity conception capable of dealing with such a situation must not only be cognitively adequate but must also be motivationally meaningful. It is precisely the role of religion in action systems to provide such a cognitively and motivationally meaningful identity conception or set of identity symbols. It is such a set of symbols that provides answers to Weber's problems of meaning and to which Durkheim referred in speaking of religious representations. It is also what in large part Freud meant when he spoke of the superego. This mode of analysis leads to a definition of religion very close to that of Clifford Geertz, who wrote: "A religion is a system of symbols which acts to establish powerful, pervasive and long-lasting moods and motivations in men by formulating conceptions of a general order of existence and clothing these conceptions with such an aura of factuality that the moods and motivations seem uniquely realistic."[14]

The conception of religion briefly sketched here—religion as the most general mechanism for integrating meaning and motivation in action systems—applies to all types of action systems, not only to whole societies or groups of them. Many smaller units (individual personalities and groups) appropriate the religious symbols of their social and cultural environment in dealing with their own religious problems, though always with some degree of individual variation. Moreover, even where prevailing religious symbol systems are rejected, the idiosyncratic solutions of individuals and groups to fundamental problems of orientation and identity may be viewed in terms of this scheme as "religious." Of course, the degree to which religious problems will be salient for any individual or group is quite variable.

Current Theoretically Relevant Research

While the theory outlined above has not previously been stated in exactly these terms, some recent research seems to be guided by a conception of religion as a control system linking meaning and motivation, a conception that is a close parallel of this theory. Three particularly interesting examples of such research will be cited. Each of them concentrates at a traditional level of social science—psychological, social, or cultural—but it is noteworthy that they all transcend the discipline boundaries in trying to understand religion.

Analysis of historical figures. The first is the application of detailed psychological analysis to significant figures in religious history. Erik H. Erikson, in *Young Man Luther,*[15] has overcome a tendency toward psychological reductionism that was evident in some earlier work of this sort. He is careful to place Luther's life history in its proper social, historical, and religious context. In doing so, he shows how Luther was able to solve his own problem of identity, which had its roots deep in his unconscious conflicts, through constructive innovation with respect to religious symbolism. However, Erikson's knowledge of the deep motivational forces involved does not lead him to deny the contribution of the religious reformulation itself. Rather, he emphasizes the fusing and forming power of the symbols to synthesize motivational conflicts and control destructive impulses.

Erikson also contributes to the broader problem of religious change by indicating that Luther's solution, once it was embodied in communicable symbolic form, could be appropriated by others in the same society that had analogous identity problems arising from social-historical matrices similar to Luther's own. Moreover, although the argument is not worked out in detail, Erikson implies that Luther was able to contribute to certain social and cultural identity problems of Germany in particular and of Western civilization in general. This detailed analysis of the mechanism involved in a major example of religious change, although it involves only one among several types of change, is an important contribution to one of our least understood problems.

Small-group research. The second new line of research has to do with the analysis of religious phenomena in small groups, as illustrated in Philip E. Slater's *Microcosm*.[16] The small-group situation provides a laboratory within which the symbolic processes involved in group formation, as hypothesized by Durkheim and Freud, can be empirically synthesized. Slater shows how the group and its leader become foci for the unconscious anxieties, hopes, and fears of the members in the initial situation of uncertainty and lack of definition. These feelings are handled initially by the development of projective symbols, which are redolent with the mysterious potency of the unconscious feelings; that is, they are highly magical and sacred. However, over time, as more and more of the group process becomes consciously understood and as the deeper feelings about the group and the leader are worked through, the group itself becomes "secularized" and the quality of the sacred is relegated to certain group ideals and symbols of group solidarity.

Slater's comparison of this process of group development with the long-term process of religious evolution is highly suggestive. Particularly important is the perception of the changing role of symbolism with respect to the meaning-motivation balance as the group itself undergoes new experiences and changes in structure. Also of great general significance is Slater's observation that social and psychological aspects of group process interpenetrate at every point and that a purely psychological or a purely sociological theoretical framework would result in an inadequate understanding of the process at work.

Analysis of language as symbolic action. A third area of promising research is the analysis of language as symbolic action as it has been developed by Kenneth Burke in his *Rhetoric of Religion*[17] and other works. Burke's theory of artistic form (defined as "the arousing and fulfilling of expectations"), which is based on the Aristotelian theory of catharsis, emphasizes the working through of emotional tensions in symbolic form; thus, it is very close to the theory of religion developed above. Burke has pointed out that the tensions may be social as well as psychological, though they must be presented in personal terms if they are to have emotional impact. He has also pointed out the function of social and psychological control that such symbolic working through performs.

Perhaps Burke's chief contribution is his insistence on the special formal qualities of language and symbolism generally. Language does not merely reflect or communicate social and psychological realities. Rather, language contains within itself a "principle of perfection,"[18] which operates relatively independently of other factors. That is, a terminology, once established, has certain "entelechial" implications. For example, once the terms *king, society,* and *god* come into existence, there is the logical possibility that someone will ask what a perfect king, society, or god is and from this analysis actually draw conclusions about existing kings, societies, or ideas of god. Regardless of the many actual social and psychological blocks to carrying through such analyses, the fact is that the possibility of pushing toward terminological perfection is always present, and under certain circumstances it will actually be pursued. This is one of the chief reasons why cultural symbol systems cannot be treated entirely reductionistically. In *The Rhetoric of Religion* Burke has applied these insights with great brilliance to two key religious documents: the first three chapters of Genesis and Augustine's *Confessions*.

Religion and Society

An interest in the social consequences of religious belief and action is probably as old as the interest in religion itself. In the sixteenth century Machiavelli gave, in his *Discourses,* a functional analysis of Roman religion that had considerable influence. Spinoza, Montesquieu, Rousseau, and Comte continued and developed the analysis of the political significance of religious commitment and the related problems of the influence of religion on personal morality and social solidarity. In one of the earliest quantitative studies in sociology, Durkheim introduced a "religious variable" in his study of suicide.[19] Subsequently many studies of varying breadth and quality have included a religious variable, thus advancing our knowledge of the influence or lack of influence of religion on some aspect of social existence; however, a comprehensive survey of the results obtained is still lacking.

The man who contributed most to the systematic understanding of the interrelations between religion and society and who stimulated more research (both quantitative and nonquantitative) than any other scholar was undoubtedly Max Weber. The most influential single hypothesis in this field is certainly his thesis on the influence of the Protestant ethic on the rise of modern society.[20] Although the cumulated argument and evidence on this thesis are too massive to review here, one recent study by Gerhard Lenski[21] is worth mentioning, not only because it sheds light on the Protestant Ethic thesis in contemporary America but also because it is perhaps the most successful attempt to apply the methods of survey research to the sociology of religion. Lenski was concerned with the influence of religious affiliations and beliefs on attitudes toward work, authority, education, and a variety of other matters in a large American city, and he found this influence to be considerable. Weber's ideas on the non-Western religions have been applied much more sporadically,[22] but as the comparative horizon of the sociology of religion widens, these ideas seem likely to attract more attention. In this same connection, a revival of interest in religious evolution as providing the soundest classificatory system for comparative work can also be expected.

Religious Evolution

Although foreshadowings of the idea of religious evolution can be traced as far back as classical times, the first extensive effort in this direction was that of Giovanni Battista Vico in the eighteenth century. Elaborate schemes of religious evolution with copious empirical illustration were developed in the nineteenth century by Hegel, Comte, and Spencer. In more modest and judicious form, evolutionary ideas provided the basis of the sociology of religion of Durkheim and Weber.[23] Though long neglected and in some quarters excoriated, the idea of religious evolution has recently been revived.[24] It provides the natural link between the kind of theory of religion sketched in this article and the comparative study of religion.

If one defines religion as a control system linking meaning and motivation by providing an individual or a group with the most general model that it has of itself and its world, then it becomes apparent that such a control system can vary in degree of complexity in ways that are not entirely random with respect to the degree of complexity of the social system of which it is a part. Since it has been clear for a long time that levels of social and cultural complexity are best understood in an evolutionary framework, it seems inevitable that religion too must be considered in such a framework.

Here it is possible only to enumerate some of the most important dimensions along which religious evolution can be expected to occur. The central focus of religious evolution is the religious symbol system itself. Here the main line of development is from compact to differentiated symbolism, that is, from a situation in which world, self, and society are seen to involve the immediate expression of occult powers to one in which the exercise of religious influence is seen to be more indirect and "rational." This is the process of the "disenchantment of the world" that was described by Weber. Part of this process is the gradual differentiation of art, science, and other cultural systems as separate from religious symbolism. Furthermore, changes in the nature and position of religious symbolism effect changes in the conception of the religious actor. The more differentiated symbol systems make a greater demand on the individual for decision and commitment. To support this growing religious individualism, specifically religious group structures are required, whereas at earlier stages religion tends to be a dimension of all social groups. Finally, the capacity for religion to provide ideals and models for new lines of social development increases with the growing symbolic, individual, and social differentiation.

An adequate theory of religious evolution would have to go hand in hand with a general theory of social evolution. For example, the varying saliency of law, custom, and religion as agencies of social control in different societies, which was long ago pointed out by Montesquieu, could probably best be explicated by a general analysis of the evolution of control systems. Moreover, the contribution that a theory of religious evolution could make to a general conception of social evolution is also considerable. Such an approach would begin to indicate the ways in which changes in social structure impinge on the integation of established cultural meanings with the deeper levels of individual personalities, and how shifts in that meaning-motivation balance can in turn help or hinder social differentiation.

NOTES

1 James Frazer, *The Golden Bough: A Study in Magic and Religion,* 3d ed., rev. & enl. 13 vols. (New York: St. Martins, 1955). First published in 1890, an abridged edition was published in 1922 and reprinted in 1955.

2 Robert R. Marett, *The Threshold of Religion,* 4th ed. (London: Methuen, 1929). First published in 1900.

3 Rudolph Otto, *The Idea of the Holy: An Inquiry Into the Nonrational Factor in the Idea of the Divine and Its Relation to the Rational,* 2d ed. (London: Oxford Univ. Press, 1950). First published as *Das Heilige* in 1917.

4 Gerardus van der Leeuw, *Religion in Essence and Manifestation: A Study in Phenomenology* (New York: Macmillan Co., 1938), p. vi. First published as *Phänomenologie der Religion* in 1933, and reissued in paperback by Harper & Row in 1963.

5 Talcott Parsons, *The Structure of Social Action: A Study in Social Theory with Special Reference to a Group of Recent European Writers* (Glencoe, Ill.: Free Press, 1949). First published in 1937.

6 See the discussion of collective effervescence in Emile Durkheim, *The Elementary Forms of the Religious Life* (London: Allen & Unwin, 1954), bk. 2, chap. 7. First published as *Les formes élémentaires de la vie religieuse, le système totémique en Australie* in 1912.

7 See the discussion of funeral ritual in Durkheim, *op. cit.,* bk. 3, chap. 5.

8 Sigmund Freud, *Totem and Taboo,* in *The Standard Edition of the Complete Psychological Works of Sigmund Freud,* vol. 13 (London: Hogarth Press, 1959), pp. ix–162. First published in German in 1913.

9 Freud, "Group Psychology and the Analysis of the Ego," in *The Standard Edition, op. cit.,* vol. 18, pp. 67–143. First published in German in 1921.

10 Freud, "The Ego and the Id," in *The Standard Edition, op. cit.,* vol. 19, pp. 19–63. First published in German in 1923.

11 Freud, *Moses and Monotheism: Three Essays,* in *The Standard Edition, op. cit.,* vol. 23. First published in German from 1934 to 1938.

12 Freud, "The Future of an Illusion," in *The Standard Edition, op. cit.*, vol. 21, pp. 5–58. First published in German in 1927.

13 For a relevant, though partial, exposition, see Karl W. Deutsch, *The Nerves of Government: Models of Political Communication and Control* (New York: Free Press, 1963).

14 Clifford Geertz, "Religion as a Cultural System," in Michael Banton, ed., *Anthropological Approaches to the Study of Religion*, A.S.A. Monographs, vol. 3 (London: Tavistock Press, 1966), p. 4. First presented at the Conference on New Approaches in Social Anthropology, Jesus College, Cambridge, England, in 1963.

15 Erik H. Erikson, *Young Man Luther: A Study in Psychoanalysis and History*, Austen Riggs Monograph no. 4 (New York: Norton, 1962). First published in 1958.

16 Philip E. Slater, *Microcosm* (New York: John Wiley, 1966).

17 Kenneth Burke, *The Rhetoric of Religion: Studies in Logology* (Boston: Beacon Press, 1961).

18 *Ibid.*, epilogue.

19 Durkheim, *Suicide: A Study in Sociology* (Glencoe, Ill.: Free Press, 1954). First published in French in 1897.

20 Max Weber, *The Protestant Ethic and the Spirit of Capitalism*, trans. by Talcott Parsons (London: Allen & Unwin, 1930). First published in German in 1904–5.

21 Gerhard E. Lenski, *The Religious Factor: A Sociological Study of Religion's Impact on Politics, Economics, and Family Life*, rev. ed. (Garden City, N.Y.: Doubleday & Co., 1963).

22 See the incomplete review in Robert N. Bellah, "Reflections on the Protestant Ethic Analogy in Asia," *Journal of Social Issues* 19 (1963): 52–60.

23 Durkheim, *The Elementary Forms of the Religious Life, op. cit.*, and Weber, *The Sociology of Religion*, trans. Ephriem Fischoff (Boston: Beacon Press, 1963), first published in German as bk. 2, chap. 4 of *Wirtschaft und Gesellschaft* in 1922.

24 Bellah, "Religious Evolution," *American Sociological Review* 29 (1964): 358–74.

2 Religious Evolution

"Time in its aging course teaches all things."
—Aeschylus, *Prometheus Bound*

THOUGH one can name precursors as far back as Herodotus, the systematically scientific study of religion begins only in the second half of the nineteenth century. According to Chantepie de la Saussaye, the two preconditions for this emergence were that by the time of Hegel religion had become the object of comprehensive philosophical speculation and that by the time of Henry Thomas Buckle history had been enlarged to include the history of civilization and culture in general.[1] In its early phases, partly under the influence of Darwinism, the science of religion was dominated by an evolutionary tendency already implicit in Hegelian philosophy and early nineteenth-century historiography. The grandfathers of modern sociology, Auguste Comte and Herbert Spencer, contributed to the strongly evolutionary approach to the study of religion as, with many reservations, did Emile Durkheim and Max Weber.

But by the third decade of the twentieth century the evolutionary wave was in full retreat both in the general field of science of religion and in the sociology of religion in particular. Of course, this was only one aspect of the general retreat of evolutionary thought in social science, but nowhere did the retreat go further or the intensity

Part of this paper was given as a lecture at the University of Chicago in October 1963. Some of the ideas were worked out in a seminar on social evolution which I gave with Talcott Parsons and S. N. Eisenstadt at Harvard University in the spring of 1963. The basic conception, however, goes back much further. A long unpublished paper on this subject was written in Montreal in 1956 while I was at the Institute of Islamic Studies at McGill University. In a sense the paper contains the precipitate of my early involvement with Marxism in that it attempts to sketch a broad meaningful pattern of social development, even though its theoretical presuppositions are very different from historical materialism.

of the opposition to evolution go deeper than in the field of religion. An attempt to explain the vicissitudes of evolutionary conceptions in the field of religion would be an interesting study in the sociology of knowledge but beyond the scope of this brief paper. Here I can only say that I hope that the present attempt to apply the evolutionary idea to religion evidences a serious appreciation of both nineteenth-century evolutionary theories and twentieth-century criticisms of them.

Evolution at any system level I define as a process of increasing differentiation and complexity of organization that endows the organism, social system, or whatever the unit in question may be with greater capacity to adapt to its environment, so that it is in some sense more autonomous relative to its environment than were its less complex ancestors. I do not assume that evolution is inevitable, irreversible, or must follow any single particular course. Nor do I assume that simpler forms cannot prosper and survive alongside more complex forms. What I mean by evolution, then, is nothing metaphysical but the simple empirical generalization that more complex forms develop from less complex forms and that the properties and possibilities of more complex forms differ from those of less complex forms.

A brief handy definition of religion is considerably more difficult than a definition of evolution. An attempt at an adequate definition would, as Clifford Geertz has recently demonstrated, require a paper in itself for adequate explanation.[2] So, for limited purposes only, let me define religion as a set of symbolic forms and acts that relate man to the ultimate conditions of his existence. The purpose of this definition is to indicate exactly what I claim has evolved. It is not the ultimate conditions, or, in traditional language, God that has evolved, or is it man in the broadest sense of *homo religiosus*. I am inclined to agree with Mircea Eliade when he holds that primitive man is as fully religious as man at any stage of existence, though I am not ready to go along with him when he implies *more* fully.[3]

Neither religious man nor the structure of man's ultimate religious situation evolves, then, but rather religion as symbol system. Erich Voegelin, who I suspect shares Eliade's basic philosophical position, speaks of a development from compact to differentiated symbolization.[4] Everything already exists in some sense in the religious symbol system of the most primitive man; it would be hard to find anything later that is not "foreshadowed" there, as for example, the monotheistic God is foreshadowed in the high gods of some primitive peoples. Yet just as obviously the two cannot be equated. Not only in their idea of God but in many other ways the monotheistic religions of Judaism, Christianity, and Islam involve a much more differentiated symbolization of, and produce a much more complex relation to the ultimate conditions of human existence than do primitive religions. At least the existence of that kind of difference is the thesis I wish to develop. I hope it is clear that there are a number of other possible meanings of the term "religious evolution" with which I am not concerned. I hope it is also clear that a complex and differentiated religious symbolization is not therefore a better or a truer or a more beautiful one than a compact religious symbolization. I am not a relativist and I do think judgments of value can reasonably be made between religions, societies, or personalities. But the axis of that judgment is not provided by social evolution and if progress is used in an essentially ethical sense, then I for one will not speak of religious progress.

Having defined the ground rules under which I am operating let me now step back from the subject of religious evolution and look at a few of the massive facts of human religious history. The first of these facts is the emergence in the first millennium B.C. all across the Old World, at least in centers of high culture, of the phenomenon of religious rejection of the world characterized by an extremely negative evaluation of man and society and the exaltation of another realm of reality as alone true and infinitely valuable. This theme emerges in Greece through a long development into Plato's classic formulation in the *Phaedo* that the body is the tomb or prison of the soul, and that only by disentanglement from the body and all things worldly can the soul unify itself with the unimaginably different world of the divine. A very different formulation is found in Israel, but there too the world is profoundly devalued in the face of the transcendent God with whom alone is there any refuge or comfort. In India we find perhaps the most radical of all versions of world rejection, culminating in the great image of the Buddha, that the world is a burning house and man's urgent need is a way to escape from it. In China, Taoist ascetics urged the transvaluation of all the accepted values and withdrawal from human society, which they condemned as unnatural and perverse.

Nor was this a brief or passing phenomenon. For over two

thousand years great pulses of world rejection spread over the civilized world. The *Qur'an* compares this present world to vegetation after rain, whose growth rejoices the unbeliever, but it quickly withers away and becomes as straw.[5] Men prefer life in the present world but the life to come is infinitely superior; it alone is everlasting.[6] Even in Japan, usually so innocently world-accepting, Shōtoku Taishi declared that the world is a lie and only the Buddha is true, and in the Kamakura period the conviction that the world is hell led to orgies of religious suicide by seekers after Amida's paradise.[7] And it is hardly necessary to quote Revelations or Augustine for comparable Christian sentiments. I do not deny that there are profound differences among these various rejections of the world; Max Weber has written a great essay on the different directions of world rejection and their consequences for human action.[8] But for the moment I want to concentrate on the fact that they were all in some sense rejections, and that world rejection is characteristic of a long and important period of religious history. I want to insist on this fact because I want to contrast it with an equally striking fact, namely the virtual absence of world rejection in primitive religions, in religion prior to the first millennium B.C. and in the modern world.[9]

Primitive religions are on the whole oriented to a single cosmos; they know nothing of a wholly different world relative to which the actual world is utterly devoid of value. They are concerned with the maintenance of personal, social, and cosmic harmony and with attaining specific goods—rain, harvest, children, health—as men have always been. But the overriding goal of salvation that dominates the world rejecting religions is almost absent in primitive religion, and life after death tends to be a shadowy semiexistence in some vaguely designated place in the single world.

World rejection is no more characteristic of the modern world than it is of primitive religion. Not only in the United States but through much of Asia there is at the moment something of a religious revival, but nowhere is this associated with a great new outburst of world rejection. In Asia apologists, even for religions with a long tradition of world rejection, are much more interested in showing the compatibility of their religions with the developing modern world than in totally rejecting it. And it is hardly necessary to point out that the American religious revival stems from motives quite opposite to world rejection.

One could attempt to account for this sequence of presence and absence of world rejection as a dominant religious theme without ever raising the issue of religious evolution, but I think I can account for these and many other facts of the historical development of religion in terms of a scheme of religious evolution. An extended rationale for the scheme and its broad empirical application must await publication in book form. Here all I can attempt is a very condensed overview.

The scheme is based on several presuppositions, the most basic of which I have already referred to: That religious symbolization of what Geertz calls "the general order of existence"[10] tends to change over time, at least in some instances, in the direction of more differentiated, comprehensive, and in Weber's sense, more rationalized formulations. A second assumption is that conceptions of religious action, of the nature of the religious actor, of religious organization, and of the place of religion in the society tend to change in ways systematically related to the changes in symbolization. A third assumption is that these several changes in the sphere of religion, which constitute what I mean by religious evolution, are related to a variety of other dimensions of change in other social spheres that define the general process of sociocultural evolution.

Now, for heuristic purposes at least, it is also useful to assume a series of stages that may be regarded as relatively stable crystallizations of roughly the same order of complexity along a number of different dimensions. I shall use five stages that, for want of better terminology, I shall call primitive, archaic, historic, early modern, and modern.[11] These stages are ideal types derived from a theoretical formulation of the most generally observable historical regularities; they are meant to have a temporal reference but only in a very general sense.

Of course the scheme itself is not intended as an adequate description of historical reality. Particular lines of religious development cannot simply be forced into the terms of the scheme. In reality there may be compromise formations involving elements from two stages that I have for theoretical reasons discriminated; earlier stages may, as I have already suggested, strikingly foreshadow later developments; and more developed may regress to less developed stages. And of course no stage is ever completely abandoned; all earlier stages continue to coexist with and often within later ones. So what I shall present is not intended as a procrustean bed into which the facts of history are to be forced but a theoretical construction against which historical facts may be illuminated. The logic is much the same as that involved in conceptualizing stages of the life cycle in personality development.

Primitive Religion

Before turning to the specific features of primitive religion let us go back to the definition of religion as a set of symbolic forms and acts relating man to the ultimate conditions of his existence. Godfrey Lienhardt, in his book on Dinka religion, spells out this process of symbolization in a most interesting way:

> I have suggested that the Powers may be understood as images corresponding to complex and various combinotions of Dinka experience which are contingent upon their particular social and physical environment. For the Dinka they are the grounds of those experiences; in our analysis we have shown them to be grounded in them, for to a European the experiences are more readily understood than the Powers, and the existence of the latter cannot be posited as a condition of the former. Without these Powers or images or an alternative to them there would be for the Dinka no differentiation between experience of the self and of the world which acts upon it. Suffering, for example, could be merely "lived" or endured. With the imaging of the grounds of suffering in a particular Power, the Dinka can grasp its nature intellectually in a way which satisfies them, and thus to some extent transcend and dominate it in this act of knowledge. With this knowledge, this separation of a subject and an object in experience, there arises for them also the possibility of creating a form of experience they desire, and of freeing themselves symbolically from what they must otherwise passively endure.[12]

If we take this as a description of religious symbolization in general, and I think we can, then it is clear that in terms of the conception of evolution used here the existence of even the simplest religion is an evolutionary advance. Animals or prereligious men could only "passively endure" suffering or other limitations imposed by the conditions of their existence, but religious man can to some extent "transcend and dominate" them through his capacity for symbolization, and thus can attain a degree of freedom relative to his environment that was not previously possible.[13]

Now though Lienhardt points out that the Dinka religious images make possible a "differentiation between experience of the self and of the world which acts upon it," he also points out earlier that the Dinka lack anything closely resembling our conception of the " 'mind,' as mediating and, as it were, storing up the experiences of the self."[14] In fact, aspects of what we would attribute to the self are "imaged" among the divine Powers. Again, if Lienhardt is describing something rather general, and I think there is every reason to believe he is, then religious symbolization relating man to the ultimate conditions of his existence is also involved in relating him to himself and in symbolizing his own identity.[15]

Granted then that religious symbolization is concerned with imaging the ultimate conditions of existence, whether external or internal, we should examine at each stage the kind of symbol system involved, the kind of religious action it stimulates, the kind of social organization in which this religious action occurs, and the implications for social action in general that the religious action contains.

Marcel Mauss, criticizing the heterogeneous sources from which Lucien Lévy-Bruhl had constructed the notion of primitive thought, suggested that the word "primitive" be restricted to Australia, which was the only major culture area largely unaffected by the neolithic.[16] That was in 1923. In 1935 Lévy-Bruhl, heeding Mauss's stricture, published a book called *La Mythologie Primitive,* in which the data are drawn almost exclusively from Australia and immediately adjacent islands.[17] While Lévy-Bruhl finds material similar to his Australian data in all parts of the world, nowhere else does he find it in as pure a form. The differences between the Australian material and that of other areas are so great that Lévy-Bruhl is tempted to disagree with Durkheim that Australian religion is an elementary form of religion and term it rather "prereligion,"[18] a temptation that for reasons already indicated I would firmly reject. At any rate, W. E. H. Stanner, by far the most brilliant interpreter of Australian religion in recent years, goes far to confirm the main lines of Lévy-Bruhl's position without committing himself on the more broadly controversial aspects of the assertions of either Mauss or Lévy-Bruhl (indeed without so much as mentioning them). My description of a primitive stage of religion is a theoretical abstraction, but it is heavily indebted to the work of Lévy-Bruhl and Stanner for its main features.[19]

The *religious symbol system* at the primitive level is characterized by Lévy-Bruhl as *"le monde mythique,"* and Stanner directly translates the Australians' own word for it as "the Dreaming." The

Dreaming is a time out of time, or in Stanner's words, "everywhen," inhabited by ancestral figures, some human, some animal.[20] Though they are often of heroic proportions and have capacities beyond those of ordinary men as well as being the progenitors and creators of many particular things in the world, they are not gods, for they do not control the world and are not worshiped.[21]

Two main feautres of this mythical world of primitive religion are important for the purposes of the present theoretical scheme. The first is the very high degree to which the mythical world is related to the detailed features of the actual world. Not only is every clan and local group defined in terms of the ancestral progenitors and the mythical events of settlement, but virtually every mountain, rock, and tree is explained in terms of the actions of mythical beings. All human action is prefigured in the Dreaming, including crimes and folly, so that actual existence and the paradigmatic myths are related in the most intimate possible way.

The second main feature, not unrelated to the extreme particularity of the mythical material, is the fluidity of its organization. Lienhardt, though describing a religion of a somewhat different type, catches the essentially free-associational nature of primitive myth when he says,

> We meet here the typical lack of precise definition of the Dinka when they speak of divinities. As Garang, which is the name of the first man, is sometimes associated with the first man and sometimes said to be quite different, so Deng may in some sense be associated with anyone called Deng, and the Dinka connect or do not connect usages of the same name in different contexts according to their individual lights and to what they consider appropriate at any given moment.[22]

The fluid structure of the myth is almost consciously indicated by the Australians in their use of the word Dreaming: this is not purely metaphorical, for as Ronald Berndt has shown in a careful study, men do actually have a propensity to dream during the periods of cult performance. Through the dreams they reshape the cult symbolism for private psychic ends and, what is even more interesting, dreams may actually lead to a reinterpretation in myth that in turn causes a ritual innovation.[23] Both the particularity and the fluidity, then, help account for the hovering closeness of the world of myth to the actual world. A sense of gap, that things are not all they might be, is there, but it is hardly experienced as tragic and is indeed on the verge of being comic.[24]

Primitive *religious action* is characterized not, as we have said, by worship, nor, as we shall see, by sacrifice, but by identification, "participation," acting out. Just as the primitive symbol system is myth par excellence, so primitive religious action is ritual par excellence. In the ritual the participants become identified with the mythical beings they represent. The mythical beings are not addressed or propitiated or beseeched. The distance between man and mythical being, which was at best slight, disappears altogether in the moment of ritual when everywhen becomes now. There are no priests and no congregation, no mediating representative roles and no spectators. All present are involved in the ritual action itself and have become one with the myth.

The underlying structure of ritual, which in Australia always has themes related to initiation, is remarkably similar to that of sacrifice. The four basic movements of the ritual as analyzed by Stanner are offering, destruction, transformation, and return-communion.[25] Through acting out the mistakes and sufferings of the paradigmatic mythical hero, the new initiates come to terms symbolically with, again in Stanner's words, the "immemorial misdirection" of human life. Their former innocence is destroyed and they are transformed into new identities now more able to "assent to life, as it is, without morbidity."[26] In a sense the whole gamut of the spiritual life is already visible in the Australian ritual. Yet the symbolism is so compact that there is almost no element of choice, will, or responsibility. The religious life is as given and as fixed as the routines of daily living.

At the primitive level *religious organization* as a separate social structure does not exist. Church and society are one. Religious roles tend to be fused with other roles, and differentiations along lines of age, sex, and kin group are important. While women are not as excluded from the religious life as male ethnographers once believed, their ritual life is to some degree separate and focused on particularly feminine life crises.[27] In most primitive societies age is an important criterion for leadership in the ceremonial life. Ceremonies are often handed down in particular moieties and clans, as is only natural when the myths are so largely concerned with ancestors. Specialized shamans or medicine men are found in some tribes but are not a necessary feature of primitive religion.

As for the *social implications* of primitive religion, Durkheim's analysis still seems to be largely acceptible.[28] The ritual life does reinforce the solidarity of the society and serves to induct the young into the norms of tribal behavior. We should not forget the innovative aspects of primitive religion, that particular myths and ceremonies are in a process of constant revision and alteration, and that in the face of severe historic crisis rather remarkable reformulations of primitive material can be made.[29] Yet on the whole the religious life is the strongest reinforcement of the basic tenet of Australian philosophy, namely that life, as Stanner puts it, is a "one possibility thing." The very fluidity and flexibility of primitive religion is a barrier to radical innovation. Primitive religion gives little leverage from which to change the world.

Archaic Religion

For purposes of the present conceptual scheme, as I have indicated, I am using primitive religion in an unusually restricted sense. Much that is usually classified as primitive religion would fall in my second category, archaic religion, which includes the religious systems of much of Africa and Polynesia and some of the New World, as well as the earliest religious systems of the ancient Middle East, India, and China. The characteristic feature of archaic religion is the emergence of true cult with the complex of gods, priests, worship, sacrifice, and in some cases divine or priestly kingship. The myth and ritual complex characteristic of primitive religion continues within the structure of archaic religion, but it is systematized and elaborated in new ways.

In the archaic *religious symbol system* mythical beings are much more definitely characterized. Instead of being great paradigmatic figures with whom men in ritual identify but with whom they do not really interact, the mythical beings are more objectified, conceived as actively and somtimes willfully controlling the natural and human world, and as beings with whom men must deal in a definite and purposive way; in a word they have become gods. Relations among the gods are a matter of considerable speculation and systematization, so that definite principles of organization, especially hierarchies of control, are established. The basic worldview is still, like the primitives', monistic. There is still only one world with gods dominating particular parts of it, especially important being the high gods of the heavenly regions whose vision, knowledge, and power may be conceived as very extensive indeed.[30] But though the world is one it is far more differentiated, especially in a hierarchical way, than was the monistic worldview of the primitives: archaic religions tend to elaborate a vast cosmology in which all things divine and natural have a place. Much of the particularity and fluidity characteristic of primitive myth is still to be found in archaic religious thinking. But where priestly roles have become well established a relatively stable symbolic structure may be worked out and transmitted over an extended period of time. Especially where at least craft literacy[31] has been attained, the mythical tradition may become the object of critical reflection and innovative speculation that can lead to new developments beyond the nature of archaic religion.

Archaic *religious action* takes the form of cult in which the distinction between men as subjects and gods as objects is much more definite than in primitive religion. Because the division is sharper the need for a communication system through which gods and men can interact is much more acute. Worship and especially sacrifice are precisely such communication systems, as Henri Hubert and Marcel Mauss so brilliantly established in their great essay on sacrifice.[32] There is no space here for a technical analysis of the sacrificial process;[33] suffice it to say that a double identification of priest and victim with both gods and men effects a transformation of motives comparable to that referred to in the discussion of primitive religious action. The main difference is that instead of a relatively passive identification in an all-encompassing ritual action, the sacrificial process, no matter how stereotyped, permits the human communicants a greater element of intentionality and entails more uncertainty relative to the divine response. Through this more differentiated form of religious action a new degree of freedom as well, perhaps, as an increased burden of anxiety enters the relations between man and the ultimate conditions of his existence.

Archaic *religious organization* is still by and large merged with other social structures, but the proliferation of functionally and hierarchically differentiated groups leads to a multiplication of cults, since every group in archaic society tends to have its cultic aspect. The emergence of a two-class system, itself related to the increasing density of population made possible by agriculture, has its religious aspect. The upper-status group, which tends to monopolize political and military power, usually claims a superior religious status as well. Noble families are proud of their divine descent and often have special priestly functions. The divine king who is the chief link between his people and the gods is only the extreme case of the general tendency of archaic societies. Specialized priesthoods attached to cult centers may differentiate out but are usually kept subordinate to the political elite, which at this stage never completely divests itself of religious leadership. Occasionally priesthoods at cult centers located interstitially relative to political units—for example, Delphi in ancient Greece—may come to exercise a certain independence.

The most significant limitation on archaic religious organization is the failure to develop differentiated religious collectivities including adherents as well as priests. The cult centers provide facilities for sacrifice and worship to an essentially transient clientele that is itself not organized as a collectivity, even though the priesthood itself may be rather tightly organized. The appearance of mystery cults and related religious confraternities in the ancient world is usually related to a reorganization of the religious symbol and action systems, which indicates a transition to the next main type of religious structure.

The *social implications* of archaic religion are to some extent similar to those of primitive religion. The individual and his society are seen as merged in a natural-divine cosmos. Traditional social structures and social practices are considered to be grounded in the divinely instituted cosmic order, and there is little tension between religious demand and social conformity. Indeed, social conformity is at every point reinforced with religious sanction. Nevertheless the very notion of well-characterized gods acting over against men with a certain freedom introduces an element of openness that is less apparent at the primitive level. The struggle between rival groups may be interpreted as the struggle between rival deities or as a deity's change of favor from one group to another. Through the problems posed by religious rationalization of political change new modes of religious thinking may open up. This is clearly an important aspect of the early history of Israel, and it occurred in many other cases as well. The Greek preoccupation with the relation of the gods to the events of the Trojan War gave rise to a continuous deepening of religious thought from Homer to Euripides. In ancient China the attempt of the Chou to rationalize their conquest of the Shang led to an entirely new conception of the relation between human merit and divine favor. The breakdown of internal order led to messianic expectations of the coming of a savior king in such distant areas as

Egypt on the one hand and Chou-period China on the other. These are but a few of the ways in which the problems of maintaining archaic religious symbolization in increasingly complex societies drove toward solutions that began to place the archaic pattern itself in jeopardy.

Historic Religion

The next stage in this theoretical scheme is called historic simply because the religions included are all relatively recent; they emerged in societies that were more or less literate and so have fallen chiefly under the discipline of history rather than that of archaeology or ethnography. The criterion that distinguishes the historic religions from the archaic is that the historic religions are all in some sense transcendental. The cosmological monism of the earlier stage is now more or less completely broken through and an entirely different realm of universal reality, having for religious man the highest value, is proclaimed. The discovery of an entirely different realm of religious reality seems to imply a derogation of the value of the given empirical cosmos: at any rate the world rejection discussed above is, in this stage for the first time, a general characteristic of the religious system.

The *symbol systems* of the historic religions differ greatly among themselves but share the element of transcendentalism that sets them off from the archaic religions; in this sense they are all dualistic. The strong emphasis on hierarchical ordering characteristic of archaic religions continues to be stressed in most of the historic religions. Not only is the supernatural realm "above" this world in terms of both value and control but both the supernatural and earthly worlds are themselves organized in terms of a religiously legitimated hierarchy. For the masses, at least, the new dualism is above all expressed in the difference between this world and the life after death. Religious concern, focused on this life in primitive and archaic religions, now tends to focus on life in the other realm, which may be either infinitely superior or, in certain situations with the emergence of various conceptions of hell, infinitely worse. Under these circumstances the religious goal of salvation (or enlightenment, release, and so forth) is for the first time the central religious preoccupation.

In one sense historic religions represent a great "demythologization" relative to archaic religions. The notion of the one God who has neither court nor relatives, who has no myth himself, and who is the sole creator and ruler of the universe, the notion of self-subsistent being, or of release from the cycle of birth and rebirth, are all enormous simplifications of the ramified cosmologies of archaic religions. Yet all the historic religions have, to use Voegelin's term, mortgages imposed on them by the historical circumstances of their origin. All of them contain, in suspension as it were, elements of archaic cosmology alongside their transcendental assertions. Nonetheless, relative to earlier forms the historic religions are all universalistic. From the point of view of these religions a man is no longer defined chiefly in terms of what tribe or clan he comes from or what particular god he serves but rather as a being capable of salvation. That is to say that it is for the first time possible to conceive of man as such.

Religious action in the historic religions is thus above all action necessary for salvation. Even where elements of ritual and sacrifice remain prominent they take on a new significance. In primitive ritual the individual is put in harmony with the natural divine cosmos. His mistakes are overcome through symbolization as part of the total pattern. Through sacrifice archaic man can make up for his failures to fulfill his obligations to men or gods. He can atone for particular acts of unfaithfulness. But historic religion convicts man of a basic flaw far more serious than those conceived of by earlier religions. According to Buddhism, man's very nature is greed and anger from which he must seek a total escape. For the Hebrew prophets, man's sin is not particular wicked deeds but his profound heedlessness of God, and only a turn to complete obedience will be acceptable to the Lord. For Muhammad the *kafir* is not, as we usually translate, the "unbeliever," but rather the ungrateful man who is careless of the divine compassion. For him only Islam, willing submission to the will of God, can bring salvation.

The identity diffusion characteristic of both primitive and archaic religions is radically challenged by the historic religious symbolization, which leads for the first time to a clearly structured conception of the self. Devaluation of the empirical world and the empirical self highlights the conception of a responsible self, a core self, or a true self, deeper than the flux of everyday experience, facing a reality over against itself, a reality which has a consistency belied by the fluctuations of mere sensory impressions.[34] Primitive man can only accept the world in its manifold givenness. Archaic man can through sacrifice fulfill his religious obligations and attain peace with the gods. But the historic religions promise man for the first time that he can understand the fundamental structure of reality and through salvation participate actively in it. The opportunity is far greater than before but so is the risk of failure.

Perhaps partly because of the profound risks involved, the ideal of the religious life in the historic religions tends to be one of separation from the world. Even when, as in the case of Judaism and Islam, the religion enjoins types of worldly participation that are considered unacceptable or at least doubtful in some other historic religions, the devout are still set apart from ordinary worldlings by the massive collections of rules and obligations to which they must adhere. The early Christian solution, which, unlike the Buddhist, did allow the full possibility of salvation to the layman, nevertheless in its notion of a special state of religious perfection idealized religious withdrawal from the world. In fact the standard for lay piety tended to be closeness of approximation to the life of the religious.

Historic religion is associated with the emergence of differentiated religious collectivities as the chief characteristic of its *religious organization*. The profound dualism with respect to the conception of reality is also expressed in the social realm. The single religio-political hierarchy of archaic society tends to split into two at least partially independent hierarchies, one political and one religious. Together with the notion of a transcendent realm beyond the natural cosmos comes a new religious elite that claims direct relation to the transmundane world. Even though notions of divine kingship linger on for a very long time in various compromise forms, it is no longer possible for a divine king to monopolize religious leadership. With the emergence of a religious elite alongside the political one the problem of legitimizing political power enters a new phase. Legitimation now rests upon a delicate balance of forces between the political and religious leadership. But the differentiation between religious and political that exists most clearly at the level of leadership tends also to be pushed down into the masses so that the roles of believer and subject become distinct. Even where, as in the case of Islam, this distinction was not supported by religious norms, it was soon recognized as an actuality.

The emergence of the historic religions is part of a general shift from the two-class system of the archaic period to the four-class system characteristic of all the great historic civilizations up to modern times: a political-military elite, a cultural-religious elite, a rural lower-status group (peasantry), and an urban lower-status group (merchants and artisans). Closely associated with the new religious developments was the growth of literacy among the elite groups and in the upper segments of the urban lower class. Other social changes, such as the growth in the market resulting from the first widespread use of coinage and the development of bureaucracy and law as well as new levels of urbanization, are less directly associated with religion but are part of the same great transformation that got under way in the first millennium B.C. The distinction between religious and political elites applies to some extent to the two great lower strata. From the point of view of the historic religions the peasantry long remained relatively intractable and were often considered religiously second-class citizens, their predilection for cosmological symbolization rendering them always to some degree religiously suspect. The notion of the peasant as truly religious is a fairly modern idea. On the contrary it was the townsman who was much more likely to be numbered among the devout, and Max Weber has pointed out the great fecundity of the urban middle strata in religious innovations throughout the several great historical traditions.[35] Such groups developed new symbolizations that sometimes threatened the structure of the historic religions in their early form, and in the one case where a new stage of religious symbolization was finally achieved they made important contributions.

The *social implications* of the historic religions are implicit in the remarks on religious organization. The differentiation of a religious elite brought a new level of tension and a new possibility of conflict and change onto the social scene. Whether the confrontation was between Israelite prophet and king, Islamic ulama and sultan, Christian pope and emperor, or even between Confucian scholar-official and his ruler, it implied that political acts could be judged in terms of standards that the political authorities could not finally control. The degree to which these confrontations had serious social consequences of course depended on the degree to which the religious group was structurally independent and could exert real pressure. S. N. Eisenstadt has made a comprehensive survey of these differences;[36] for our purposes it is enough to note that they were nowhere entirely absent. Religion, then, provided the ideology and social cohesion for many rebellions and reform movements in the historic civilizations, and consequently played a more dynamic and especially a more purposive role in social change than had previously been possible. On the other hand, we should not forget that in most of the historic civilizations for long periods of time religion performed the functions we have noted from the beginning: legitimation and reinforcement of the existing social order.

Early Modern Religion

In all of the previous stages the ideal type was based on a variety of actual cases. Now for the first time it derives from a single case, or at best a congeries of related cases: namely, the Protestant Reformation. The defining characteristic of early modern religion is the collapse of the hierarchical structuring of both this and the other world. The dualism of the historic religions remains as a feature of early modern religion but takes on a new significance in the context of more direct confrontation between the two worlds. Under the new circumstances salvation is not to be found in any kind of withdrawal from the world but in the midst of worldly activities. Of course elements of this existed in the historic religions from the beginning, but on the whole the historic religions as institutionalized had offered a mediated salvation. Either conformity to religious law, participation in a sacramental system, or performance of mystical exercises was necessary for salvation. All of these to some extent involved a turning away from the world. Further, in the religious two-class systems characteristic of the institutionalized historic religions, the upper-status groups—the Christian monks or Sufi shaykhs or Buddhist ascetics—could through their pure acts and personal charisma store up a fund of grace that could then be shared with the less worthy. In this way too salvation was mediated rather than immediate. What the Reformation did was in principle, with the usual reservations and mortgages to the past, break through the whole mediated system of salvation and declare salvation potentially available to any man no matter what his station or calling might be.

Since immediate salvation seems implicit in all the historic religions it is not surprising that similar reform movements exist in other traditions, notably Shinran Shonin's version of Pure Land Buddhism, but also certain tendencies in Islam, Buddhism, Taoism, and Confucianism. But the Protestant Reformation is the only attempt that was successfully institutionalized. In the case of Taoism and Confucianism the mortgage of archaic symbolization was so heavy that what seemed a new breakthrough easily became regressive. In the other cases, notably in the case of the Jōdo Shinshū, the radical implications were not sustained and a religion of mediated salvation soon reasserted itself. Religious movements of the early modern type may be emerging in a number of the great traditions today, perhaps even in the Vatican Council, and there are also secular movements with features strongly analogous to what I call early modern religion. But all of these tendencies are too uncertain to rely on in constructing an ideal type.

Early modern *religious symbolism* concentrates on the direct relation between the individual and transcendent reality. A great deal of the cosmological baggage of medieval Christianity is dropped as superstition. The fundamentally ritualist interpretation of the sacrament of the Eucharist as a reenactment of the paradigmatic sacrifice is replaced with the antiritualist interpretation of the Eucharist as a commemoration of a once-and-for-all historical event. Even though in one sense the world is more devalued in early Protestantism than in medieval Christianity, since the reformers reemphasized the radical separation between divine and human, still by proclaiming the world as the theater of God's glory and the place wherein to fulfill his command, the Reformation reinforced positive autonomous action in the world instead of a relatively passive acceptance of it.

Religious action was now conceived to be identical with the whole of life. Special ascetic and devotional practices were dropped as well as the monastic roles that specialized in them; instead the service of God became a total demand in every walk of life. The stress was on faith, an internal quality of the person, rather than on particular acts clearly marked "religious." In this respect the process of identity unification that I have designated as a central feature of the historic religions advanced still further. The complex requirements for the attainment of salvation in the historic religions, though ideally they encouraged identity unification, could themselves become a new form of identity diffusion, as Luther and Shinran were aware. Assertion of the capacity for faith as an already received gift made it possible to undercut that difficulty. It also made it necessary to accept the ambiguity of human ethical life and the fact that salvation comes in spite of sin, not in its absolute absence. With the acceptance of the world not as it is but as a valid arena in which to work out the divine command, and with the acceptance of the self as capable of faith in spite of sin, the Reformation made it possible to turn away from world rejection in a way not possible in the historic religions. All of this was possible, however, only within the structure of a rigid orthodoxy and a tight though voluntaristic religious group.

I have already noted that early modern religion abandoned hierarchy as an essential dimension of its religious symbol system.[37] It did the same in its *religious organization.* Not only did it reject papal authority, but it also rejected the old form of the religious distinction between two levels of relative religious perfection. This was replaced with a new kind of religious two-class system: the division between elect and reprobates. The new form differed from the old one in that the elect were really a vanguard group in the fulfillment of the divine plan rather than a qualitative religious elite. The political implications of Protestantism had much to do with the overthrow of the old conception of hierarchy in the secular field as well. Where Calvinistic Protestantism was powerful, hereditary aristocracy and kingship were either greatly weakened or abandoned. In fact the Reformation is part of the general process of social change in which the four-class system of peasant societies began to break up in Europe. Especially in the Anglo-Saxon world Protestantism greatly contributed to its replacement by a more flexible multicentered mode of social organization based more on contract and voluntary association. Both church and state lost some of the reified significance they had in medieval times and later on the continent. The roles of church member and citizen were two among several. Both church and state had their delimited spheres of authority, but with the full institutionalization of the common law neither had a right to dominate each other or the whole of society. Nonetheless, the church acted for a long time as a sort of cultural and ethical holding company, and many developments in philosophy, literature, and social welfare took their initiative from clerical or church groups.[38]

The *social implications* of the Protestant Reformation are among the more debated subjects of contemporary social science. Lacking space to defend my assertions, let me simply say that I stand with Weber, Merton, *et al.,* in attributing very great significance to the Reformation, especially in its Calvinistic wing, in a whole series of developments from economics to science, from education to law. Whereas in most of the historic civilizations religion stands as virtually the only stable challenger to the dominance of the political elite, in the emerging early modern society religious impulses give rise to a variety of institutional structures, from the beginning or very soon becoming fully secular, which stand beside and to some extent compete with and limit the state. The direct religious response to political and moral problems does not disappear, but the impact of religious orientations on society is also mediated by a variety of worldly institutions in which religious values have been expressed. Weber's critics, frequently assuming a premodern model of the relation between religion and society, have often failed to understand the subtle interconnections he was tracing. But the contrast with the historic stage, when pressures toward social change in the direction of value realization were sporadic and often utopian, is decisive.

In the early modern stage for the first time pressures to social change in the direction of greater realization of religious values are actually institutionalized as part of the structure of the society itself. The self-revising social order expressed in a voluntaristic and democratic society can be seen as just such an outcome. The earliest phase of this development, especially the several examples of Calvinist commonwealths, was voluntaristic only within the elect vanguard group and otherwise was often illiberal and even dictatorial. The transition toward a more completely democratic society was complex and subject to many blockages. Close analogies to the early modern situation occur in many of the contemporary developing countries, which are trying for the first time to construct social systems with a built-in tendency to change in the direction of greater value realization. The leadership of these countries varies widely between several kinds of vanguard revolutionary movements with distinctly illiberal proclivities to elites committed to the implementation of a later, more democratic, model of Western political society.

Modern Religion

I am not sure whether in the long run what I call early modern religion will appear as a stage with the same degree of distinctness as the others I have distinguished or whether it will appear only as a transitional phase, but I am reasonably sure that, even though we must speak from the midst of it, the modern situation represents a stage of religious development in many ways profoundly different from that of historic religion. The central feature of the change is the collapse of the dualism that was so crucial to all the historic religions.

It is difficult to speak of a *modern religious symbol system.* It is indeed an open question whether there can be a religious symbol system analogous to any of the preceding ones in the modern situation, which is characterized by a deepening analysis of the very nature of symbolization itself. At the highest intellectual level I would trace the fundamental break with traditional historic symbolization to the work of Kant. By revealing the problematic nature of the traditional metaphysical basis of all the religions, and by indicating that it is not so much a question of two worlds as it is of as many worlds as there are modes of apprehending them, he placed the whole religious problem in a new light. However simple the immediate result of his grounding religion in the structure of ethical life rather than in a metaphysics claiming cognitive adequacy, it nonetheless pointed decisively in the direction that modern religion would go. The entire modern analysis of religion, including much of the most important recent theology, though rejecting Kant's narrowly rational ethics, has been forced to ground religion in the structure of the human situation itself.

In this respect the present paper is a symptom of the modern religious situation as well as an analysis of it. In the worldview that has emerged from the tremendous intellectual advances of the last two centuries there is simply no room for a hierarchic dualistic religious symbol system of the classical historic type. This is not to be interpreted as a return to primitive monism: it is not that a single world has replaced a double one but that an infinitely multiplex one has replaced the simple duplex structure. It is not that life has become again a "one possibility thing" but that it has become an infinite possibility thing. The analysis of modern man as secular, materialistic, dehumanized, and in the deepest sense areligious seems to me fundamentally misguided, for such a judgment is based on standards that cannot adequately gauge the modern temper.

Though it is central to the problems of modern religion, space forbids a review of the development of the modern analysis of religion on its scholarly and scientific side. Hence I shall confine myself to some brief comments on directions of development within Protestant theology. In many respects Friedrich Schleiermacher is the key figure in early nineteenth-century theology who saw the deeper implications of the Kantian breakthrough. The development of "liberal theology" in the later nineteenth century, partly on the basis of Schleiermacher's beginnings, tended to fall back into Kant's overly rational limitations. Against this, Barth's reassertion of the power of the traditional symbolism was bound to produce a vigorous response, but unfortunately, due to Barth's own profound ambiguity on the ultimate status of dogma, the consequences were in part simply a regressive reassertion of the adequacy of the early modern theological formulation. By the middle of the twentieth century, however, the deeper implications of Schleiermacher's attempt were being developed in various ways by such diverse figures as Paul Tillich, Rudolf Bultmann, and Dietrich Bonhoeffer.[39] Tillich's assertion of "ecstatic naturalism," Bultmann's program of "demythologization," and Bonhoeffer's search for a "religionless Christianity," though they cannot be simply equated with each other, are efforts to come to terms with the modern situation. Even on the Catholic side the situation is beginning to be recognized.

Interestingly enough, indications of the same general search for an entirely new mode of religious symbolization, though mostly confined to the Protestant West, also appear in that most developed of the non-Western countries, Japan. Uchimura Kanzō's nonchurch Christianity was a relatively early indication of a search for new directions, and is being developed even further today. Even more interesting perhaps is the emergence of a similar development out of the Jōdo Shinshū tradition, at least in the person of Ienaga Saburo.[40] This example indeed suggests that highly "modern" implications exist in more than one stand of Mahayana Buddhism and perhaps several of the other great traditions as well. Although in my opinion these implications were never developed sufficiently to dominate a historical epoch as they did in the West in the last two centuries, they may well prove decisive in the future of these religions.

So far what I have been saying applies mainly to intellectuals, but at least some evidence indicates that changes are also occurring at the level of mass religiosity.[41] Behind the 96 per cent of Americans who claim to believe in God[42] there are many instances of a massive reinterpretation that leaves Tillich, Bultmann, and Bonhoeffer far behind. In fact, for many churchgoers the obligation of doctrinal orthodoxy sits lightly indeed, and the idea that all creedal statements must receive a personal reinterpretation is widely accepted. The dualistic worldview certainly persists in the minds of many of the devout, but just as surely many others have developed elaborate and often pusedoscientific rationalizations to bring their faith in its experienced validity into some kind of cognitive harmony with the twentieth-century world. The wave of popular response that some of the newer theology seems to be eliciting is another indication that not only the intellectuals find themselves in a new religious situation.[43]

To concentrate on the church in a discussion of the modern religious situation is already misleading, for it is precisely the characteristic of the new situation that the great problem of religion as I have defined it, the symbolization of man's relation to the ultimate conditions of his existence, is no longer the monopoly of any groups explicitly labeled religious. However much the development of Western Christianity may have led up to and in a sense created the modern religious situation, it just as obviously is no longer in control of it. Not only has any obligation of doctrinal orthodoxy been abandoned by the leading edge of modern culture, but every fixed position has become open to question in the process of making sense out of man and his situation. This involves a profounder commitment to the process I have been calling religious symbolization than ever before. The historic religions discovered the self; the early modern religion found a doctrinal basis on which to accept the self in all its empirical ambiguity; modern religion is beginning to understand the laws of the self's own existence and so to help man take responsibility for his own fate.

This statement is not intended to imply a simple liberal optimism, for the modern analysis of man has also disclosed the depths of the limitations imposed by man's situation. Nevertheless, the fundamental symbolization of modern man and his situation is that of a dynamic multidimensional self capable, within limits, of continual self-transformation and capable, again within limits, of remaking the world, including the very symbolic forms with which he deals with it, even the forms that state the unalterable conditions of his own existence. Such a statement should not be taken to mean that I expect, even less that I advocate, some ghastly religion of social science. Rather, I expect traditional religious symbolism to be maintained and developed in new directions, but with growing awareness that it is symbolism and that man in the last analysis is responsible for the choice of his symbolism. Naturally, continuation of the symbolization characteristic of earlier stages without any reinterpretation is to be expected among many in the modern world, just as it has occurred in every previous period.

Religious action in the modern period is, I think, clearly a continuation of tendencies already evident in the early modern stage. Now less than ever can man's search for meaning be confined to the church. But with the collapse of a clearly defined doctrinal orthodoxy and a religiously supported objective system of moral standards, religious action in the world becomes more demanding than ever. The search for adequate standards of action, which is at the same time a search for personal maturity and social relevance, is in itself the heart of the modern quest for salvation, if I may divest that word of its dualistic associations. How the specifically religious bodies are to adjust their time-honored practices of worship and devotion to modern conditions is of growing concern in religious circles. Such diverse movements as the liturgical revival, pastoral psychology, and renewed emphasis on social action are all efforts to meet the present need. Few of these trends have gotten much beyond the experimental stage but we can expect the experiments to continue.

In the modern situation as I have defined it, one might almost be tempted to see in Thomas Paine's "My mind is my church" or in Thomas Jefferson's "I am a sect myself" the typical expression of *religious organization* in the near future. Nonetheless it seems unlikely that collective symbolization of the great inescapabilities of life will soon disappear. Of course the "free intellectual" will continue to exist as he has for millennia, but such a solution can hardly be very general. Private voluntary religious association in the West achieved full legitimation for the first time in the early modern situation, but in the early stages especially, discipline and control within these groups was very intense. The tendency in more recent periods has been to continue the basic pattern but with a much more open and flexible pattern of membership. In accord with general trends I have already discussed, standards of doctrinal orthodoxy and attempts to enforce moral purity have largely been dropped. The assumption in most of the major Protestant denominations is that the church member can be considered responsible for himself. This trend seems likely to continue, with an increasingly fluid type of organization in which many special purpose subgroups form and disband. Rather than interpreting these trends as significant of indifference and secularization, I see in them the increasing acceptance of the notion that each individual must work out his own ultimate solutions and that the most the church can do is provide him a favorable environment for doing so, without imposing on him a prefabricated set of answers.[44] And it will be increasingly realized that answers to religious questions can validly be sought in various spheres of "secular" art and thought.

Here I can only suggest what I take to be the main *social implication* of the modern religious situation. Early modern society, to a considerable degree under religious pressure, developed, as we have seen, the notion of a self-revising social system in the form of a democratic society. But at least in the early phase of that development social flexibility was balanced against doctrinal (Protestant orthodoxy) and characterological (Puritan personality) rigidities. In a sense those rigidities were necessary to allow the flexibility to emerge in the social system, but it is the chief characteristic of the more recent modern phase that culture and personality themselves have come to be viewed as endlessly revisable. This has been characterized as a collapse of meaning and a failure of moral standards. No doubt the possibilities for pathological distortion in the modern situation are enormous. It remains to be seen whether the freedom modern society implies at the cultural and personality as well as at the social level can be stably institutionalized in large-scale societies. Yet the very situation that has been characterized as one of the collapse of meaning and the failure of moral standards can also, and I would argue more fruitfully, be viewed as one offering unprecedented opportunities for creative innovation in every sphere of human action.

Conclusion

The schematic presentation of the stages of religious evolution just concluded is based on the proposition that at each stage the freedom of personality and society has increased relative to the environing conditions. Freedom has increased because at each successive stage the relation of man to the conditions of his existence has been conceived as more complex, more open and more subject to change and development. The distinction between conditions that are really ultimate and those that are alterable becomes increasingly clear though never complete. Of course this scheme of religious evolution has implied at almost every point a general theory of social evolution, which has had to remain largely implicit.

Let me suggest in closing, as a modest effort at empirical testing, how the evolutionary scheme may help to explain the facts of alternating world acceptance and rejection that were noted near the beginning of the paper. I have argued that the world acceptance of the primitive and archaic levels is largely to be explained as the only possible response to a reality that invades the self to such an extent that the symbolizations of self and world are only very partially separate. The great wave of world rejection of the historic religions I have interpreted as a major advance in what Lienhardt calls "the differentiation between experience of the self and of the world which acts upon it." Only by withdrawing cathexis from the myriad objects of empirical reality could consciousness of a centered self in relation to an encompassing reality emerge. Early modern religion made it possible to maintain the centered self without denying the multifold empirical reality, and so made world rejection in the classical sense unnecessary. In the modern phase knowledge of the laws of the formation of the self, as well as much more about the structure of the world, has opened up almost unlimited new directions of exploration and development. World rejection marks the beginning of a clear objectification of the social order and sharp criticism of it. In the earlier world-accepting phases religious conceptions and social order were so fused that it was almost impossible to criticize the latter from the point of view of the former. In the later phases the possibility of remaking the world to conform to value demands has served in a very different way to mute the extremes of world rejection. The world acceptance of the last two stages is shown in this analysis to have a profoundly different significance from that of the first two.

Construction of a wide-ranging evolutionary scheme like the one presented here is an extremely risky enterprise. Nevertheless such efforts are justifiable if, by throwing light on perplexing developmental problems, they contribute to modern man's efforts at self-interpretation.

NOTES

1 Chantepie de la Saussaye, *Manuel d'Histoire des Religions,* French translation directed by H. Hubert and I. Levy (Paris: Colin, 1904), author's introduction.

2 Clifford Geertz, "Religion as a Cultural System," in Michael Banton, ed., *Anthropological Approaches to the Study of Religion* (New York: Praeger, 1966).

3 Mircea Eliade, *Patterns in Comparative Religion* (New York: Sheed & Ward, 1958), pp. 459–65.

4 Erich Voegelin, *Order and History,* Vol. I: *Israel and Revelation* (Baton Rouge: La. State Univ. Press, 1956), p. 5.

5 *Qur'an* 57, 19–20.

6 *Qur'an* 87, 16–17.

7 On these developments see Ienaga Saburo, *Nihon Shisoshi ni okeru Hitei no Ronri no Hattatsu* (The Development of the Logic of Negation in the History of Japanese Thought) (Tokyo: 1940).

8 Max Weber, "Religious Rejections of the World and Their Directions," in Hans H. Gerth and C. Wright Mills, eds., *From Max Weber* (New York: Oxford Univ. Press, 1946).

9 One might argue that the much-discussed modern phenomenon of alienation is the same as world rejection. The concept of alienation has too many uses to receive full discussion here, but it usually implies estrangement from or rejection of only selected aspects of the empirical world. In the contemporary world a really radical alienation from the whole of empirical reality would be discussed more in terms of psychosis than religion.

10 Geertz, *op. cit.*

11 These stages are actually derived from an attempt to develop a general schema of sociocultural evolution during the seminar in which I participated, together with Talcott Parsons and S. N. Eisenstadt. This paper must, however, be strictly limited to religious evolution, which is in itself sufficiently complex without going into still broader issues.

12 Godfrey Lienhardt, *Divinity and Experience* (London: Oxford Univ. Press, 1961), p. 170.

13 One might argue that it was language and not religion that gave man the capacity to dominate his environment symbolically, but this seems to be a false distinction. It is very unlikely that language came into existence "first" and that men then "thought up" religion. Rather, we would suppose that religion in the sense of this paper was from the beginning a major element in the *content* of linguistic symbolization. Clearly the relations between language and religion are very important and require much more systematic investigation.

14 Lienhardt, *op. cit.,* p. 149.

15 This notion was first clearly expressed to me in conversation and in unpublished writings by Eli Sagan.

16 In his discussion of Lévy-Bruhl's thesis on primitive mentality, reported in *Bulletin de la Société française de Philosophie,* Séance du 15 Febrier 1923, 23e année (1923), p. 26.

17 Lucien Lévy-Bruhl, *La Mythologie Primitive* (Paris: Alcan, 1935). This volume and Lévy-Bruhl's last volume, *L'Experience Mystique et les Symboles Chez les Primitifs* (Paris: Alcan, 1938), were recently praised by Evans-Pritchard as unsurpassed in "depth and insight" among studies of the structure of primitive thought in his introduction to the English translation of Robert Hertz, *Death and the Right Hand* (New York: Free Press, 1960), p. 24. These are the only two volumes of Lévy-Bruhl on primitive thought that have not been translated into English.

18 Lévy-Bruhl, *La Mythologie Primitive, op. cit.,* p. 217.

19 Of Stanner's publications the most relevant are a series of articles published under the general title "On Aboriginal Religion" in *Oceania,* 30–33 (1959–63), and "The Dreaming" in T. A. G. Hungerford, ed., *Australian Signpost* (Melbourne: Cheshire, 1956), and reprinted in William Lessa and Evon Z. Vogt, eds., *Reader in Comparative Religion* (Evanston, Ill.: Row, Peterson, 1958). (References to "The Dreaming" are to the Lessa and Vogt volume.) Outside the Australian culture area, the new world provides the most examples of the type of religion I call primitive. Navaho religion, for example, conforms closely to the type.

20 Stanner, "The Dreaming," *op. cit.,* p. 514.

21 This is a controversial point. For an extensive bibliography see Eliade, *op. cit.,* p. 112. Eliade tends to accept the notion of high gods in Australia, but Stanner says of the two figures most often cited as high gods: "Not even by straining can one see in such culture heroes as Baiame and Darumulum the true hint of a Yahveh, jealous, omniscient and omnipotent." "The Dreaming," *op. cit.,* p. 518.

22 Lienhardt, *op. cit.,* p. 91.

23 Ronald Berndt, *Kunapipi* (Melbourne: Cheshire, 1951), pp. 71–84.

24 Stanner, "On Aboriginal Religion I," *Oceania,* 30 (December 1959): 126; Lienhardt, *op. cit.,* p. 53.

25 Stanner, *op. cit.,* p. 118. The Navaho ritual system is based on the

same principles and also stresses the initiation theme. See Katherine Spencer, *Mythology and Values: An Analysis of Navaho Chantway Myths* (Philadelphia: American Folklore Society, 1957). A very similar four-act structure has been discerned in the Christian eucharist by Dom Gregory Dix in *The Shape of the Liturgy* (Westminster: Dacre Press, 1943).

26 Stanner, "On Aboriginal Religion II," *Oceania,* 30 (June 1960): 278. Of ritual Stanner says: "Personality may almost be seen to change under one's eyes." "On Aboriginal Religion I," *op. cit.,* p. 126.

27 Catherine Berndt, *Women's Changing Ceremonies in Northern Australia* (Paris: Herman, 1950).

28 Emile Durkheim, *The Elementary Forms of the Religious Life* (Glencoe, Ill.: The Free Press, 1947).

29 Anthony Wallace, "Revitalization Movements," *American Anthropologist,* 58 (April 1956): 264–79.

30 Raffaele Pettazzoni, *The All-Knowing God* (London: Methuen, 1956).

31 By "craft literacy" I mean the situation in which literacy is limited to specially trained scribes and is not a capacity generally shared by the upper-status group. For an interesting discussion of the development of literacy in ancient Greece see Eric Havelock, *Preface to Plato* (Cambridge: Harvard Univ. Press, 1963).

32 Henri Hubert and Marcel Mauss, "Essai sur la nature et la fonction du Sacrifice," *L'Année Sociologique,* 2 (1899).

33 Two outstanding recent empirical studies are E. E. Evans-Pritchard, *Nuer Religion* (London: Oxford, 1956), esp. chaps. 8–11, and Lienhardt, *op. cit.,* esp. chaps. 7 and 8.

34 Buddhism, with its doctrine of the ultimate nonexistence of the self, seems to be an exception to this generalization, but for practical and ethical purposes, at least, a distinction between the true self and the empirical self is made by all schools of Buddhism. Some schools of Mahayana Buddhism give a metaphysical basis to a notion of "basic self" or "great self" as opposed to the merely selfish self caught up in transience and desire. Further, it would seem that *nirvana,* defined negatively so as rigorously to exclude any possibility of transience or change, serves fundamentally as an identity symbol. Of course the social and psychological consequences of this kind of identity symbol are very different from those following from other types of identity symbolization.

35 Max Weber, *The Sociology of Religion,* trans. Ephriam Fischoff (Boston: Beacon Press, 1963), pp. 95–98, etc.

36 S. N. Eisenstadt, "Religious Organizations and Political Process in Centralized Empires," *Journal of Asian Studies,* 21 (May 1962): 271–

94, and also his *The Political Systems of Empires* (New York: Free Press, 1963).

37 God, of course, remains hierarchically superior to man, but the complex stratified structure of which purgatory, saints, angels, and so on, are elements is eliminated. Also, the strong reassertion of covenant thinking brought a kind of formal equality into the God-man relation without eliminating the element of hierarchy. Strictly speaking then, early modern (and modern) religion does not abandon the idea of hierarchy as such, but retains it in a much more flexible form, relative to particular contexts, and closely related to new emphases on equality. What is abandoned is rather a single overarching hierarchy, summed up in the symbol of the great chain of being.

38 Of course, important developments in modern culture stemming from the recovery of classical art and philosophy in the Renaissance took place outside the mainstream of religious development. However, the deep interrelations between religious and secular components of the Renaissance should not be overlooked. Certainly the clergy in the Anglo-Saxon world were among the foremost guardians of the classical tradition in literature and thought. The most tangible expression of this was the close relation of higher education to the church, a relation that was not seriously weakened until the late nineteenth century in America.

39 Paul Tillich, *The Courage to Be* (New Haven: Yale Univ. Press, 1952); Karl Jaspers and Rudolf Bultmann, *Myth and Christianity* (New York: Noonday Press, 1958); Dietrich Bonhoeffer, *Letters and Papers from Prison* (London: SCM Press, 1954). Numerous other works of these three theologians could be cited.

40 Robert N. Bellah, "Ienaga Saburo and the Search for Meaning in Modern Japan," in Marius Jansen, ed., *Japanese Attitudes toward Modernization* (Princeton: Princeton Univ. Press, 1965).

41 There are a few scattered studies such as Gordon Allport, James Gillespie, and Jacqueline Young, "The Religion of the Post-War College Student," *The Journal of Psychology,* 25 (January 1948): 3–33, but the subject does not lend itself well to investigation via questionnaires and brief interviews. Richard V. McCann in his Harvard doctoral dissertation, "The Nature and Varieties of Religious Change," 1955, utilized a much subtler approach involving depth interviewing and discovered a great deal of innovative reinterpretation in people from all walks of life. Unfortunately, lack of control of sampling makes it impossible to generalize his results.

42 Will Herberg, *Protestant, Catholic, Jew* (Garden City, N.Y.: Doubleday & Co., 1955), p. 72.

43 Bishop J. A. T. Robinson's *Honest to God* (Philadelphia: Westminster Press, 1963), which states in straightforward language the posi-

tions of some of the recent Protestant theologians mentioned above, has sold (by November 1963) over 300,000 copies in England and over 71,000 in the United States, with another 50,000 on order, and this in the first few months after publication. (Reported in *Christianity and Crisis,* 23 [November 11, 1963]: 201.)

44 The great Protestant stress on thinking for oneself in matters of religion is documented in Gerhard Lenski, *The Religious Factor* (Garden City, N.Y.: Doubleday & Co., 1961), pp. 270–73.

PART TWO

Religion in the Modernization Process

THE CHAPTERS in Part II are concerned with the role of religion in the great transition from traditional peasant society to modern industrial society. It therefore expands on the treatment of early modern religion, the fourth stage of religious evolution as outlined in Part I. The role of Protestantism in the development of the modern West, especially as it was brilliantly formulated in the work of Max Weber, lies in the background of all the chapters in this section. But whereas Weber concentrated mainly on the role of religion in man's economic life, the major area to which religion is related in these chapters is the political. Chapters 3 and 4 attempt a general consideration of the role of Protestantism and its functional analogues in non-Western societies. Chapter 5 is an attempt to deal anew with the great problem with which Weber dealt in the last chapter of his *Religion of China,* the contrasting social implications of Western Christianity and Chinese Confucianism. Chapters 6 and 7 deal with Japanese religion in the modernization process and Chapter 8 treats Islam in the same context. Chapter 9 is concerned with the relation between religion and national integration in the United States. The idea of a civil religion developed in that chapter can itself be extended in comparative perspective. Some hints of such a perspective are to be found in the earlier chapters in this section, but this is still largely a job for the future. A major essay of mine that treats the problems of religion and modernization is the epilogue to a book that I edited, *Religion and Progress in Modern Asia.* More monographic consideration of some aspects of the Japanese case can be found in *Tokugawa Religion* and in my articles on Ienaga Saburō and Watsuji Tetsurō.*

**See the Bibliography for full citation of these articles.*

3 Reflections on the Protestant Ethic Analogy in Asia

THE WORK of Max Weber, especially the so-called "Protestant Ethic hypothesis," continues to exercise an impressive influence on current research in the social sciences, as a glance at recent journals and monographs will quickly show.[1] The great bulk of this research is concerned with refining the Weberian thesis about the differential effects of Protestant compared with Catholic religious orientations in the sphere of economic activity. In recent years, however, there have been increasing though still scattered attempts to apply Weber's argument to material drawn from various parts of Asia. The present paper will not undertake to review these attempts with any completeness. Rather, it will be devoted to a selective consideration of several different approaches to the problem with a view to determining some of their possibilities and limitations.

Perhaps the commonest approach has been to interpret the Weber hypothesis in terms of the economists' emphasis on the importance of entrepreneurship in the process of economic development. Weber's "Protestant Ethic" is seen as an ideological orientation tending to lead those who hold it into an entrepreneurial role where they then contribute to economic growth. I will consider shortly how serious this oversimplification of Weber's view distorts his intention. At any rate, those who have taken this interpretation have proceeded to analyze various Asian religious groups to see whether examples of

This chapter grew out of a paper presented in April 1962 at the annual meeting of the Association for Asian Studies held in Boston. It is an effort to place the argument of my book Tokugawa Religion *in a broader perspective by considering a number of Asian cases where analogies to Weber's Protestant Ethic thesis had been claimed. To some extent the argument of this chapter is a response to and an acceptance of some of the criticisms of* Tokugawa Religion *that appeared in Japanese reviews, particularly that of Maruyama Masao.*

this-worldly asceticism, the religious significance of work in a calling, and so forth, have been associated with successful economic activity. Cases in which the association has been claimed include in Japan Jōdo and Zen Buddhists and the Hōtoku and Shingaku movements; in Java the Santri Muslims; in India the Jains, Parsis, and various business or merchant castes, and so forth.[2] David C. McClelland has recently subsumed a number of such examples under the general rubric of "Positive Mysticism," within which he finds Weber's Protestant example to be merely a special case.[3]

Whether or not the claim to have discovered a religious ethic analogous to Weber's type case can be substantiated in all of these Asian examples, this general approach has much to recommend it. For one thing it calls attention to the motivational factor that historians, economists and sociologists have often overlooked. For another it calls attention to subtle and nonobvious connections between cultural and religious beliefs and behavioral outcomes. This latter point is one that some readers of Weber have consistently failed to understand, Kurt Samuelson being merely one of the more recent examples. The latter claims, in refutation of Weber, that since the Puritan fathers did not espouse a materialistic dog-eat-dog capitalism their theology could not possibly have led to its development.[4] Milton Singer, on the other hand, proves himself a more discerning pupil of Weber when he argues that economic development is not supported merely by "materialistic" values but may be advanced by an "ethic of austerity," based perhaps in the case of India on the tradition of religious asceticism.[5]

But the application of the "entrepreneurship model" or motivational approach to Weber's thesis has certain grave limitations. Some of the difficulty lies in the original essay itself when it is not grasped in its proper relation to the whole of Weber's work. One of the most serious of these limitations is the emphasis on the importance of the motivational factor at the expense of the historical and institutional setting.

However important motivational factors may be, they have proven time and again to be highly sensitive to shifts in institutional arrangements. The consequences for economic development depend as much on the institutional channeling of motivation as on the presence of absence of certain kinds of motivation. For example, the entrepreneurial potential of the Japanese samurai, who from at least the sixteenth century comprised what most observers would agree was the most achievement-oriented group in Japan, could not be realized until the Meiji period when legal restraints on their entering trade were abolished and their political responsibilities eliminated. Chinese merchants who made an indifferent showing within the institutional limitations of imperial China turned into a vigorous capitalist class under more favorable conditions in Southeast Asia. Clifford Geertz has shown how the Muslim Santri group in Java, characterized by a long merchant tradition and a favorable religious ethic, began to burgeon into entrepreneurship under favorable economic conditions early in this century, only to wither on the vine when economic conditions worsened markedly during the Great Depression.[6] Gustav Papanek in a recent paper has indicated how several relatively small "communities" (quasi castes) of traditional traders were able to spearhead Pakistan's remarkable industrial growth in recent years by taking advantage of highly favorable economic conditions that had not previously existed.[7] On the basis of such examples one might argue that there exists in most Asian countries a small but significant minority that has the motivation necessary for entrepreneurial activity. If this is the case, then, it would be advisable to consider motivation in close connection with institutional structure and its historical development.

In *The Protestant Ethic and the Spirit of Capitalism,* Weber himself seems to lean rather heavily on the motivational variable, and this may be what has led some of his readers astray. In the later comparative studies in the sociology of religion, however, we get a much more balanced view and an implicit correction of emphasis in the earlier work. Following Weber's comparative studies a number of students have undertaken what might be called an "institutional approach," attempting to discern institutional factors favorable or unfavorable to economic development. Examples of this kind of study are Albert Feuerwerker's monograph, *China's Early Industrialization,*[8] my *Tokugawa Religion,* about the inadequacies of which I will speak in a moment, Joseph Elder's dissertation on India,[9] and perhaps the most comprehensive in scope and historical coverage, Clifford Geertz's work on Java contained in a number of published and unpublished writings.[10] In all of these studies Weber's emphasis on the religious ethic continues to receive a central focus. It is seen, however, not simply in relation to personal motivation but also as embodied in or related to a wide range of institutional structures. Feuerwerker writes, ". . . one institutional breakthrough is worth a dozen textile mills or shipping companies established within the framework of the traditional society and its system of values."[11] And Geertz says in a similar vein:

> The extent and excellence of a nation's resources, the size and skill of its labor force, the scope and complexity of its productive "plant," and the distribution and value of entrepreneurial abilities among its population are only one element in the assessment of its capacity for economic growth; the institutional arrangements by means of which these various factors can be brought to bear on any particular economic goal is another. . . . It is for this reason that economic development in "underdeveloped" areas implies much more than capital transfers, technical aid, and ideological exhortation: it demands a deep going transformation of the basic structure of society and, beyond that, perhaps even in the underlying value-system of which that structure operates.[12]

My study of Tokugawa Japan, taking a somewhat more optimistic approach to traditional society, stressed the extent to which traditional Japanese institutions were or could under certain circumstances be made to be favorable to economic development. In so doing I drew a number of parallels between certain aspects of "rationalization" in Japan and the rationalization Weber was talking about in the West. It was precisely on this point that Maruyama Masao's review in the April 1958 issue of *Kokka Gakkai Zasshi* was sharply critical.[13] Without denying that a number of the mechanisms I discussed—for example, the concentration of loyalty in the emperor—may have been effective in bringing about certain social changes contributing to economic growth, he points out that they were far from rational in Weber's sense, and indeed had profoundly irrational consequences in subsequent Japanese development, not the least of which were important economic inefficiencies.

With Maruyama's strictures in mind one is perhaps better able to deal with some remarks of Milton Singer near the end of his sensitive and illuminating review article on Weber's *Religion of India:*

> To evaluate Weber's conclusions is not easy. In view of the complexity of Hinduism, and of Asian religions generally, any characterization of them or any comparison of them with Western religion is going to involve large simplifications. Certainly Weber has brilliantly constructed a characterization based on an impressive knowledge of both textual and contextual studies. But one may wonder whether the construction does justice to elements of Asian religions. Some of these are: a strand of this-worldly asceticism; the economic rationality of merchants, craftsmen, and peasants; the logically-consistent system of impersonal determinism

in Vedānta and Buddhism, with direct consequences for a secular ethic; the development of "rational empirical" science; religious individualism; and personal monotheism. Weber is certainly aware of all these elements and discusses them in his study. . . . But in the construction of the "Spirit" he does not give very much weight to these elements. With the evidence today before us of politically independent Asian states actively planning their social, economic, and scientific and technical development, we would attach a good deal more importance to these elements and see less conflict between them and the religious "spirit."[14]

For Maruyama the mere *presence* of rational elements, for which I argued in the Japanese case along lines quite parallel to those of Singer, is simply not enough if they exist passively side by side with irrational elements (as they do in both Japanese and Indian cases), and are not pushed though "methodically and systematically" to their conclusion as they were in Weber's paradigmatic case of Protestantism. If Maruyama is right, and I am coming increasingly to believe that he is, then it becomes necessary to press beyond both the motivational and the institutional approaches and to view matters in an even broader perspective as the above quotation from Geertz already hinted.

Concretely, this means that we are forced to take seriously Weber's argument for the special significance of Protestantism. The search through Asia for religious movements that here and there have motivational or institutional components analogous to the Protestant Ethic ultimately proves inadequate. The Protestant Reformation is not after all some mere special case of a more general category. It stands in Weber's whole work, not in the *Protestant Ethic* essay alone, as the symbolic representative of a fundamental change in social and cultural structure with the most radical and far-reaching consequences. The proper analogy in Asia then turns out to be, not this or that motivational or institutional component, but reformation itself. What we need to discern is the "transformation of the basic structure of society" and its "underlying value-system," to use Geertz's language. Before trying to discover some examples of this structural approach to the Protestant Ethic analogy in Asia, it is necessary to note briefly that we see here an example of what must occur in any really serious confrontation with Asian examples: we are forced back to a reconsideration of the European case which gives us so many of the conscious and unconscious categories of our investigation.

The first consideration is that the development in Europe is neither even nor uniform. Developments in different countries and at different times have very different significance. As Reinhard Bendix has so clearly indicated, it was Weber's growing discernment of the failure of structural transformation in important sectors of German society that led him to the Protestant Ethic problem.[15] As every reader of the famous essay knows, the material is derived from England primarily, not from Germany where the Reformation remained abortive in important respects and its structural consequences stunted. This is indeed the background for Weber's profound cultural pessimism. Interestingly enough, one of the first Japanese to penetrate deeply into the structure of Western culture, Uchimura Kanzō, made a similar diagnosis. Writing in 1898 he said:

> One of the many foolish and deplorable mistakes which the Satsuma-Chōshū Government have committed is their having selected Germany as the example to be followed in their administrative policy. Because its military organization is well-nigh perfect, and its imperialism a gift of its army, therefore they thought that it ought to be taken as the pattern of our own Empire. . . .
>
> Germany certainly is a great nation, but it is not the greatest, neither is it the most advanced. It is often said that Art, Science, and Philosophy have their homes in Germany, that Thought has its primal spring there. But it is not in Germany that Thought is realized to the fullest extent. Thought may originate in Germany, but it is actualized somewhere else. The Lutheran Reformation bore its best fruit in England and America.[16]

These suggestions about European developments, which serve here without adequate elaboration, have a further important implication. Germany is certainly one of the most economically developed nations in the world, yet it lagged, according to Weber, in some of the structural transformations which he discovered to be crucial in the development of modern society. Once the crucial breakthroughs have been accomplished it becomes possible for other nations to take some of them over piecemeal without the total structure being transformed—possible, but at great cost, as the German case indicates.

These considerations bring us back to Maruyama's criticism of my work and the criticism of a number of Japanese intellectuals of American analyses of Japan in general.[17] Japan too, comparatively speaking, is one of the world's most economically advanced nations. Looking at economic growth as our sole criterion, Japan appears as a rather unambiguous success story. But to Japanese intellectuals, who feel as acutely as Weber did the failure of modern Japan to carry through certain critical structural transformations that are associated with modern society, the evaluation of Japan's modern history is much more problematic. It would be convenient for social scientists and policymakers if economic growth were an automatic index to successful structural tranformation. This does not, however, seem to be the case. Indeed, where economic growth is rapid and structural change is blocked or, as in the Communist cases, distorted, social instabilities result that under present world conditions are serious enough to have potentially fatal consequences for us all. A broader perspective than has often been taken would seem then to be in order.

As examples of the structural approach, which I believe to be the most adequate application of the Weberian problem to Asia, I may cite again the work of Clifford Geertz on Indonesia, and especially a very suggestive recent article on Bali,[18] together with a highly interesting study of recent religious and social developments in Ceylon by Michael Ames.[19] In the Balinese case only the beginnings of the questioning of traditional assumptions are evident and the degree to which rationalization at the value level will have social consequence is not yet clear. In Ceylon Ames documents the existence of movements of religious reform that have gone far in changing some of the most fundamental assumptions of tradtional Buddhism, replacing them with orientations supporting social reform. The degree to which the structural reform itself has gotten under way is not as yet clear. In Japan a century of ideological ferment has given rise to a number of tendencies and potentialities which need much more clarification, a problem on which I am currently working.[20]

There are indications from a number of Asian countries that traditional elements are being reformulated as part of new nationalist ideologies. Joseph Elder has presented some evidence that the Indian caste ethic is being transformed into a universalistic ethic of occupational responsibility detached from its earlier anchorage in the hereditary caste structure.[21] Such examples would seem to support Singer's argument quoted above, as indeed in a sense they do. But it should not be forgotten that these reformulations have occurred under Western impact (not infrequently under Protestant Christian impact as Ames shows in Ceylon), and involve fundamental alterations in pattern even when based on traditional material, making them often formally similar to Western paradigms. This is not to imply that Asian cultures are inherently imitative but rather that modern Western societies are not fortuitous cultural sports. Since they represent the earliest versions of a specific structural type of society, it is inevitable that Asian societies should in some patterned way come to resemble them as they shift toward that type. Another set of problems arising from the structural approach have to do with the extent to which nationalism or communism can supply the ideological underpinning, the cultural reformation if you like, for the necessary structural transformations. Unfortunately, it is not possible to review here all the relevant work done on these topics.

In conclusion let me say that the whole range of problems having to do with social change in Asia would be greatly illuminated if we had a comprehensive social taxonomy based on evolutionary principles of the sort that Durkheim called for in 1895.[22] Among recent sociologists I can think only of S. N. Eisenstadt as having made significant contributions toward this end.[23] With such a taxonomy in hand we would be in a much stronger position to interpret the meaning of the results obtained by those currently concentrating on motivational and institutional research. We might also be in a better position to clear up profound problems both of science and policy that hover around the definition of the concept of modernization.

NOTES

1 For example the current (Apiil 1962) issue of the *American Sociological Review* contains two articles explicitly claiming to shed light on "the Weberian hypothesis." Among last year's more important books in which the influence of Weber's work is very evident are Gerhard Lenski's *The Religious Factor* (New York: Doubleday & Co., 1961) and David C. McClelland's *The Achieving Society* (Princeton: Van Nostrand, 1961). One might also mention Kurt Samuelson's scurrilous attack, *Religion and Economic Action* (New York: Basic Books, 1961). That Weber can at this date generate such irrational hostility is in itself a kind of indication of his importance.

2 The influence of Jōdo Buddhism and the Hōtoku and Shingaku movements in Japan was discussed by Robert N. Bellah in *Tokugawa Religion* (Glencoe, Ill.: Free Press, 1957), chap. 5. The Zen case in Japan was discussed by David C. McClelland, *op. cit.*, pp. 369–70, under the mistaken impression that the samurai in the Meiji period were devotees of Zen Buddhism. The Santri Muslims of Java were treated by Clifford Geertz in *The Religion of Java* (Glencoe, Ill.: Free Press, 1960), and more especially in terms of the present context in "Religious Belief and Economic Behavior in a Central Javanese Town: Some Preliminary Considerations," *Economic Development and Cultural Change* 4, no. 2 (1956). McClelland has discussed the Jains and the Parsis in *op. cit.*, pp. 368–69, and Milton Singer has discussed several Indian examples in "Cultural Values in India's Economic Development," *The Annals* 305 (May 1956): 81–91. The latter article received further comment from John Goheen, N. M. Srinivas, D. G. Karve, and Milton Singer in "India's Cultural Values and Economic Development: A Discussion," *Economic Development and Cultural Change* 7, no. 1 (1958): 1–12. Nakamura Hajime, in a brief article, "The Vitality of Religion in Asia," in Herbert Passin, ed., *Cultural Freedom in Asia* (Rutland, Vt.: Charles Tuttle, 1956), pp. 53–66, argued for the positive influence of a number of Asian religious currents on economic development. In his more comprehensive *The Ways of Thinking of Eastern Peoples* (Honolulu: East-West Center Press, 1965), a translation of

Tōyōjin no Shii Hōhō, 2 vols. (Tokyo: Misuzu Shobō, 1949), Nakamura takes a position very close to that of Weber. The types of argument put forward in this very partial listing of work on this problem are quite varied. In particular, Clifford Geertz was careful to point out that the Santri religious ethic seemed suited to a specifically precapitalist small trader mentality that Weber argued was very different from the spirit of capitalism. This distinction could perhaps be usefully applied to many of the above cases of traditional merchant groups that seem to have some special religious orientation supporting their occupational motivations.

3 McClelland, *op. cit.,* pp. 367–73, 391.

4 Samuelson, *op. cit.,* pp. 27–48.

5 Milton Singer, "India's Cultural Values and Economic Development: A Discussion," *Economic Development and Cultural Change* 7, no. 1: 12.

6 Clifford Geertz, "The Social Context of Economic Change: An Indonesian Case Study," mimeographed (Cambridge: M.I.T. Center for International Studies, 1956), pp. 94–119.

7 Gustav Papanek, "The Development of Enterpreneurship," *The American Economic Review* 52, no. 2 (May 1962).

8 Albert Feuerwerker, *China's Early Industrialization* (Cambridge: Harvard Univ. Press, 1958).

9 Joseph Elder, *Industrialization in Hindu Society: A Case Study in Social Change* (Ph.D. diss. Harvard Univ., 1959).

10 In addition to Geertz's writings already cited, see especially "The Development of the Javanese Economy: A Socio-Cultural Approach," mimeographed (Cambridge: M.I.T. Center for International Studies, 1956).

11 Feuerwerker, *op. cit.,* p. 242.

12 Geertz, "The Developments of the Javanese Economy," *op. cit.,* pp. 105–6.

13 Maruyama Masao, in *Kokka Gakkai Zasshi* (The Journal of the Association of Political and Social Sciences) 72, no. 4 (April 1958).

14 Milton Singer, in *American Anthropologist* 63, no. 1 (1961): 150.

15 Reinhard Bendix, *Max Weber: An Intellectual Portrait* (New York: Doubleday & Co., 1960), chap. II.

16 Uchimura Kanzō, *Uchimura Kanzō Zenshū,* vol. 16 (Tokyo: Iwanami Shoten, 1933), pp. 361–62.

17 Some illuminating remarks on this topic are to be found in John Whitney Hall's "Changing Conceptions of the Modernization of Japan," in Marius B. Jansen, ed., *Changing Japanese Attitudes Toward Modernization* (Princeton: Princeton Univ. Press, 1965).

18 Geertz, "Internal Conversion in Contemporary Bali," in John Bastin

and R. Roolvink, eds., *Malayan and Indonesian Studies* (New York: Oxford Univ. Press, 1964).

19 Michael Ames, "An Outline of Recent Social and Religious Changes in Ceylon," *Human Organization* 22, no. 1 (1963): 45–53.

20 Robert N. Bellah, "Ienaga Saburo and the Search for Meaning in Modern Japan," in Marius B. Jansen, ed., *op. cit.,* is the first study concerned with this problem that I have completed.

21 Joseph Elder, *op. cit.*

22 Emile Durkheim, *The Rules of Sociological Method* (Glencoe, Ill.: Free Press, 1950), chap. 4.

23 See S. N. Eisenstadt, *From Generation to Generation* (Glencoe, Ill.: Free Press, 1956), and especially *The Political Systems of Empires* (Glencoe, Ill.: Free Press, 1963).

4 Meaning and Modernization

MODERNIZATION, whatever else it involves, is always a moral and a religious problem. If it has sometimes been hailed as an exhilarating challenge to create new values and meanings, it has also often been feared as a threat to an existing pattern of values and meanings. In either case the personal and social forces called into play have been powerful.

One very widespread response to the modern has been to see it as disturbing and disorienting, as creating an unsatisfactory situation that must be mastered or overcome. In considering a few examples of this response we might begin with the Japanese case, where "overcoming the modern" was actually a widespread slogan during the Second World War. The phrase "overcoming the modern" (*kindai no chōkoku*) was used by Japanese intellectuals to describe their war aims. Occasionally they spoke of "using the modern to overcome the modern," by which they meant using technology and science as means, particularly in the form of modern armaments, to overcome the modern spirit, which they took to be embodied particularly in Anglo-American culture. In opposition to the modern spirit they exalted the "Japanese spirit" (*Nihon Seishin*), a notion difficult to define but compounded of primordial religiosocial images focussing on the person of the divine emperor. The Second World War was viewed as an almost eschatological conflict in which the Japanese spirit would overcome the modern spirit. In this context "overcoming the modern" is almost an epitome of rightist reactionary thought in modern Japan. But just a few years ago one of Japan's leading left-wing, "progressive" intellectuals, Takeuchi Yoshimi, turned again to the phrase "overcoming the modern."[1] In

This chapter was read at the annual meeting of the American Sociological Association in Chicago in September 1965. It represents an elaboration of the general point of view presented in the previous chapter and in particular a recognition of the disruptive and destructive aspects of the modernization process.

spite of the "bad taste in the mouth" that Takeuchi says that phrase still has because of its association with fascism and militarism during the war, he argues that the modern remains a problem, an unsolved problem, for Japan. For him the solution is not a return to the past, though he recognizes certain important resources deep in the Asian past, but the creation of a new kind of society in the future. These are simply indications of the profound dissatisfaction with modern culture and society that has appeared both on the Right and on the Left in modern Japan. Many nonpolitical intellectuals have pointed to the same thing. For example Natsume Soseki, modern Japan's greatest novelist, spoke of the "spiritual breakdown" that he claimed was the inevitable result of contact with the modern West.

Turning to the Islamic world we can find an extreme but by no means isolated case of the deeply disturbing nature of the modern and the Western in the reaction of the young Hasan al Banna, founder of the Muslim Brotherhood, to life in Cairo as he found it when at the age of 17 he left his delta village to study in the capital. In his memoirs he writes:

> After the last war [World War I] and during this period which I spent in Cairo, there was an increase in spiritual and ideological disintegration, in the name of intellectual freedom. There was a deterioration of behavior, morals, and deeds, in the name of individual freedom. . . . Books, newspapers, and magazines appeared whose only aim was to weaken or to destroy the influence of any religion on the masses. . . . Young men were lost, and the educated were in a state of doubt and confusion. . . .[2]

All this he blamed on the destructive and degenerative influence of modern Western culture and social forms.

The Indonesian intellectual, Soedjatmoko, speaks of a "crisis of identity" following contact with the modern world. Traditional social structures and established customs begin to break down, but modern society is felt to be strange and unattractive. He says:

> The image of one's self, the answer to who am I, and who I want to be, has become blurred and fractured. Questions like: to whom or to what to be loyal, after whom to model one's self, which pattern of behavior to adopt or adjust to, have all lost their obvious answers, and no new satisfactory ones are readily available.[3]

Of course we do not need to go as far as Africa and Asia to find examples of dissatisfaction and dismay in the face of the modern.

Such a response has been widespread in the West. Joseph Conrad expresses the mood of general uneasiness when he describes the modern age as one "in which we are camped like bewildered travellers in a garish, unrestful hotel." Perhaps the deepest revulsion against the modern to be found anywhere in the world occurred in Germany, with its roots deep in the nineteenth century, culminating in the Hitler period. The folkish ideology that grew out of the Romantic movement equated "modern" with "Western" and "Jewish" to characterize the alien, polluted, mobile, restless, and destructive spirit that was undermining the old, pure, spiritual German folk.[4] In France, alongside somewhat less creative responses to the political and industrial revolutions of modern times, was the emergence of sociology itself in the work of Henri Saint-Simon and Auguste Comte as an effort to reconcile order, which in their view characterized the Middle Ages but has since become disrupted, and progress. And it is interesting to note that for the first sociologists the only solution was to be found in a new religion: for Saint-Simon the "New Christianity," for Comte the "Religion of Humanity."[5]

With these random examples in hand—and they could be multiplied a thousandfold—let us turn to a somewhat more abstract consideration of the modern, not as a form of political or economic system, but as a spiritual phenomenon or a kind of mentality. We can take a cue from Alfred North Whitehead, who said that "The new mentality is even more important than the new science and the new technology." This new mentality, which was found among small groups of enlightened spirits all over Europe in the sixteenth and seventeenth centuries and was to some extent socially institutionalized in Holland and England by the end of the seventeenth century, can best be characterized as a new attitude toward the phenomenon of change. Change was seen as something not to be feared but to be welcomed, to be responsibly and intelligently guided. This new attitude toward change implied a new attitude toward authority. The direction of change was not to be decided by reference to any fixed or given authority in the past, but only through reason and discussion, through intelligent inquiry and tentative consenus. To establish this new mentality of an open orientation to change required a great social-psychological revolution. When successful, this social-psychological revolution has produced social and personality systems capable of combining continuity and change, identity and openness to even deep-going structural reorganization. In S. N.

Eisenstadt's terms, these personalities and societies have the capacity to "absorb change" without either stagnation or breakdown.[6]

It is not my intention to imply that these ideas have been easy to institutionalize, or that they have in any society been more than incompletely institutionalized. Quite the contrary. I want to emphasize precisely how difficult it has been to put these ideas into operation, ideas that seem to contradict the basic presuppositions of all of the traditional cultures. The notion that conscious directional change is a primary human responsibility presents enormous problems for social as well as psychic and perhaps even biological balance. It seems to violate one of the cardinal requirements for organized action of any sort, namely the need for continuity, for stability of orientation—in a word, for identity. We must not forget that in all the great traditional civilizations the notion of change was charged with horror and fear and was contrasted with that which is eternal, which does not change, and which alone is of value, as in the Christian idea of God. The radical quality of Buddhism resided in its horrifying assertion that all is change. In that case the only good can be nirvana, the blowing out of the flickering candle. The great problem for the modern conception of change, then, was how to integrate it with a conception of identity, a conception traditionally provided by religion. It is this problem with which the modern social-psychological revolution has been concerned.

We can, following Max Weber, identify one of the earliest and the deepest going phases of this social-psychological revolution in the West with the Protestant Reformation. The Reformation, especially in its Calvinist and sectarian forms, reformulated the deepest level of identity symbols, which as in all tradtional societies were expressed as religious symbols, in order to open up entirely new possibilities of human action. God's will was seen not as the basis and fulfillment of a vast and complex natural order that men must largely accept as it is—the conception of medieval Christianity as of most traditional religion—but as a mandate to question and revise every human institution in the process of building a holy community. Here we have the inner-worldly asceticism or this-worldly activism that expressed itself not only in economic action, which Weber emphasized so much, but in every social and cultural realm from politics to science, from the family to education. Particularly worth noting is that it was on Protestant soil that the modern ideology of science first took root. All the early publicists of science in the sixteenth and seventeenth century were Protestants, men like Petrus Ramus, Bernard Palissy, Bacon, Comenius, and Hartlib. None of them were important scientists, but they were the early architects of an entirely new conception of the relation between science and society that made the conquest of nature a central social goal and the building of a new civilization a scientific endeavor.[7] The "priesthood of all believers," the new Protestant principle in church policy, was applied to secular politics in the course of the Puritan Revolution in England and eventuated in the secular democratic theory of John Locke. Thus, already by the late seventeenth century in the Protestant milieu of England, the modern secular ideology of liberalism had emerged in embryonic form with its twin principles of progress and democracy, the secular translations of the Protestant innerworldly asceticism and priesthood of all believers.

In England, and generally wherever Anglo-Saxon culture has gone, this new secular ideology did not involve a repudiation of religion but went hand in hand with new popular forms of Protestantism, such as Methodism, which swept the English-speaking world in the eighteenth century. On the whole, such movements operated more to bring modern liberal values to social strata previously unaffected by them than to oppose modernization,[8] though under certain social conditions an antimodern Protestantism could develop, as in the case of some recent fundamentalist groups. Nevertheless the basically positive attitude of ascetic Protestantism toward modernization has contributed to the relatively smooth course of development in areas where it predominated and to the absence of social movements evidencing a high degree of emotional rejection of modernity. Analogous reform movements have occurred in a number of the world religions, but have on the whole remained minority movements contributing only minimally to the solution of the ideological and religious problems of moderization, though in the future they may be more significant.[9]

The embryonic ideology of liberalism was taken up and developed in eighteenth-century France under the influence of English thought and institutions. The thinkers of the French Enlightenment were, however, in contrast to their English mentors, apt to be antireligious or at least anti-clerical, for traditional Catholicism provided a much less adequate basis for liberalism than did Protestantism. English deism, which tended at home to become domesticated in the denominational form of Unitarianism, came to be a much more radical alternative to the established church in France. When the ideas of the Enlightenment finally achieved power in the revolution of 1789, what eventuated was a new secular religion of liberalism, briefly establishing its headquarters in the cathedral of Notre Dame. For more than a century we can discern abortive attempts to establish a promodern religious alternative in France in opposition to the Catholic establishment, which remained deeply committed to the old regime both intellectually and politically.

We have already mentioned Saint-Simon and Comte in this connection and we must classify Emile Durkheim's efforts to supply a moral basis for the secular state as a less grandiose contribution in the same direction. The degree to which these liberal secular religions were actually institutionalized in France would be worth study, but it is also notable that they had some export appeal in other societies burdened with a powerful antimodern religious establishment. Positivism made a strong impression in Latin America in the nineteenth century, particularly in Brazil and Mexico,[10] and Durkheim contributed to the ideology of the secularizing Turkey of the 1920s through his influence on Ziya Gokalp.[11] In none of these cases was there a mass following of the new ideology, but the role of these liberal secular religions as the ideology of the modernizing elite was nonetheless significant. In recent years the significance of such movements in the Catholic world has been greatly lessened because of the sustained reforming tendencies within the Catholic church that have operated to bring it into a much more positive relation to the modernization process.

Liberalism, which we may call the primary ideology of modernization, was largely successful in the Anglo-Saxon world and in France, where, though it met powerful opposition, it also established deep roots. During the course of the nineteenth century, however, liberalism was either initially rejected or suffered serious defeats after some early success in the nations of Central, Southern, and Eastern Europe. These setbacks of liberalism were occurring at precisely the time that these societies were undergoing ever more extensive changes in the scientific, economic, and organizational spheres. In the face of actual material and social transformation, an intransigent religious or ideological traditionalism became less and less possible. But where the early modern social-psychological revolution had not taken place and a religious orientation favorable to modernization had not become established, the ideology of liberalism did not meet with a favorable reception. It was indeed quickly linked to the disruptive anxiety-producing changes that were going on and denounced as responsible for them. These reactions can be likened to psychological resistance, and led to the formation of defensive counterideologies.

Germany was the first underdeveloped country in the sense that she was the first country to feel powerful pressure to change emanating from the alien early modernizing societies of the West. And it is in Germany that we can see clearly for the first time the emergence of the great countermodernizing ideologies that would be subsequently important in all the developing nations—both European and otherwise—in the nineteenth and twentieth centuries. These ideologies can be grouped under two main headings: romantic nationalist on the one hand and radical socialist on the other, with, naturally, the possibility of various combinations. Of course liberalism had its nationalist and its social ameliorative aspects, but these were not absolutized or used as the basis for rejection of important features of modern society as they tended to be in the new nineteenth-century ideologies. Modern critics of modernization, if we can use that term to differentiate them from the traditional critics who are always with us, can be found before the nineteenth century, particularly in France. The great examples are Blaise Pascal in the seventeenth century and Jean Jacques Rousseau in the eighteenth. Rousseau is particularly interesting because he made a major contribution to liberal thought at the same time that he contained seeds of the romantic and radical reactions against it. But in spite of these and other forerunners (for example the English and French "Utopian Socialists"), the systematic formulation of romantic nationalism and radical socialism developed in nineteenth-century Germany, the crisis land of European modernization.

Though both romantic nationalism and radical socialism are quite critical of aspects of modern society, both desiring a more tightly integrated, less differentiated, and less individualistic society, though in quite different ways, they can nonetheless be called secondary ideologies of modernization. Both have been used to sanction large-scale social change. Whether they further or hinder modernization depends partly on economic and political conditions that are not directly the subject of this paper. But their modernizing potential needs to be kept in mind. Especially where neither religious reform nor secular liberalism have any appeal they may be the only possible ideologies of modernization.

Romantic nationalism, unlike the civil nationalism of Anglo-French thought, stresses solidarity on the basis of primordial identities of language, ethnic origin, or religion. In cases where there is a clear religious difference between the developing society and more modernized politically or culturally dominant societies impinging on it, religion may be a salient feature of the nationalist ideology, as in the case of nineteenth-century Russia, some East European nations, most Islamic nations, and India. Where religion is a divisive issue within the society or its universalism appears to threaten national particularism, religion may not be a primary theme in the ideology, or some primitive national religion may be emphasized or created for the occasion. Germany, where religious divisions between Lutherans, Calvinists, and Catholics went very deep, is such an example, though the attempt to resurrect early German mythology, even with the help of Richard Wagner, was never entirely successful. In Japan, where the old national religion, Shintō, was still functioning, the artificial revival of old religious symbolism was considerably more effective. But even where conventionally religious symbolism was not prominent the emotional totalism characteristic of the secondary ideologies of modernization was expressed in pseudosacred symbolism and ritual. In general the technique of romantic nationalism in the face of the disturbances and disruptions of modernization has been to reemphasize the real or supposed unity and solidarity of the hallowed past.

The radical socialist ideology on the other hand plays on the deep tensions existing in the traditional society. In all traditional societies there are disfavored strata and groups with a traditional suspicion and hostility toward the established authorities and their charisma. In the disturbed conditions brought on by rapid modernization these suspicions and hostilities easily become exacerbated, and if there is a tradition of chiliastic hope, this too may be intensified. Radical socialism is precisely the ideology that tends to exploit the "sacrilegious, 'atheistic' hostility" that Edward Shils says established charisma always calls forth.[12] Of course inevitably socialism generates its own countercharisma and as an antireligion functions to some extent as a religion itself, a religion of millennial hope, though this aspect may have to be sharply curtailed once it becomes the established ideology.

Even before the First World War, at least in Germany and Japan, there was experimentation with the possibility of fusing the two secondary ideologies of nationalism and socialism into a social nationalism or a national socialism.[13] Subsequent history has shown this a most potent ideological mixture and much of the world at the moment is dominated by one or another version of it. The term "national socialism" calls to mind the especially malignant German example, but the term could also be meaningfully applied to the benign regime in postwar India, or in a different way to China. Indeed, the term "national communism" is gradually becoming established in Western political usage as somehow preferable to "international communism." The point is that a combination of national solidarity on the basis of sentimental primordial imagery with a determination to overcome inherited injustice and to build a new society makes a powerful motivational basis for directed social change. The degree to which such a combination may become authoritarian or militaristic, or on the contrary may include a large measure of liberalism, depends in part on a range of social factors that I am deliberately excluding from this paper.

I am not proposing a religious or ideological explanation of modernization to replace technological or economic or political explanations. Rather, I have attempted to show the following things: 1) Modernization inevitably disturbs the preexisting structure of meaning and motivation in any society where it seriously gets under way. 2) In premodern societies religion plays an important role in propagating meaningful orientations toward the world and in regulating personal feelings, and contributes directly and indirectly to individual stability and social solidarity. 3) Various religious groups have led the way to modern social and cultural forms, opposed the development of those forms, or gradually adjusted to them, but it has been impossible for religion to remain entirely indifferent to modernization. 4) In some Protestant countries as early as the eighteenth century there developed a differentiation between a basically promodern religious orientation and the nontotalistic social and political ideology of liberalism. This situation is the one most likely to favor the emergence of voluntaristic, pluralistic democracy. 5) Where this situation did not occur there emerged a) a totalistic, semireligious liberalism as in the French Revolution, or b) what I have called the secondary ideologies of modernization, romantic nationalism, and radical socialism. In these cases, since existing religions were unable to restructure the traditional patterns of meaning and motivation so as to make them favorable for modernization, the new ideologies have had to take on a religious character and provide this restructuring themselves. The success of a modernizing society in the economic, political, scientific, and other fields is partly dependent on its success in the field of meaning and motivation, though what happens there is of course heavily influenced by other aspects of the modernization process. Finally let me say that "success" in modernization is always relative and transient because modernization itself is so endlessly subversive of every fixed position, no matter how great an achievement it may have been originally. There are no grounds for complacency that any society has in any final sense "solved" the problems of meaning and modernization.

NOTES

1 Takeuchi Yoshimi, "Kindai no Chōkoku," in *Kindai Nihon Shisō-shi Kōza* (Symposium on the History of Modern Japanese Thought), Vol. 7 (Tokyo: Chikuma Shobo, 1959), pp. 225–81.

2 Christina Phelps Harris, *Nationalism and Revolution in Egypt* (The Hague: Mouton, 1964), p. 146.

3 Soedjatmoko, "Cultural Motivations to Progress: the 'Interior' and the 'Exterior' View," in Robert N. Bellah, ed., *Religion and Progress in Modern Asia* (New York: Free Press, 1965), p. 2.

4 Several excellent books on this subject have recently become available: Fritz Stern, *The Politics of Cultural Despair* (Berkeley: and Los Angeles: The Univ. of Calif. Press, 1961); George L. Mosse, *The Crisis of German Ideology: Intellectual Origins of the Third Reich* (New York: Grosset & Dunlap, 1964); Peter G. J. Pulzer, *The Rise of Political Anti-Semitism in Germany and Austria* (New York: John Wiley, 1964).

5 Henri Saint-Simon, "New Christianity," in *Henri Comte de Saint-Simon: Selected Writings,* trans. Felix Markham (Oxford: Blackwell, 1952), pp. 76–116; Auguste Comte, *System of Positive Polity,* trans. J. H. Bridges *et al.,* 4 vols. (London: Longmans, Green, 1875–77). *Nouveau Christianisme* was first published in 1825; *Systeme de Politique Positive* in 1851–54.

6 S. N. Eisenstadt, "Modernization and Conditions of Sustained Growth," *World Politics,* 16 (1964): 576–94.

7 Joseph Ben-David, "The Scientific Role: The Conditions of Its Establishment in Europe," *Minerva* 4, no. 1 (1965): 41.

8 This point has been made by Benton Johnson in several papers. For example see "Do Holiness Sects Socialize in Dominant Values?," *Social Forces,* 39 (1961): 309–16.

9 For a slightly more expanded comparative treatment of religious reformism see Robert N. Bellah, ed., *op. cit.,* pp. 207–12.

10 See Leopoldo Zea, "Positivism and Porfirism in Latin America," in F. S. C. Northrup, ed., *Ideological Differences and World Order* (New Haven: Yale Univ. Press, 1949).

11 Ziya Gokalp, *Turkish Nationalism and Western Civilization,* trans. Niyazi Berkes (New York: Columbia Univ. Press, 1959).

12 Edward Shils, "Charisma, Order and Status," *American Sociological Review,* 30 (1965): 210.

13 A brief comparative treatment of some aspects of the problem of national socialism can be found in Eugen Weber, *Varieties of Fascism* (Princeton: Van Nostrand, Anvil, 1964).

5 Father and Son in Christianity and Confucianism

ARISTOTLE, in the first book of the *Politics,* briefly discusses the relation between the family and religious symbolism. He says that the earliest form of social organization is the family, that the earliest form of political organization is simply an extension of the family in which the patriarch of an extended family is king, and finally, that men speak of Zeus being the father of gods and men, or of the gods having a king, on the analogy of their own way of life.[1] Though noting that "He who thus considers things in their first growth and origin, whether a state or anything else, will obtain the clearest view of them,"[2] Aristotle apparently considers this peculiar relation between the family and the early modes of organization of gods and men as sufficiently obvious to warrant no great amount of time spent explaining it. It must be admitted that Aristotle's insight provides a fundamental reference point for us even today, and that in fact the analysis of the problem has not gone as much beyond Aristotle as might be imagined. However, our evident advantage over Aristotle in the systematic understanding of human behavior and in the amount of comparative data available to us should allow us to push the analysis considerably further. This essay is intended as a brief reconnaissance in that direction.

Aristotle's notion that men think of the gods on the analogy of their own way of life is perhaps close to what some modern psychiatrists mean when they speak of religion as a projection. Freud

This chapter was first read at the annual meeting of the American Society for the Study of Religion in New York City in 1960. It represents an effort to bring out the psychological as well as the sociological dimension in the comparison between Christianity and Confucianism. The reader might compare the connections between personality, family structure, political structure, and religion pointed out in this chapter with the parallel patterns in Japan and the Islamic world presented in the following three chapters.

very significantly contributed to our understanding of the relation between the family and religious symbolism when he traced the structure of conflicts within the family that might give rise to such projection. In the Oedipus complex Freud had found the nucleus of all neurosis. In *Totem and Taboo* he asserted that the major aspects of human society and culture found their origin in the same place. Religion, morals, and society, he said, arise out of and are means of dealing with problems and conflicts within the family, especially "one single concrete point—man's relation to his father."[3] In particular he held that the function of religious symbolism and religious ritual is to give expression to the love and fear, respect and guilt, and obedience and rebellion generated in man's relation to his father in a way that will not be socially disruptive. For example, he analyzed the totemic sacrifice as a symbolic substitute for the actual murder of the father. In the ritual, the hostile impulses together with the guilt feelings could both be appeased in such a way that cultural values and social norms would be reinforced rather than destroyed.

In *The Future of an Illusion* Freud stated even more clearly the projective function of religion and dealt with it mainly as a defense against anxiety generated in the process of growing up in a family. On the basis of Freud's general view a number of psychologists and anthropologists have dealt with religion as a fairly direct projective mechanism that can be explained almost entirely in terms of the typical family structure in a given society and the way in which it channels the anxieties of growing children. The work of Abram Kardiner is perhaps the best known example of such an approach, and a number of interesting studies of religion in various primitive societies have been made from this point of view.

While accepting the Freudian analysis in general terms and adopting Freud's insistence on the importance of the father-son relationship as at least a convenient focus for investigation, I would argue that the relation between the family and religious symbolism is not quite so simple as the projective hypothesis might lead us to assume. In particular I would argue that religious symbolism cannot be treated as merely a dependent variable of family structure. Elements of motivation derived from family experiences are very profoundly involved in religion, but it is my thesis that in the religious sphere these motivational elements may be reformulated in such a way as to affect dramatically the structure of the family itself and the motivation of people in family and society generally. Interestingly enough, Freud, who earlier seems to have been supporting a rather straightforward projective interpretation, in *Moses and Monotheism* is clearly cognizant of the creative historical role of religion and of the consequences for personality and society that changes in religious symbolism might have.

As a stimulus for the tentative explorations that will be presented here, it is useful to compare two diverse examples of religions in which the family or family symbolism are evidently central, though in contrasting ways: Christianity and Confucianism. It seems obvious that no great religion has concentrated more on familial symbolism than has Christianity. Above all, the father-son relation is symbolically absolutely central. And yet Christian civilization as compared to the other great civilizations has not placed an especial stress on the family, and one could argue that the father-son tie, though certainly important, is less so than in Islamic, Indian, or East Asian society. And it is clear that modern Western society, which has grown out of traditional Christian civilization, is based less exclusively on the family than any other known society.

In contrast, China, of all the great civilizations, made the family most central. The family has been the core of Chinese society for millennia, and the breakup of the traditional family system in this century has been accompanied by the drastic disruption and perhaps end of classical Chinese civilization. And yet in Chinese religious symbolism familial figures are far from central. Though there is no civilization that has placed greater emphasis on the father-son tie, it is not reflected in the ultimate religious symbolism. For example, the *Tao* was never even anthropomorphic, much less a father, and *T'ien* was only vestigially and nonessentially paternal, at least from mid-Chou times. It would seem that in dealing with these two cases, where the relation between the actual position of the family and the place of familial symbolism in religion is not exactly what one would have expected on the basis of the projective hypothesis, an investigation may be useful in elucidating the problem at hand.

Let us begin by analyzing the place of familial symbolism in Christianity and some of its motivational implications. Freud (in *Totem and Taboo* and especially in *Moses and Monotheism*) provides a useful starting point for analysis.

The story of Adam's fall states narratively what the doctrine of original sin states essentially about the sinful nature of man. In

Totem and Taboo Freud chose characteristically to state narratively in terms of the archetypal father-murder in the primal horde his own theory of the essential disturbance in human nature, which he elsewhere described more analytically in terms of the Oedipal conflicts inevitable in the process of growing up in a family. In analyzing Christianity he identified original sin with the archetypal father-murder and interpreted Christ as bringing redemption from original sin by sacrificing his own life and thus allaying the guilt of the company of brothers responsible (hereditarily) for committing the original crime. It is a case of a life for a life. Christ's death obtains satisfaction through the law of talion for the murder of the father. But in accordance with the law of ambivalence that always displays itself in Oedipal situations, the very act that atones most completely for the original crime is in a way the complete fulfillment of the wishes that motivated the crime. For through the atonement the son becomes united with the father in such a way that he effectively replaces the father not only as redeemer but as creator. But a further consequence of this development, which displays again the characteristic ambivalence, is that the atoning death is also a father-murder, for if Christ is God then it is God who has been murdered. The Christian Eucharist gathers up all these motives and repeats them in a continual symbolic reenactment of the original deed. Freud attributes the effectiveness of Christianity to the relatively undisguised manner in which this complex of motives was acknowledged.

Before dealing with the limitations in Freud's analysis, let us consider whether it sheds light on the meaning of Christ for Christians in New Testament and later times. It is in Paul perhaps that we can find the most explicit confirmation of Freud's interpretation. Paul says, "For as by one man's disobedience many were made sinners, so by one man's obedience many will be made righteous" (Rom. 5:19). Through Adam sin and death came into the world just as through Christ have come acquittal and life. The pattern of implications that Paul sets up in his parallelisms between Adam and Christ can leave but one conclusion: Christ was obedient to his father unto death; Adam was disobedient to his father unto murder. Or at any rate Adam's disobedience, his denial of God's authority, opened the door to a sinfulness in man that could and eventually did reach the extreme of the murder of God.

The same motivational components are clearly revealed in an important counterplot in the Gospels in which Judas portrays a parody of Christ. Judas was certainly a father murderer, for in accordance with Jewish ideas of the time a man's spiritual master was to be treated as a father to whom, if anything, more honor and reverence was due than to the literal father.[4] Furthermore, at least by implication, Judas was not only one of the company of brothers to harbor murderous impulses. Peter was dismayed to discover in himself a degree of betrayal that he had not thought possible. In order to expiate his crime Judas goes willingly to his death, that is, he commits suicide. Through the starkest contrast he illustrates the motivational components that are involved in the crucifixion of the innocent Christ.

Christ is not just victim; he is also hero. He accepts the Father's command to do what is required even though he must suffer. He willingly gives his life for the sake of others: "Greater love has no man than this, that a man lay down his life for his friends" (John 15:13). He struggles with death and overcomes it. Many writers through the centuries have emphasized this heroic aspect of Christ. Aquinas, for example, wrote that Christ gave us an example "by overcoming bravely the sufferings of the flesh" and in love exposing himself to the dangers of death.[5] None goes further than Calvin in stressing the heroic accomplishments of Christ undertaken in spite of the dread arising from his sensitive nature. Calvin says,

> Nothing had been done if Christ had only endured corporeal death. In order to interpose between us and God's anger, and satisfy his righteous judgment, it was necessary that he should feel the weight of divine vengeance. Whence also it was necessary that he should engage, as it were, at close quarters with the powers of hell and the horrors of eternal death.[6]

Calvin expressly rejects a passive interpretation of Christ's sacrifice:

> Nor are we to understand that by the curse which he endured he was himself overwhelmed, but rather that by enduring it he repressed, broke, annihilated all its force.[7]

Through withstanding the worst, Christ won the right to sit at the right hand of the Father. He who emptied himself and took the form of a servant became the One to whom every knee shall bow. Thus Christ does not merely expiate the original crime. As Freud said, he also fulfills, though of course innocently in Christian terms, part of the motivation behind the original crime, namely the desire to replace the Father, to participate in his power rather than be simply subjected to it.

Freud posited the effectiveness of Christianity in the fact that Christians identify with Christ and participate in the working through of the motives involved in his life and sacrificial death. Of course this is merely Freud's way of expressing what is thoroughly evident in the New Testament and later Christian thought. The Gospel is indeed the message that Christ's victory over death is mankind's victory, that all men can and indeed actually do participate in it. Christ is the only begotten Son of God. But through Christ all men can become sons of God. Augustine says:

> For God doth this thing, out of sons of men He maketh sons of God; because out of the Son of God He hath made the Son of Man. Mark what this participation is. There hath been promised to us a participation of Divinity.[8]

Paul speaks of the church as the body of Christ, thus emphasizing the participation of the believers in the divine life. The identification with Christ, however, to be real must be total. As Augustine says,

> Whatever He hath suffered, therein we also have suffered; and that which we suffer, He also suffers in us. . . . In Him we are dead, and in Him we are risen again; and He dieth in us and in us riseth again; for He is the unity of the Head and the Body.[9]

Paul asks the brethren "to present your bodies as a living sacrifice, holy and acceptable to God" (Rom. 12:1), and Augustine says that the cross is for the whole of life.[10]

It is precisely in the Eucharist, the center of the Christian liturgy from the earliest times, that the sacrificial identification of the church with the body of Christ was made most plainly manifest. Again it is Augustine who says,

> This is the sacrifice of Christians: we, being many, are one body in Christ. And this also is the sacrifice which the Church continually celebrates in the sacrament of the altar, known to the faithful, in which she teaches that she herself is offered in the offering she makes to God.[11]

In fact without the Eucharist it is hardly possible to speak of a Church at all, and yet there could be no Eucharist until Christ had sacrificed Himself. The church had to lose Christ in order to become Christ, a point recognized in the fourth Gospel where Jesus says in his farewell speech, "Nevertheless I tell you the truth: it is to your advantage that I go away, for if I do not go away, the Counselor will not come to you; but if I go, I will send him to you" (John 16:7).

The descent of the Counselor or Holy Spirit into the assembled believers on the day of Pentecost marks the foundation of the Church. Through the recurrent Eucharist the Church celebrates both the loss of the beloved object and its own identification with that object. The psychological mechanisms involved in the process of identification with the lost object were first pointed out by Freud in his brilliant paper "Mourning and Melancholia," and later even more explicitly in *The Ego and the Id,*[12] though he did not have the Eucharist in mind.

Having sampled briefly some of the implications of the father-son symbolism in Christian belief and ritual, what are we to make of it? It would seem that Freud's analysis in terms of Oedipal themes has much to recommend it. Nevertheless it becomes obvious upon reflection that the Christian symbolism is not *explained* by the Oedipus complex. If it were simply a direct projection of the Oedipus complex, then since the Oedipus complex is universal so would be Christian symbolism. But this is clearly far from the case. Christian symbolism is in fact highly unique, emerging from a particular historical context and bearing a particular historical role, a fact that Freud seems to have recognized. The particular qualities of the Christian symbolism emerge in the first instance from the Christian notion of God, around which the whole symbolic structure hangs. This notion is neither general nor obvious and has, in fact, emerged only once in history, and that once historically traceable to Israel at the moment of the Mosaic revelation.[13] There the notion of one God, rejecting all magic and known through his ethical demands rather than any philosophical speculation, was first clearly discerned.

As the recent work of George Mendenhall[14] and others has pointed out, the social analogies on which the Mosaic covenant was based were political and not familial. God was conceived in terms of the Near Eastern great king, not as a father. Though memories of the Abrahamic covenant with its more patriarchal conception of fatherhood with respect to Yahweh was eschewed and any suggestions of the more naturalistic relations with divinity found in the widespread Near Eastern fertility cults was violently rejected. God was to be known through his will, which gradually became codified as his law. In the face of such an overwhelming and demanding God the temptation to respond with an obsessive-compulsive legalism was strong. Nevertheless the sense of God's love and faithfulness was not lost, and by the time of Jesus references to God as Father or Father in Heaven were not infrequent.

Whatever may have been Jesus' own understanding of his role and mission, and this is in dispute among New Testament scholars, the early church soon proclaimed his divine Sonship. In this way, for the first time in the history of Israel, the family symbolism was taken up explicitly into the religious sphere and worked out there. The life and death of Jesus then provided a pattern or model for the working through of the father-son relationship with such a father as the God of Israel. The church emerged as the body of those who identified with Jesus and participated in his action. As such it was a collectivity of a different kind from that of the Jewish community, bound together by its hereditary connection with the patriarchs and its adherence to the law. This new religious collectivity that was the Christian church had enormous sociological consequences that we will return to briefly later. Here we can only state that the radical extent to which this new collectivity involved elements of familial motivation, transformed on the religious plane, has something to do with its dynamism. It must of course be noticed that this familial motivation is not just projection, for the religious symbolism differs drastically from the fundamental family pattern. There is no mother, for the one God is a Father.[15] Any other solution would have involved a violation of Israel's idea of God and so have been no solution at all.

If we are right that the Oedipus complex itself cannot explain the difference between Christian symbolism and that of other religions—including, as we shall see, Confucianism—perhaps marked differences in family structure of the sort that anthropologists have studied in primitive societies can explain the difference. Let us compare briefly the Jewish family at the time of Christ with the Chinese family and then consider whether Confucian religious symbolism is illuminated by such a contrast.

Filial piety, according to George Foot Moore, was considered by the Jews at the time of Christ as "among all the commandments the 'weightiest of the weighty.' "[16] The fifth of the Ten Commandments was of course, "Honor thy father and thy mother, that thy days may be long upon the land which the Lord thy God giveth thee" (Exod. 20:12). Custom provided detailed forms of reverence in word and act that a son owed his parents. A son who strikes a parent or who is stubborn and rebellious may be put to death according to the Mosaic law.[17] Only in one instance was disobedience countenanced: a son should not transgress one of the commandments of the law even if bidden to do so by a parent.

With the exception of the last point the teaching of Confucianism was in agreement with that of Judaism. This is not surprising, as the family systems in China and Palestine were superficially not markedly dissimilar. Both Confucian and Jewish families were patrilineal and patrilocal, with a strong emphasis on the authority of the father and a relatively subordinate position for women. Again, if we were to follow the hypothesis that religious symbolism is essentially projected from the family situation, we should expect to find in Confucianism a set of religious symbols broadly similar to that found in Judaism or early Christianity.[18] Unfortunately this is not the case.

We have already noted that the main characteristics of Yahweh in the Old Testament were formed on a political analogy rather than on a familial one. While the political analogy is also of great importance in Chinese religious thought there was no Chinese equivalent to Yahweh. There were a number of highest terms only partially integrated with each other. Some like *T'ien* and *Shang Ti* have a clearly anthropomorphic background, and may have originally meant the ancestor or ancestors of the tribe (who dwell in heaven, *T'ien*).[19] But by late Chou times these terms were largely depersonalized. *T'ien,* which remains an important concept up to modern times, is frequently joined with *Ti,* "earth," and joined or not tends to mean the order of nature. Therefore, even when *T'ien* is said to have a *ming,* "decree," what is implied is an impersonal normative pattern, not a personal ethical command. There is no conception of a creator deity. In addition to these terms of anthropomorphic origin there were several terms with a quality of ultimacy that never had any personal referent, such as *Tao* and later *T'ai Ch'i* ("Supreme Ultimate"). If Marcel Granet's admittedly speculative analysis is correct, *Tao,* literally "the way," may originally have been derived from *Wang Tao,* the magicopolitical action or "way" of the king whereby he orders the social and cosmic universe.[20] At any rate, in the *Analects Tao* clearly means the way of the former kings or the way of the ancestors and only later does it take on its more philosophical significance.

In short, the Chinese conception differs radically from that of

Judaism or Christianity. Confucianism tends to view the universe as a single social cosmic totality in which the *Tao* of heaven, earth, and man are the same. For example, the twenty-second chapter of the *Chung Yung* tells us that a man of utmost sincerity "may form a trinity with heaven and earth." The Reverend James Legge translates "he may with heaven and earth form a ternion," and says in a note, "*ts'an* is a 'file of three,' and I employ 'ternion' to express the idea, just as we use 'quaternion' for a file of four. What is it but extravagance thus to file man with the Supreme Power?"[21] And so in Legge's instinctive reaction we see the difference between the Jewish and Christian view of the divine human relation and that of the Chinese.

The *Lü-shih Ch'un Ch'iu* says, "Heaven, Earth and all things are like the body of one man, and this is what is called the Great Unity."[22] In early texts such as the *Shih Ching* and the *Shu Ching* the king is not infrequently referred to as the "One man." It is in this context that we can understand how the ruler came to be called the "son of Heaven." An early etymology for the character for *wang* or "king" (which happens to be false etymologically but valuable symbolically) interprets the three horizontal lines of which it is composed as Heaven, Man, and Earth and the vertical line that unites them as the king.[23] The ruler is to maintain order in society by taking as his model the orderly pattern of the heavens. Because the conception of heaven was so impersonal the conception of a son of heaven did not indicate much in the way of personal relationship. Nor did it when Chuang Tzu appropriated the term for the Taoist adept.[24]

What I am trying to indicate is that though familial symbolism did appear in a religious context, it was not basic. It was not meant to indicate a pattern of relationships that was *essentially* personal and familial but rather to enrich with familial symbolism a pattern that had other bases. Thus when Tung Chung-shu in the Han period says, "What produces (man) cannot (itself) be man, for the creator of man is Heaven. The fact that men are men derives from Heaven," and even, "Man's vigor is directed to love (*jen*) through the transforming influence of Heaven's will (*chih*)," we assume a pattern of relationship between Heaven and man not dissimilar to that with which we are familiar. But on closer inspection we find this to be not quite the case. For example, we are told that "Heaven has Five Elements. . . . Wood produces fire, fire earth, earth metal, metal water, and water wood. Such is their father and son (relationship)." And again, "Man's likes and dislikes are influenced by Heaven's warmth and purity. Man's joy and anger are influenced by Heaven's cold and heat. . . . The duplicate of Heaven lies in man, and man's feelings and nature derive from Heaven."[25] Here we see that the relationship of Heaven and man is one of organic correspondences, hardly the Jewish or Christian conception. Perhaps it is wrong to call the Chinese notion impersonal. In the Chinese view the whole cosmos is a closely interrelated community or organism with a continuous flow of sympathy between its parts. But the analogy of biological organism is far closer to the essence of the position than is that of familial relationship.

I do not, however, want to overstate my case. Familial symbolism, though not particularly central, is fairly constant in the East Asian religious tradition, and occasionally attains an unmistakable seriousness, as for example in the following passage from the seventeenth-century Japanese Confucian Kaibara Ekken:

> All men may be said to owe their birth to their parents, but a further inquiry into their origins reveals that men come into being receiving their principle of life from heaven and earth. Thus all men in the world are children born of heaven and earth, and heaven and earth are the great parents of us all. The Book of History says, "Heaven and earth are the father and mother of all things" (T'ai-shih 1). Our own parents are truly our parents; but heaven and earth are the parents of everyone in the world. Moreover, though we are brought up after birth through the care of our own parents and are sustained on the graciousness of the ruler, still if we go to the root of the matter, we find that we sustain ourselves using the things produced by heaven and earth for food, dress, housing, and implements. Thus, not only do all men at the outset come into being receiving their principle of life from heaven and earth, but from birth till the end of life they are kept in existence by the support of heaven and earth. Man surpasses all other created things in his indebtedness to the limitless bounty of heaven and earth. It will be seen therefore that man's duty is not only to do his best to serve his parents, which is a matter of course, but also to serve heaven and earth throughout his life in order to repay his immense debt. That is one thing all men should keep in mind constantly.[26]

Nevertheless I doubt if any Confucian would have felt comfortable with the following statement of Karl Barth:

> It is therefore not as if the Father-Son relationship were itself a reality

originally and properly creaturely, as if God in some hidden source of His essence were nevertheless something other than Father and Son, and as if therefore these names were optional and ultimately meaningless symbols, symbols the original and proper, non-symbolic content of which consisted in the said creaturely reality. On the contrary, it is precisely in God that the Father-Son relationship, like all creaturely relationships, has its original and proper reality. The mystery of the generation is originally and properly not a creaturely but a divine mystery, perhaps we ought to say outright, *the* divine mystery.[27]

The Confucian would simply not see the necessity for drawing the line between creaturely and divine in that way. This consideration leads us to the core of familial symbolism in Confucianism.

We have seen that heaven and earth may be considered the parents of men and that the ruler is called the son of Heaven. The ruler may also be called the parent of the people.[28] But all of these usages are rather peripheral. The core of familial involvement in Confucianism is not really in one sense symbolic at all, for it is the family itself. My subject here is the family in a religious context, but for Confucianism the family in many respects *is* the religious context. Honor thy father and thy mother is very nearly the whole of it. At least there is the fairly clear assumption that if that is achieved everything else will follow naturally. For example, the *Hsiao Ching* (*Classic of Filial Piety*) says,

Serving parents when alive with love and affection and when dead with grief and sorrow—this completely exhausts the basic duties of living men (chap. 18).
Filial piety is the root of virtue and that from which teaching comes (chap. 1).
Filial piety is heaven's pervading principle, earth's fundamental meaning, and the people's duty (chap. 7).

The relative vagueness and impersonality of religious concepts such as *T'ien* and *Tao* is certainly not unrelated to the fact that the religious sphere par excellence is the highly personal domestic scene itself. It is father and mother who have the first claim on reverence and it is father and mother who, after their death, will form the center of the family cultus. It is the family cult that is in the foreground. It is the family cult that monopolizes the drama and the intense personal feelings of the religious life. Other objects of religious reverence are mediated to the individual only through the family and have but a reflected light, so to speak. A passage from

Nakae Toju, a seventeenth-century Japanese Confucianist who made filial piety almost into a cosmic principle, illustrates the point:

When we seek to investigate origins [we find that] our body is received from our parents, our parents' bodies are received from heaven and earth, heaven and earth are received from the universe (*taikyo*), and therefore since basically our body is a branch and transformation of the universe and the gods (*shimmei*), we are clearly one with the universe and the gods.[29]

Since one's relation to the universe is mediated through the parents, one's primary religious obligation is filial piety. It is thus that one expresses one's unity with the universe.

A consideration of the family cultus itself is extremely revealing for our purposes. It is interesting that nearly one-fourth of the *Li Chi,* by far the most important early source on ritual practice, is devoted to mourning rites. In order to give indication of what these involved I would like to quote a rather extended passage from the *Li Chi:*

Immediately after his father's death, (the son put off his cap, and) kept his hair, with the pin in it, in the bag (of silk); went barefoot, with the skirt of his dress tucked up under his girdle; and wailed with his hands across his breast. In the bitterness of his grief, and the distress and pain of his thoughts, his kidneys were injured, his liver dried up, and his lungs scorched, while water or other liquid did not enter his mouth, and for three days fire was not kindled (to cook anything for him). On this account the neighbors prepared for him gruel and rice-water, which were his (only) meat and drink. The internal grief and sorrow produced a change in his outward appearance; and with the severe pain in his heart, his mouth could not relish any savoury food, nor his body find ease in anything pleasant.

Someone may ask, "Why does the dressing not commence till three days after death?" and the answer is:—When his parent is dead, the filial son is sad and sorrowful, and his mind is full of trouble. He crawls about and bewails his loss;—how can he hurriedly take (the corpse) and proceed to dress it? Therefore, when it is said that the dressing does not begin till after three days, the meaning is, that (the son) is waiting that time to see if (his father) will come to life. When after three days there is no such return, the father is not alive, and the heart of the filial son is still more downcast. . . .

On the third day there was the (slighter) dressing (of the corpse). . . . At the moving of the corpse, and lifting up of the coffin, (the son) wailed and leaped, times without number. Such was the bitterness of his heart, and the pain of his thoughts, so did his grief and sorrow fill his mind and agitate his spirit, that he bared his arms and leaped, seeking by the movement of his limbs to obtain some comfort to his heart and relief to his spirit.

In presenting the sacrifice (of repose) in the ancestral temple, (the son) offered it (to his parent) in his disembodied state, hoping that his shade would peradventure return (and enjoy it). When he came back to the house from completing the grave, he did not venture to occupy his chamber, but dwelt in the mourning shed, lamenting that his parent was now outside. He slept on the rushes, with a clod for his pillow, lamenting that his parent was in the ground. Therefore he wailed and wept, without regard to time; he endured the toil and grief for three years. His heart of loving thoughts showed the mind of the filial son, and was the real expression of his human feelings.[30]

Though the more extreme aspects of the procedure were greatly modified in later times, the mourning observances remained extremely important. The three-year (actually twenty-seven months) period was strictly observed by the literati, and government officials left office temporarily to do so.

Before making some interpretative remarks let us consider a few examples of what the *Li Chi* has to say about sacrifices to the ancestral tablets, the so-called ancestor worship, which is both an attenuated form of the mourning ritual and the basic periodic ritual of the family cult:

King Wan, in sacrificing, served the dead as if he were serving the living. He thought of them dead as if he did not wish to live (any longer himself). On the recurrence of their death-day, he was sad; in calling his father by the name elsewhere forbidden, he looked as if he saw him. So sincere was he in sacrificing that he looked as if he saw the things which his father loved, and the pleased expression of his face: such was King Wan! The lines of the ode (II, v, ode 2),

When early dawn unseals my eyes,
Before my mind my parents rise,

might be applied to King Wan. On the day after the sacrifice, when the day broke, he did not sleep, but hastened to repeat it; and after it was finished, he still thought of his parents. On the day of sacrifice his joy and sorrow were blended together. He could not but rejoice in the opportunity of offering the sacrifice; and when it was over, he could not but be sad.

When a filial son is about to sacrifice, he is anxious that all preparations should be made beforehand; and when the time arrives, that everything necessary should be found complete; and then, with a mind free from all preoccupation, he should address himself to the performance of his sacrifice.

. . . He sets forth the stands with the victims on them; arranges all the ceremonies and music; provides the officers for the various ministries. These aid in sustaining and bringing in the things, and thus he declares his mind and wish, and in his lost abstraction of mind seeks to have communion with the dead in their spiritual state, if peradventure they will enjoy his offerings, if peradventure they will do so. Such is the aim of the filial son (in his sacrifices).[31]

This do in remembrance of me. If the ancestral sacrifices be compared to the Eucharist then the mourning rites are concerned with Calvary itself. For the death of the father is the death of the son's most religiously significant object. Freud said that the death of a man's father is the most poignant moment in his life. The Confucians made it the most religiously significant as well. All the ambivalence that is normally found in Oedipal situations is revealed in the mourning rites: love and hostility, respect and fear. The aggression against the self and the guilt this indicates are of course normal in the grief work, but the intensity of the reaction probably displays the extent of the unconscious aggression against the father, unconscious because so profoundly disapproved of in this society. The three-year mourning period gives a socially approved opportunity to accomplish the grief work and internalize the lost object. This transition is crucial socially as well as psychologically since upon the death of one's father one becomes in a new sense the head of a family and the family cult. Only then, in a sense, has one really become a father, even though one may have married and had children long before.

The Chinese, of course, have no monopoly on filial piety. Legge, for all his misgivings, could still write, "We are justified in looking on the long-continued existence and growth of the [Chinese] nation as a verification of the promise attached to our fifth commandment, 'Honour thy father and mother, that thy days may be long in the land which Jehovah thy God giveth thee.' "[32] But as we will have occasion to see in a moment, the place of filial piety in Christianity had quite different consequences than in Confucianism.

We have now completed a cursory glance at father-son symbolism in the context of Christianity and Confucianism. While there are common elements the configurations in the two instances are quite different. Let us briefly consider some of the spheres in which these differences expressed themselves.

In the sphere of religious organization the early church saw a rich development of familial symbolism. Abbot, the word for the head of a monastic community, is from the Aramaic for father. Pope, which in the early church was synonymous with bishop, is from the Greek for father. These terms, together with the common term "father" for priest, were used to indicate the appropriately familial relationships that should obtain within the Christian community. The power that made the priests "fathers," however, was not derived from the natural family as such but delegated from God through Christ. Even when the demands of the church contravened those of the natural family the church could claim a higher right to be a true family than could the natural family, in terms of Christian assumptions. This is one of the practical implications of Karl Barth's point mentioned above, that creaturely paternity derives from divine.

No such conception is possible on Confucian assumptions and there is no basis for a structurally independent religious community. For the Confucian any religious community that caused disturbance to actual family relations could only be a perversion. Chu Hsi points this out as follows:

> Beneath Heaven, it is only this normative Principle that unto the end we cannot but follow. The Buddhists and Taoists, for example, even though they would destroy the social relationships [by becoming monks], are nevertheless quite unable to escape them. Thus, lacking (the relationship of) father and son, they nevertheless on the one hand pay respect to their own preceptors (as if they were fathers), and on the other treat their acolytes as sons. The elder among them become elder brother preceptors, while the younger become younger brother preceptors. They are thereby clinging to something false, whereas it is the (Confucian) sages and worthies who have preserved the reality.[33]

For Chu Hsi it is not conceivable that these religious communities could have a higher basis of legitimation than the family. Rather, he perceives them as subject to the pervasive family principle itself, but in a perverted and destructive way.

Again, while Christianity can, in accordance with its basic assumptions, validly use familial terms for religious offices, it can equally well reject such terms. The Reformers rejected the mediatorial function of the clergy and held that Christians are directly related to the triune God without intermediaries.[34] The Reformed churches consequently dropped the use of paternal terminology for their clergy lest any suggestion of spiritual hierarchy remain. Whether the familial terminology is used or dropped the legitimation of Christian assumptions must be divine authority.

The Christian attitude toward political and familial authority is again based on the premise of the derivative nature of such authority, as is well brought out in the following passage from Calvin:

> The end of this precept [the fifth commandment] is, that since the Lord God desires the preservation of the order he has appointed, the degrees of pre-eminence fixed by him ought to be inviolably preserved. The sum of it, therefore, will be that we should reverence them whom God has exalted to any authority over us, and should render them honour, obedience and gratitude.[35]

It is on the basis of authority derived from God that parents and rulers should be reverenced. Calvin goes on to develop his point with considerable warmth:

> For to those, to whom he gives any pre-eminence, he communicates his own authority, as far as is necessary for the preservation of that pre-eminence. The titles of Father, God, and Lord, are so eminently applicable to him, that, whenever we hear either of them mentioned, our minds cannot but be strongly affected with a sense of majesty. Those, therefore, on whom he bestows these titles, he illuminates with a ray of his splendour, to render them all honourable in their respective stations. Thus in a father we ought to recognize something Divine; for it is not without reason that he bears one of the titles of the Deity. Our prince, or our Lord, enjoys an honour somewhat similar to that which is given to God.[36]
>
> Wherefore it ought not to be doubted that God here lays down a universal rule for our conduct; namely, that to everyone, whom we know to be placed in authority over us by his appointment, we should render reverence, obedience, gratitude, and all the other services of our power. Nor does it make any difference, whether they are worthy of this honour, or not. For whatever is their character, yet it is not without the appointment of the Divine providence, that they have attained that station, on account of which the supreme Legislator has commanded them to be honoured. He has particularly enjoined reverence to our parents, who have brought us into this life, which nature itself ought to teach us. For those who violate the parental authority are monsters. Therefore the Lord commands all those, who are disobedient to their parents, to be put to death, as having rendered themselves unworthy to enjoy the light, by their disregarding those by whose means they were introduced to it.[37]

Calvin seems to be determined to use every argument in support of absolute authority. The penalty of disobedience to one illumined by a ray of His splendor is death. He goes on to an involved discussion of the promise of long life attached to the fifth commandment, and then near the end of his discussion adds as a sort of afterthought what is in fact a delayed action bomb that places what went before in a new light:

> But it must be remembered by the way, that we are commanded to obey them "in the Lord;" and this is evident from the foundation before laid; for they preside in that station to which the Lord has exalted them by communicating to them a portion of his honour. Wherefore the submission exercised towards them ought to be a step towards honouring the Supreme Father. Therefore, if they instigate us to any transgression of the law, we may justly consider them not as parents, but as strangers, who attempt to seduce us from obedience to our real Father. The same observation is applicable to princes, lords and superiors of every description. For it is infamous and absurd, that their eminence should avail to depreciate the pre-eminence of God, upon whom it depends, and to which it ought to conduct us.

Unillumined by a ray of His splendor our fathers and princes are strangers.

Of course that "We must obey God rather than men" (Acts 5:29) is good New Testament doctrine, but the Reformation pushed it relentlessly through in every sphere of life. Luther, Calvin, Theodore Beza, and other Reformers disobeyed their fathers at critical junctures of their lives when they felt a divine calling to do so. They were able not only to disobey the pope but to abandon the monarchical principle in the church, when they felt it did not accord with divine intent. And it was not long before English Calvinists would behead an English king, and put a permanent crimp in the monarchical principle in the state as well.

No wonder Calvin protested his devotion to authority in such extreme language. He was unable to admit to himself how revolutionary the implications of his own position were, nor could the aging Luther. The especial violence with which both execrated the Anabaptists reveals that they had to deny in the world what they could not face in themselves. In the case of Luther, Erikson has helped us to understand the special guilt that attaches to a man who has made a great step toward freedom. Calvin, I think, had the same guilt. They had, in a sense, dared too much and they tried to repair the damage in their later years. It is clear that it was only their reliance on an absolute God which made it psychologically possible for them to question every accepted authority in their world without being completely overwhelmed in the process. They bore the guilt for their followers, who could proceed to carry through the implications of their teaching with much less inner conflict.

When we look at the Confucian attitude toward political and familial authority, there does not seem to be any point of leverage in the Confucian symbol system from which disobedience to parents could be justified. This does not mean parents could not be criticized. When they did not live up to the pattern of their ancestors there was indeed a positive duty to remonstrate, but they could not be disobeyed. Thus the *Li Chi* says:

> If a parent have a fault, (the son) should with bated breath, and bland aspect, and gentle voice, admonish him. If the admonition do not take effect he will be the more reverential and the more filial; and when the father seems pleased, he will repeat the admonition. If he should be displeased with this, rather than allow him to commit an offense against any one in the neighborhood or countryside, (the son) should strongly remonstrate. If the parent be angry and (more) displeased, and beat him till the blood flows, he should not presume to be angry and resentful, but be (still) more reverential and more filial.[38]

By suffering patiently and by being even more reverential and filial the son can silently reproach his father. But that is all, at least all that is legitimate within the framework of the Confucian system.

It is true that rebellion against tyrannical rulers has a classical justification in Confucianism, notably in the famous passages in Mencius. Nevertheless there was a strong tendency in Confucianism, especially in neo-Confucianism, to regard political rebellion as virtually in the same category as disobedience to parents. It is notable that major rebellions were usually justified initially in terms of some Taoist or Buddhist ideology, and only when successful was the Confucian stamp of approval received. Of course there was the obligation, as in the case of the family, to remonstrate with an erring superior. But there was little in the Confucian position to justify going beyond that. In this connection the notes of the censor Tso Kuang-tou written to his sons, just before he was tortured to death by the emperor on a trumped-up charge in 1625, are psychologically very revealing:

At this moment my pain and distress are extreme: I can no longer even walk a step. In the middle of the night the pain gets still worse. If I want water to drink, none is at hand. Death! Death! Only thus can I make recompense to the Emperor and to the two imperial ancestors. . . . The bones of my whole body are broken, and my flesh is bloodlogged. . . . This loyal heart came to be at odds with powerful villains and brought about this sore calamity. All sorts of punishments I have willingly endured. Since I have already argued at the risk of my life, why need I shrink from running against the spear and dying? My body belongs to my ruler-father. I am lucky I shall not die in the arms of my wife and children; for I have found the proper place to die! I only regret that this blood-filled heart has not been able to make recompense to my ruler, and that my aged parents cannot once again see my face. This will be my remorse in Hades! . . . My misery is extreme; my pain is extreme. Why do I live on? Why do I cling to life? Death! Only thus can I make recompense to the Emperor and to the two imperial ancestors in Heaven.[39]

There is in such an attitude a truly heroic loyalty that refuses to waver even at such a moment. The roots of the strength and endurance of a great civilization are displayed in these words. But at the same time the Confucian phrasing of the father-son relationship blocks any outcome of Oedipal ambivalence except submission—submission not in the last analysis to a person but to a pattern of personal relationships that is held to have ultimate validity. An outcome that could lead to creative social innovation as in the Protestant case was precluded by the absence of a point of transcendent loyalty that could provide legitimation for it. In the West, from the time of the Mosaic revelation, every particular pattern of social relations was in principle deprived of ultimacy. In China filial piety and loyalty became absolutes. In the West it was God alone who in the last analysis exercised power. In China the father continued to dominate.

Before concluding I would like to suggest two other lines of inquiry that we might pursue if there were time. It is a generally admitted fact that in East Asia there is no literary genre that we might call tragic. There are conquering heroes and there are suffering heroes, but there are no tragic heroes in the Western sense, men whose agony calls into question the justice of the cosmos itself; in a word, there is no Chinese Job. This is not unrelated, it seems to me, to the patterns of father-son symbolism we have been suggesting. The particularly tragic note in the West seems to require a double motion that never quite gets started in China. In the first motion the world is criticized from the point of view of God, but then by a subtle reversal it is God himself who is questioned. Christianity, it is claimed, overcomes the tragic. Perhaps so, but as long as it carries near the heart of its critical narrative the words "My God, My God, Why hast thou forsaken me?" it does not destroy the tragic. However much exegetical effort one makes to explain this away, the fact remains that it is a question. Even when the question is in a sense answered it is not blotted out. The capacity to ask questions of the ultimate is perhaps a consequence of shifting the locus of ultimacy from the natural social order to a transcendent reference point. From the point of view of the transcendent, everything natural has only relative value and can be questioned. But the questioning leads to the question of the ultimate itself.[40]

One last point. Both Christianity and Confucianism repress rather drastically certain forms of aggression. Communism is to be explained in part as an aggressive parody of the religion of divine love. In the Orozco mural at Dartmouth College this is stunningly illustrated in the giant figure of Christ, who stands, legs apart, his left hand raised in a clenched fist salute, his right hand holding the axe with which he has just cut down the cross, and behind him an immense pile of broken idols and symbols of the religions of the world. In its origin Communism can be understood only in relation to the Christian symbolizations that preceded it, and its appeal in various Western countries has been partly conditioned by the variety of Christianity prevailing in them. I would suggest that Chinese Communism must be understood in terms of the particular background of Confucian symbolization. It has apparently succeeded in tapping at last the age-long repressed aggression of sons against fathers, as is indicated by the symbolic denunciation of the father that forms the high point of Chinese Communist "reeducation." But it could do so only by bringing in a basic reference point that transcends the given social and familial order. The capacity of Communism to do this derives in part from its own Christian lineage. And so Christianity, in parody form at least, has come closer in the last fifteen years to the missionaries' dream of "total evangelization" than in the whole preceding century of effort. The subtle dialectic between surviving elements of the Confucian tradition and crypto-Christian Communism helps to explain the dynamism of current Chinese society.

The burden of this brief comparison is that we must take seriously the content and structure of historical religious symbols. The Oedipus complex and the patriarchal family help us to understand much in the Christian and Confucian cases, but they do not explain the differences between them. In fact we have seen on closer inspection that the phrasing and outcome of the Oedipus complex and the structure of the family may themselves be profoundly affected by particular modes of religious symbolization.

NOTES

1 Aristotle, *Politics,* 1252b, 1259b.

2 *Ibid.,* 1252a.

3 Sigmund Freud, *Totem and Taboo,* trans. James Strachey (New York: Norton, 1952), p. 157.

4 George Foot Moore, *Judaism,* vol. 2 (Cambridge: Harvard Univ. Press, 1927), p. 134.

5 Thomas Aquinas, *Summa Contra Gentiles,* bk. 4, chap. 55, par. 14, 18.

6 John Calvin, *Institutes,* bk. 2, chap. 16, par. 10.

7 *Ibid.,* par. 6.

8 Augustine, in E. Przywara, *An Augustine Synthesis* (New York: Harper & Row, Harper Torchbooks, 1958), p. 305.

9 *Ibid.,* p. 287.

10 *Ibid.,* p. 290.

11 Augustine, *City of God,* X: 6.

12 Freud, *The Ego and the Id* (London: Hogarth Press, 1947), p. 36.

13 On this point see E. Voegelin, *Israel and Revolution* (Baton Rouge: Univ. of La. Press, 1956), chap. 12.

14 George Mendenhall, "Law and Covenant in Israel and the Ancient Near East," *The Biblical Archaeologist* 17 (1954).

15 The problem of female symbolism in Christianity is a complicated one and lies beyond the scope of this paper. The central point for present purposes is that none of the members of the Godhead is explicitly female. We cannot here pursue the problems that arise in connection with the Virgin Mary, the feminization of Jesus, or the church itself as a feminine symbol. On the last point, Kenneth Burke's essay on Augustine in *The Rhetoric of Religion* (Boston: Beacon Press, 1961) is especially illuminating.

16 Moore, *op. cit.,* vol. 2, p. 131.

17 *Ibid.,* p. 134.

18 The historical transformation of religious symbolism within and between Judaism and Christianity is a problem of great importance, but

a systematic treatment of it is beyond the scope of this paper. Here I can only stress the main differences between Judaism and Christianity on the one hand and Confucianism on the other.

19 A. Waley, *The Analects of Confucius* (London: Allen & Unwin, 1938), pp. 40–43; H. G. Creel *et al., Literary Chinese,* vol. 1 (Chicago: Univ. of Chicago Press, 1948), p. 66.

20 Marcel Granet, *La Pensée Chinoise* (Paris: Albin Michel, 1934), pp. 300–39.

21 James Legge, *The Chinese Classics,* vol. 1 (London: Oxford Univ. Press, 1893), p. 416.

22 Fung Yu-lan, *A History of Chinese Philosophy,* vol. 1 (Princeton: Princeton Univ. Press, 1953), p. 168.

23 Granet, *op. cit.,* p. 319.

24 *Chuang Tzu,* X.

25 Fung, *op. cit.,* vol. 2, pp. 20–21, 32.

26 Tsunoda *et al., Sources of the Japanese Tradition* (New York: Columbia Univ. Press, 1958), p. 376. Translation slightly revised after consultation with *Ekken Zenshu,* vol. 3, p. 2.

27 Karl Barth, *Church Dogmatics,* vol. 1, no. 1, p. 495.

28 Legge, *op. cit.,* vol. 3, p. 125.

29 *Okina Mondo,* ed. Iwanami, pp. 54–55.

30 Legge, trans., *Sacred Books of the East,* vol. 28, pp. 375–77. The paragraphs have been somewhat rearranged for greater clarity of exposition.

31 *Ibid.,* pp. 210–14 (with omissions).

32 Legge, *The Religions of China* (London: Hodder & Stoughton, 1880), p. 88.

33 Fung, *op. cit.,* vol. 2, p. 569.

34 E.g., Calvin, *op. cit.,* vol. 3, chap. 20, par. 37.

35 *Ibid.,* vol. 2, chap. 8, par. 35.

36 *Ibid.*

37 *Ibid.*

38 Legge, trans., *Sacred Books of the East,* vol. 27, pp. 456–57.

39 Tso Kuang-tou, trans. in Charles O. Hucker, "Confucianism and the Chinese Censorial System," in Nivison and Wright, eds., *Confucianism in Action* (Stanford: Stanford Univ. Press, 1959), p. 208.

40 The emergence of tragedy in Greece is closely related to the philosophical questioning of the inherited myth and ritual pattern from the point of view of a more transcendental conception of reality. On this point see Voegelin, *The World of the Polis* (Baton Rouge: Univ. of La. Press, 1957), chap. 10.

6 The Religious Situation in the Far East

IT IS extremely presumptuous to try to discuss so complex a subject as the religious situation in East Asia in so short a time. All I can do is raise some general considerations and give a few examples. I will try to give some idea of the order of complexity of the problems, but I cannot hope to give any solutions.

In speaking of religion today, I will be using an essentially Tillichian definition—religion as that meaningful structure through which man relates himself to his ultimate concern—and will not be concerned primarily with the largely moribund institutional structure of traditional religion in East Asia. It is the problem of how men in East Asia are attempting to make sense out of the reality in which they find themselves that I will be considering. Actually, in the case of China and Japan there is much in the situation that is the same as that which Paul Tillich discussed last time as being in the situation of contemporary Western man. For in China and Japan, too, people are having to face the human problems of a rapidly expanding rationalization, mechanization, and bureaucratization. I feel that both in the case of our society and East Asian societies, the rapid pace of modernization and industrialization holds enormous promise as well as danger. This new situation confronts us with enormous potentialities as well as constrictions. But even the potentialities are deeply disturbing and raise profound questions of meaning.

There is another aspect of the modern situation, however, that we

This chapter was first given as a public lecture at the Harvard Divinity School in the fall of 1961, just after my return from a year in Japan. It was one of a series of lectures, and the preceding one had been given by Paul Tillich, which explains several references in the chapter to him. This chapter and the following one were my first efforts to characterize the central religious and cultural issues of Japan's modernization.

do not share with East Asia. For better or for worse, the modern situation grew up out of our own Western tradition. Whether you consider it a fulfillment or a pervasion of that tradition, or some combination of the two, still you cannot deny that that is where it came from and everywhere the roots are deep in our own past. In East Asia the case is completely different. The modern situation did not arise out of the East Asian past, either as natural growth or as pathological aberration; rather, it came from without. It came often sharply, even brutally, and it had no roots in the past. Now, for a hundred years East Asia has been inundated with modern Western culture, but inevitably, because of the very nature of the modern West, not with our modern culture alone but with the whole Western tradition. The modern East Asian intellectual has to grapple not only with Einstein and Karl Marx, but just as deeply with Aristotle and Jesus Christ. So the modern situation has raised the problem of cultural identity in East Asia as it has in the West, but, I think, in a far more shocking and disturbing way. For a man, in a sense, is his past. When he sees the past radically threatened his reaction may be, and in East Asia has been, extreme.

The starting point for any analysis of the ways in which East Asian societies have responded to the problems of meaning that the last hundred years have presented to them is to consider the religious cultural structure that had developed out of the East Asian tradition and that was still functioning as a more or less coherent system when Western impingement began to intensify. We find that that religious cultural structure was defined and limited by a version, or rather several versions, of the cosmological myth through which men in the archaic societies of both East and West have everywhere related themselves to reality. By the cosmological myth I mean that set of symbolizations in which nature, society, and self are seen as fused in a more or less compact unity.

The cosmological myth was broken first in the West in the Mosaic revelation at Sinai, which proclaimed the radical transcendence of God. In the symbolization of the radical transcendence of God, a sharp differentiation between God and world and between self and society occurs for the first time, giving rise to the possibility of a new kind of universalism and individualism. In the cosmological myth these differentiations tend to be blurred. Society is viewed as an integral part of eternal being and the individual has no place to stand from which to judge it. It is not that experiences of transcendence do not occur in societies based on the cosmological myth, but that the experiences do not receive the sharp objective symbolization that occurs in biblical (and I must add Koranic) religion.

To call the religious cultural structure of East Asian society "pre-Mosaic," as it can be discerned in the early nineteenth century, would be misleading if it caused us to overlook the richly symphonic development of profound religious and cultural insights that has occurred over several thousand years in those societies. If, however, the term is used merely to point to the absence of certain fundamental differentiations that developed out of biblical religion, then it would have some meaning.

One version of the East Asian cosmological myth, which had both Confucian and Buddhist antecedents, viewed the universe as an organic system of interdependent parts. In this view the individual was seen as receiving an endless flow of blessings from his parents, his ruler, and, ultimately, from heaven and earth. In return he owes a debt of service to all from whom he has received. In particular, and very centrally in East Asian ethics, he owes filial piety to his parents and loyalty to his ruler. A slightly different version of the cosmological myth stressed the fundamental unity of the essence of all things, again an idea with both Confucian and Buddhist overtones. In this version the individual who earnestly seeks for his own true soul will discover that it is the same as the soul of heaven and earth and all things. This quest for the true soul involves elements of mysticism, but it is not, in East Asia, a world-rejecting mysticism. Having discovered his true self the individual is able all the more to operate in harmony with the social and natural context in which he find himself. Both versions contain, and at certain times strongly, intimations of transcendence and universalism, but these intimations were not strong enough to break through the compact symbolism of man, society, and nature. Therefore the historical consequences of the various versions of the cosmological myth tended largely to reinforce a society in which the basic social patterns were beyond question and the individual was submerged in a network of particular social obligations.

However profoundly they differed, both China and Japan began their modern experience still living in the power of cosmological symbolization. However different their modern experiences have been, the last hundred years have shattered, probably forever, their integrated cosmological symbolic structures, though elements of those structures survive in many new forms. The traditional symbolic structures have not as integrated entities been able to withstand the massive invasion of Western cultural forms. The radical transcendence of biblical religion was not the only factor that shattered the cosmological framework of East Asian civilization, though, as we shall see, it played a part in the process. There were also the new cosmological symbolisms of the modern West, the world immanent symbolisms of liberal utilitarianism, and Marxian Communism.

In a sense, we can almost say that in the last hundred years the pre-Mosaic East has met the post-Christian West. Those who see a deep historic resonance between Confucianism and Marxism as two examples of world immanent social salvationism are probably not entirely wrong. But in the last analysis, the differences are more decisive than the similarities. The modern Western cosmological myths have taken form against the background of the radical transcendence of biblical religion. In their very structures they presuppose and imply it. Everywhere the new Western ideologies touch the traditional East Asian symbolizations, they corrode and eventually destroy them.

The traditional symbolic patterns have not been given up without a struggle. Indeed, at certain points in modern history they have even taken on a new vigor, as for example, in Chiang Kai-shek's Confucian revival of the 1930s or the revival of the Japanese spirit before 1945. But in both cases the renewed health proved to be unnatural and ill-fated, in the end as disastrous as it was ephemeral. On the whole it seems safe to say that however many discrete traditional elements may survive, the overall integrated structure of traditional symbolization is irrevocably shattered.

I would like to trace briefly in a few examples some of the vicissitudes of that shattering process. Both because of limitations of time and of my knowledge, I will confine myself largely to examples drawn from Japan. One of the earliest positive reactions to the West in Japan (and China, too) was the idea that borrowing from the West could be fruitful in the realm of means, while maintaining the integrity of East Asian civilization. The slogan "Eastern morality and Western technology" was widely voiced in both countries. But especially for those who were already of mature age when Western thought first came flooding into the country, this attitude was not so much a conscious slogan as an unconscious assumption. This assumption is to be discovered even in many of those who seem most radical in their reception of Western ideas. Take, for example, a statement from Kono Hironaka, a leader of the Liberal party that emerged only a few years after the opening of the country, in which he recounts the decisive influence that reading John Stuart Mill's "On Liberty" had on his life:

> I was riding on horseback when I first read this work. In a flash my entire way of thinking was revolutionized. Until then I had been under the influence of the Chinese Confucianists and of the Japanese classical scholars, and I had even been inclined to advocate an "expel the barbarian" policy. Now all these earlier thoughts of mine, *excepting those concerned with loyalty and filial piety,* were smashed to smithereens. At the same moment I knew that it was human freedom and human rights that I must henceforth cherish above all else.

But by "excepting" the two cardinal Confucian virtues of loyalty and filial piety, Hironaka was leaving intact the whole organic structure of society and the universe that they imply, and so radically undercutting the possibilities of his own liberalism.

It is among the early Japanese Protestant Christians that we see the deepest assumptions of the traditional view questioned for the first time. Let us now turn to the account of Niijima Jo who is telling about what happened to him as a result of his early study of the Bible. He says:

> And Jesus Christ, who was the Son of God bearing on His body the sins of the world, delivered Himself up to death by crucifixion. That we designate Him the Saviour, I was also able to know. And when I happened to read these lines I shut the book, looked around, and asked myself who it was that created me, my parents? No! *It was not my parents, but God who created me!*

Niijima's "No!" with a single sharp blow shivers the whole crystalline structure of East Asian symbolization. It is not parents *and* ruler *and* heaven and earth to whom we owe obligations. It is in the first instance to God that we are obligated. Everything else flows from that.

In the case of Ebina Danjo, another prominent early Christian, we can see the same process from a different angle. Ebina was a young samurai warrior at the time of the collapse of the feudal system and the restoration of the emperor in 1868. As a hereditary retainer of the Yanagawa fief he had been taught that loyalty to his feudal lord was his highest obligation, but because of the new situation his whole pattern of morality came into question. Speaking of his feudal lord he says,

> . . . I had firmly decided to "offer up" my life for him. However, the Yanagawa fief was lost, the castle burnt, and my young lord had been killed. I felt terribly lonely. Because the young lord was dead, there was no one to whom I could offer my life, and this was the essence of my loneliness. To whom could I offer my life after this?

The answer to his question came in a strange way through an American schoolteacher named Janes, in whose school Ebina found himself not long after. Ebina describes what happened in his own words:

> One night I had an experience which changed the course of my entire life. This took place at a Bible study meeting at Mr. Janes' house. Mr. Janes had prayed numerous times before, but for some reason he commanded us to stand that night. My friends rose one after another since they respected Janes, but I, feeling that I could not agree with the prayer, did not think it was right for me to stand. My indecision lasted for only a moment, but during that moment I suffered intensely. On the other hand, however, something was opening in my heart. This something was gratitude. Since it was natural to have obligations to one's lord and parents I thought it permissible to repay my obligations to "heaven" but to request anything of heaven was, in my opinion, a mistake. Nevertheless I had been told to stand. For some time I failed to do this, but thinking that it would be all right if it were to thank "heaven" I finally stood. This being all that was required of me, I was convinced that even a Confucianist could do it.
>
> When Mr. Janes finished reading the Bible he became very serious and said that he would like to say a few words about prayer. I was deeply moved when he went on to say that prayer was our duty to the creator. In that instant the light dawned on me. Ah! I had been neglecting my duty. I had done something unpardonable. If it were my duty I should bend my knee; I should bow my head; as a matter of fact I should be willing to do anything. It was exactly because God had created me that it was a mistake for me to exist for myself. Just like the Ptolemaic world I was self-centered, while God existed in the periphery around me to be used by me. Then, however, God became central and I became like the world of Copernicus. My way of thinking changed in the same way that the thought concerning the heavenly systems changed. When I reached this point I was completely and profoundly humiliated . . . however, hearing God's command I became a changed person. I became a com-

pletely changed being. Speaking of the inner self, it was at that moment that I brought about the restoration of imperial rule.

This, I think, is an extraordinarily interesting portrayal of the shift from cosmological to Christian symbolism. From thanking heaven as merely one alongside other objects to which gratitude is owed and a peripheral one at that, the obligation to God becomes absolute and is symbolized in the scientific vocabulary of astronomy that Ebina was also learning from Janes at the time, as the shift from Ptolemaic to Copernican thinking.

Though only a few Japanese became Christians, many underwent experiences similar to those of the young Ebina in finding that the rapid changes occurring in the years following the opening of the country called into question the traditional morality in which they had been raised. In the face of this situation the conservative leadership of the country came forward with a reformulation of the traditional cosmological symbolism in what has become known as the Meiji emperor system. This was an attempt to rephrase the old presuppositions in a new way and to fit them to the modern context. This new ideology, interestingly enough, became evident especially in the events surrounding the promulgation of the Constitution of 1889. A constitution at all was, of course, an extremely modern thing. But in its preamble it is noted that it is the free gift of the sacred and inviolable emperor who reigns for ages eternal. In the Imperial Rescript on Education issued in 1890, and henceforth read with great solemnity on certan ceremonial occasions in every school in Japan, the lineaments of the new ideology can be easily discerned:

Know ye, Our Subjects:

Our Imperial Ancestors have founded Our Empire on a basis broad and everlasting, and have deeply and firmly implanted virtue; Our subjects ever united in loyalty and filial piety have from generation to generation illustrated the beauty thereof. This is the glory of the fundamental character of Our Empire, and herein also lies the source of Our education. Ye, Our subjects, be filial to your parents, affectionate to your brothers and sisters; as husbands and wives be harmonious, as friends, true; bear yourselves in modesty and moderation; extend your benevolence to all; pursue learning and cultivate arts, and thereby develop intellectual faculties and perfect moral powers; furthermore, advance public good and promote common interests; always respect the Constitution and observe the laws; should emergency arise, offer yourselves courageously to the State; and thus guard and maintain the prosperity of Our Imperial

Throne coeval with heaven and earth. So shall ye not only be Our good and faithful subjects, but render illustrious the best traditions of your forefathers.

The Way here set forth is indeed the teaching bequeathed by Our Imperial Ancestors, to be observed alike by Their Descendants and the subjects, infallible for all ages and true in all places. It is Our wish to lay it to heart in all reverence, in common with you, Our subjects, that we may all attain to the same virtue.

October 30, 1890

Here we can see vividly how clearly cosmological elements, for example the merging of society and nature implied in the phrase "Our Imperial Throne, coeval with heaven and earth," are juxtaposed with new ideas, such as "respect the Constitution." What seems to be happening is that the traditional cosmological symbolism is being reformulated especially around the person of the emperor, who was by no means so central in the tradition itself, in order to provide a religious legitimation for the new Japanese state. In this structure the emperor is not so much an analogue of the European king as of a fusion of European king and Christian God. Functionally, at least, this is the case; though, of course, the Japanese idea of god, understandable only in terms of the divine human continuity of the cosmological myth, is very different from the Jewish-Christian notion.

What happened when the Christian who had found a transcendent focus of loyalty entirely outside the cosmological imagination first came up against this refurbished cosmological ideology is vividly illustrated in the words of Uchimura Kanzo, describing what was to be a symbolic event of the first magnitude:

March 6, 1891

Since I wrote you last, my life has been a very eventful one. On the 9th of Jan. there was in the High Middle School where I taught, a ceremony to acknowledge the Imperial Precept on Education. After the address of the President and reading of the said Precept, the professors and students were asked to go up to the platform one by one, and *bow* to the Imperial signature affixed to the Precept, *in the manner as we used to bow before our ancestral relics as prescribed in Buddhist and Shinto ceremonies.* I was not at all prepared to meet such a strange ceremony, for the thing was the new invention of the president of the school. As I was the third in turn to go up and bow, I had scarcely time to think upon the matter. So, hesitating in doubt, I took a safer course for my Christian conscience, in the august presence of sixty professors (all non-Christians, the two other Xtian prof.'s beside myself having absented themselves) and over one thousand students, I took my stand and did *not* bow! It was an awful moment for me, for I instantly apprehended the result of my conduct. The anti-Christian sentiment which was and still is strong in the school, and which it was a very delicate affair to soothe down by meekness and kindliness on our part, found a just cause (as they suppose) for bringing forth against me accusations of insult against the nation and its Head, and through me against the Christians in general. . . .

Eventually Uchimura did agree to bow provided everyone understood that the act implied only respect, and not worship, which the principal assured him was the case. But the nationwide scandal that the event caused became so great that Uchimura was dismissed. Though the Christians on the whole equivocated and even Uchimura was not always clear on the fundamental issues, that brief, almost instinctive action of his revealed the truth about the new emperor ideology, and so became a symbolic act of great significance in modern Japanese history. Of course, the Meiji emperor system was not without its ambiguities, and it actually left considerable latitude for the liberal democratic tendencies that developed in a number of areas until about 1930. But after 1930 a virulent ideology of nationalism and imperialism, which was to lead the Japanese people to the brink of total disaster, found in the emperor system a ready-made starting point.

Japanese Christianity had social consequences out of all proportions to the small percentage of the population that became Christian, and not only in the sphere of symbolic actions. In the struggle for popular rights and the equality of women Christians were often in the forefront. Christians were also active in the early attempt to form labor unions at a time when Japan was in the grip of the industrial revolution. And it should be noted that five of the six founders of the Japanese Socialist party in 1902 were Christians.

The sometimes unexpected consequences of Christian influence are well illustrated in this letter written by Kawakami Hajime from prison in the 1930s.

I went to Tokyo to study at the age of twenty, after graduating from Yamaguchi High School. I had read the *Analects* of Confucius and Mencius, but had never laid hands on either the Buddhist scriptures or the Bible. The latter I read for the first time after going to Tokyo. But the moment I came across the passage "whoever will smite thee on thy right cheek, turn to him the other also. And whosoever shall compel thee to go a mile, go with him twain. Give to him that asketh thee, and from him that would borrow of thee turn not thou away" (Matthew 5:39–42), it had a most decisive effect upon my life. This was something beyond all reasoning. My soul cried out from within itself, "That's right. It must be so." Of course, I was unable truly to put this teaching into practice, but every time something came up these words stimulated me, encouraged me, and drove me on to "extraordinary" actions. Thus the direction of my life was set toward a concern for others as well as for myself.

Two incidents took place before I moved from Tokyo to Kyoto. One was that I went and heard some speeches appealing for aid to the victims of copper poisoning at the Ashio Mine, and donated the scarf and overcoat I was wearing. Furthermore, after going home, I packed up everything but what I had on and turned it over to them.

He then goes on to tell how upset his mother was when she learned of this as she was herself in desperate poverty and working to put him through college. The second incident I will omit and go to the last paragraph of his letter.

Looking back I realize that almost thirty years have passed since then. You might as well say that my being here in prison at the age of sixty stems from those passages in the Bible. I was given Bibles by some people at Toyotama Prison, Ichigaya Prison, and here. But I personally feel that I may be closer to the spirit of the Bible than those people who gave them to me.

Why was Kawakami in prison? Because he was arrested in 1933 as an active member of the Japanese Communist party. Until his death in 1946 Kawakami remained a convinced Marxist and Communist even while conceiving of Communist society as the fulfillment of the Sermon on the Mount. Of course Kawakami is a very special case, yet he illustrates something of the eschatological significance that Marxism has had in modern Japan. Marxism, offspring, for better or worse, of the Christian West, has been in modern Japan, together with Christianity, the great challenger of the cosmological tradition. Marxism, like Christianity, has meant for many an opportunity to break out from the choking constriction of tradition-bound social groups and to find true individuality in standing for universal principles.

Japanese intellectuals have in recent years grown increasingly critical of the Communist countries, and the Japanese generally have shown no greater proclivity to commit themselves to the Communist party than they have to the Christian church. But in the sphere of ideas Marxism has played a very great role, and one only understandable in terms of Japanese experience, not ours. Though not always with quite the clarity with which it is evident in the case of Kawakami, this role has had a strongly religious dimension.

The search for individuality that I have noted as being associated with the appeal of both Christianity and Marxism is a constant theme in modern Japanese literature. In a society in which the cosmological symbolism remains strong the individual tends to be merged in his social group. He often feels entrapped in a strangling network of social obligation. As his social roles become more differentiated and he becomes aware of a greater range of his own and world culture, his need to experience his own individuality increases. This theme of individuality, which runs through modern Japanese literature, is expressed much more in the need for it than in its fulfillment. In fact, if we could characterize this literature with a single word it would be despair, especially despair about the individual. Such despair, as Professor Tillich points out with regard to Western literature, has a religious dimension. This becomes explicit in a number of writers. For example, Natsume Soseki in one of his last novels has his hero recognize only three ways out: death, madness, or religion. But for Natsume and for many other writers the religious way, which meant for him, as for many intellectuals, Zen Buddhism, remained closed. Nevertheless, the attempt to reformulate the East Asian tradition, this time to meet not so much the problem of social ethics as the subjective problem of the experience of individuality, was undertaken by Nishida Kitaro and achieved enormous currency in his philosophy.

The Nishida philosophy, which exerted great influence in the twenties and thirties in Japan and is still very much alive today, is enormously difficult and complex, and I can only give a preliminary estimate of it at this time. Nishida's first book, *A Study of the Good,* pubilshed in 1911, is in itself an amazing achievement. Basing itself squarely on the East Asian tradition, especially on that version that I said stressed the fundamental unity of the essence of all things, in Nishida as experienced in the practice of Zen meditation, it integrates with great sophistication an immense range of Western philosophical and religious thought from Plato to the German idealists, and from Jesus to the medieval Christian mystics. While it contains many rich facets and diverse implications, I think one could still assert that Nishida philosophy is in the final analysis a neo-traditional synthesis formally similar to the Meiji emperor system.

This is not to say that I agree with the current opinion in Japan, which would characterize Nishida philosophy as the intellectual orthodoxy of its day. It is too complex and open-ended a system to be called an orthodoxy. But its function nonetheless seems to me to have been to reformulate the traditional Eastern spirituality, suitably illuminated with Western insights, so as to handle the increasingly deep crisis in meaning arising over the problem of individuality. I do not doubt that Nishida had a genuine experience of transcendence, but he caught it in a philosophical network that remained within the confines of the cosmological myth. For example, note the following passage on God (it is significant that he discusses "God," which itself gives a Western overtone to what he is saying):

> We call the foundation of this universe God. As I have stated above, I do not view God as a transcendent creator outside the universe, but I think He is directly the foundation of this reality. The relationship between God and the universe is not a relationship such as that between an artist and his work, but is the relationship between essence and phenomenon, and the universe is not a thing created by God, but is a "manifestation" of God. From the movement of the sun, moon and constellations to the inner workings of the human soul, among all there is nothing which is not a manifestation of God; at the foundation of these things, through each one we are able to worship the spiritual light of God.

Here God has been captured within the cosmos as its "foundation." The implications of this conception for religious action and the solution of the problem of individuality on this basis appear in this passage:

> This kind of deepest religion can be established on the basis that God and man are the same substance, and the true meaning of religion resides in acquiring this significance of the union of God and man. In other words, it resides in experiencing in the foundation of our consciousness the lofty universal spirit which operates, destroying the consciousness of the self. Faith is not something which must be given from without according to legend and logic, but is something which must be cultivated from within. As Jacob Boehm has said, we arrive at God

through the deepest internal life (*die innerste Geburt*). At the same time that in this internal rebirth we see God directly and we believe in Him, herein we also find the true life of the self and feel unlimited power.

Unlimited power was precisly what the modern Japanese intellectual to whom the Nishida philosophy appealed did not feel. Nishida offered him the hope of a profound realization of himself together with a complete harmonization with his world. For many it was a very attractive offer. It is difficult, however, to deny what present-day Japanese critics assert when they say that the Nishida position tended to lead away from social responsibility at just the time when the balance between democracy and militarism was most delicate. And even leaving that aside, the question remains as to what kind of individuality has been experienced if the individual, in returning from his Zen meditation hall, finds himself enmeshed in exactly the same network of social constrictions as before he went to it.

Finally, let me turn to one more Japanese thinker, Ienaga Saburo, born in 1913, and an influential intellectual in Japan today. Ienaga has been influenced by most of the currents we have discussed already, by Marxism, Christianity, and the Nishida philosophy. Like Nishida, his religious position is a reformulation of East Asian positions with Western insights, but, unlike Nishida, he seems to have grasped radical transcendence and largely escaped the cosmological limitations. Speaking of himself he says,

When I entered Higher School in the spring of 1931, just before the Manchurian incident, Marxism was still at its zenith. In the year I entered school there were two strikes arising from questions of student thought. Facing that atmosphere for the first time in my life and seeing that the nationalist morality which had been poured into me at home and at school was without authority, I felt that the ground on which I stood had crumbled. Seeking for something on which my spirit could rely, I took hold of philosophy. After the orthodox morality which had no basis outside of the historical tradition of the past had slipped from the seat of my heart, philosophy, which speaks of "what one ought to do," had for me a fresh fascination. Throwing away many years of educational precepts I was spiritually reborn. This is an incident which can be called the Copernican Revolution in my spiritual life.

Interestingly enough, it was German neo-Kantianism, as mediated through one of the leaders of the Nishida school of philosophy, which provided him with his philosophical rebirth. In his first year in the university (1934) he experienced, however, a new and deeper crisis, this time of a religious nature. "At that time, for various reasons, I felt beaten in mind and body," he writes. Faced with great anxieties about his future, he found that the "dry and lifeless university lectures without any real thought in them" could not save him from a feeling of despair. In addition, he was afflicted with steadily declining health. In this situation he says he experienced for the first time the meaning of a statement by a seventh-century Japanese Buddhist: "The world is empty and false; only the Buddha is true." But he found his religious solution especially in the thirteenth-century Buddhist leader, Shinran Shonin, who stressed the absolute incapacity of men to save themselves and the necessity for faith alone. This position Ienaga elucidates with quotations from Paul to the Romans. Since the war Ienaga has turned very much to constitutional and social reform problems. It is not always easy to see the organic relation between the religious position, which he still holds, and his present social activism. Nevertheless, it would seem that his perception of radical transcendence, as mediated in one strand of Japanese Buddhism, is related to his social concern, and that he represents, at least, the possibility of reformulations out of the Japanese tradition which will not end in the cosmological cul de sac, but will genuinely contribute to the solution of the contemporary religious and social problems.

In conclusion, let me emphasize how fragmentary this presentation has been. I have elected to bring you a few concrete examples rather than a purely abstract general characterization. In a sense none of the examples I have given can be taken as typical. They are merely a selection from among the possibilities that have emerged in the modern Japanese experience. But whatever may be the case for the moment in China, it is precisely in its wealth of possibilities that the Japanese religious situation is to be characterized.

7 Values and Social Change in Modern Japan

I

IT IS POSSIBLE to differentiate between a cultural system and a social system. This is often done unconsciously, but it can be done from a more careful, analytic point of view as well. By a cultural system I mean that collection of symbol systems that includes such areas as science, art, literature, ethics, philosophy, and so on, considering them as cultural patterns more or less in themselves. They are, of course, interrelated with a social system but are to a certain degree independent, detachable elements that, of course, can be transmitted to other social systems. They are the object of cultural history, or history of thought, or more special histories, history of literature, history of science, and so on. However, my approach is not primarily that of cultural history or history of thought, but is closer to what is called in Japanese "*Seishinshi*"[1] if that category be interpreted in a rather special way. My concern is not in the first instance with the cultural systems that I have been talking about, but with the social system itself. However, I believe that within the social system there are cultural elements that are partly constitutive of that social system; this is what I mean, and what I think a good many social scientists mean, when they speak of a social value system as being part of any social system. Consequently, social action itself is not determined just by the structure

This chapter is based on tape recordings of three lectures I gave at International Christian University in Tokyo in the late spring of 1961. For this volume the first lecture has been omitted and the others have been somewhat revised; nevertheless some traces of oral delivery survive. Not only in form but also in content this chapter represents a rather immediate reaction to the spiritual climate prevailing in Japan at the time and to some of the broader issues of modern Japanese culture and society.

of economic, political, or social relationships, but also by the structure of social values that are, of course, related to the cultural system in the pure sense of culture, but are, nevertheless, not superstructure in the Marxist sense; rather, they are actual structural parts of the social system. These social values indicate what is a good society, what is good social action, what are good social relations, what is a good person as a member of society; these values regulate individual attitudes as well as the way social relationships are phrased in any society. These values limit choices; they make some choices more likely; they make some choices almost impossible in the realm of social action. That is, the social value system creates a set of possibilities and impossibilities for social action.

A relatively flexible Marxist could even agree with me up to that point, but the next point would probably leave him behind. Namely, I do not believe that such value systems are direct reflections of economic or class forces, or that they change necessarily when economic or class forces change. In fact, I believe that they are more stable and persistent than economic or class forces, and, in fact, that change coming from the economic conditions or changes in the system of social stratification will be channeled partly by the structure of values. Hence I naturally consider the study of the value system to be a very strategic point for the analysis of any society.

The next point concerns religion and why my concentration on the study of religion. That is because I believe that religion is close to the core of any social value system. Here, of course, we are in trouble at once, because the word religion is very ambiguous and means a great many different things to a great many different people. And here again we should distinguish between cultural system in a pure sense and in a social system. What I am interested in primarily is religion insofar as it is part of the social system, not religious philosophy or theology for its own sake, though that is certainly important to study in relation to society. For example, in the case of Japan, I am not interested in what is usually meant by the religions of Japan, where you start with Buddhism and talk about the six Nara Sects and then Tendai and Shingon and so on all the way through. Rather, I am concerned with religion as it is a constitutive part of the process of social existence in Japan; this means concretely the structure of beliefs and practices focusing around the Butsudan and Kamidana,[2]—the shrine, the worship of ancestors, the respect or worship of the emperor, and so on. This is not to be considered in terms of the categories of Buddhism, Confucianism, and Shintō, because here we have a complex and blurred combination of many different cultural elements from many different cultural sources that are actually a unity in the functional life of the ordinary Japanese person. For certain purposes it is, however, of prime importance to discuss the doctrinal, philosophical positions, but that will come later.

I would argue that the basic pattern of traditional Japanese values still largely dominates Japanese society, though this is a very controversial point about which a great deal of argument has centered. This basic pattern of value is very old. It predates the Edo period, during which it was developed and elaborated, and it can perhaps be traced back to the Kamakura period. In some respects it goes back to the beginning of literate Japanese civilization, to Shōtoku Taishi and the Taika Reform. There is nothing at all unusual about this case, for the same thing can be found in other societies. Systems of social values are highly resistant to basic alteration and show a tendency to persist through long periods of time. This fact, if it is a fact, is a major concept to consider in our world today.

I have argued in *Tokugawa Religion* that Japanese modernization in its successes and its failures cannot be understood unless we take into consideration this Japanese value pattern.[8] It is time to specify its contents.

1. Value is realized in groups that are thought of as natural entities. The community (*Gemeinschaft, kyōdōtai*) is the locus of value.

2. These groups are thought to be integrated with the structure of reality and thus are endowed with a sacred quality.

3. There is a divine-human continuity in which the symbolic heads of groups have an especially important place, being especially endowed with a sacred quality. One of their functions is to relate the group to the divine ancestors and protective deities. This pattern applies at many levels, e.g., family (and its ancestor worship), village (and the local deity, *ujigami*), and ultimately the whole country at whose head is the emperor (and above him the imperial ancestors).

4. Individuals exist because of a continuous flow of blessings from spirits and ancestors through the symbolic heads of groups. The individual is obligated to work in order to repay in small measure the blessings he has received and to sacrifice himself for the group if necessary.

5. Science, ethics, philosophy—virtually all aspects of culture—are valuable only insofar as they contribute to the realization of value in the group, not as ends in themselves. Ethics consist mainly in acting as one should in one's group; there is no universal ethic.

6. In spite of how completely the individual is merged in group life there is one place where he can be relatively independent: the realm of personal expressiveness, including art, mysticism, recreation, and skill. But this sphere does not legitimize failure to fulfill group expectations. It actually helps reconcile the individual to group demands.

I think this value pattern, stated rather briefly and abstractly, is very strong even today, and it provided a very important basis of the Japanese modernization process. Within certain limitations it was, in fact, a successful basis, successful from two points of view. First of all, because of its stress on group coherence and group discipline it provided a relatively well-organized, disciplined social structure on which a modern state could be erected rather rapidly, and that modern state was then able to shape and control the energy of the society in the direction of, at least in some spheres, very rapid modernization. Secondly, the structure of values provided the energy for work necessary in a modern economy by gearing the obligation of individuals to work for the group into the structure of economic life. One characteristic of the Japanese economy for many centuries, and certainly until very recent times, is that it has been an economy based on very small units of production, units organized in terms of the old values. People have worked in these units in terms of the obligation pattern of the old values so that the traditional structure did not have to be broken down and new values developed that could support economic activity, as in other cases.

The religious and cultural basis of modernization in the West was provided by the series of developments beginning with the prophetic conception of God, moving to the organization of the Christian church and then to the turning of the church into the world in the Reformation. That whole process, of course, is essentially different from what happened in Japan. However, it is necessary to qualify such an absolutely negative comparison because, actually, the value pattern that I have outlined would imply a static quality, which is not in fact characteristic of Japanese history. Related to the complexity and development of Japanese society is a long cultural tradition of transcendence in Japan that for various reasons has been a submerged and almost drowned tradition but, nevertheless, has repeatedly had important social consequences and may continue to do so. Hence, before we can discuss the modern period we must consider this aspect of the Japanese cultural tradition.

In order to analyze what I have called the submerged tradition of transcendence in the history of Japanese values, we must turn away from the mass of everyday religion and discuss certain developments in the Japanese religious tradition in the narrower sense. In connection with this tradition of transcendence, developments must be considered that at one time or another emerged from the central traditions in the Japanese background: Buddhism, Confucianism, and Shintō. Finally, we must turn to the way the Japanese reacted to Christianity, as an indication of both the potentiality and the limitations of transcendence in that tradition.

Buddhism is the most striking example and biggest problem in what I am calling the tradition of transcendence in Japan. In this area the little book of Ienaga Saburō, *The Development of the Logic of Negation in the History of Japanese Thought,* is extremely suggestive. What Ienaga means by *hitei* ("negation") will emerge in a minute or two. He begins his discussion of the development of this phenomenon in Japan at the beginning of Japanese literate civilization with the very striking words of Shōtoku Taishi, "The world is a lie, only Buddha is truth." What Ienaga means by *hitei* is the first phrase, "The world is a lie." This is an absolute denial of the actual world (*gensei*), which is very sharply different from the pre-Buddhist tradition in Japan, which accepted the world we live in as the world without any problem. In *hitei,* of course, there is a dialectical quality of absolute denial followed by absolute affirmation: the Buddha is truth.

Of course Shōtoku Taishi is an extremely complex figure, one of the most interesting figures in Japanese history and one of the most rewarding to study, and absolute negation is not by any means the whole of his thought. In fact, the new ethic that he introduced in the seventeen articles is largely Confucian and largely affirmative (*kōtei*), but it is the affirmation of a new structure in relation to Japanese history. It is possible to interpret this moment of transcendence that comes with Shōtoku Taishi as perhaps essential in the revolution that he was involved in bringing about. In order to be able to introduce a whole new civilization into Japan, he had to have a point from which to break radically with tradition. Such a statement as "The world is a lie, only Buddha is truth" gave him a position from which he could devaluate, if he needed to, any part of Japanese tradition, and break with the restraints of that tradition. This is a moment of transcendence that played a vital role in the social process, though in this book that is not Ienaga's concern. He argues, rather, that this position of denial (*hitei*), which was grasped so clearly by Shōtoku Taishi, was only gradually understood by the Japanese people on a large scale through a long process in which they had to experience social disruption and the actual breaking apart of the traditional society.

This historical process that the Japanese people went through culminated in Kamakura Buddhism, and above all with Shinran. In him there is absolute reliance on the power of Amida, which is the direct outcome of the absolute rejection of reliance on anything in the world, including of course one's own power. This was the same time in Japanese history when Nichiren appeared, who also had his own kind of transcendent position from which he was able to consider everything, even the emperor, as subordinate to the Buddha of the Lotus Sutra. Nichiren, with his political prophecy, is an almost unique figure in East Asia and one of the very few who can be compared with the political prophets in the Old Testament.

So we have this great outpouring of the recognition of transcendence in Kamakura times together with new forms of society and new cultural forms that in many ways laid down the lines of Japanese development through the Tokugawa period. However the note of transcendence was soon lost. It was drowned out by the ground bass, so to speak, of the Japanese tradition of this-worldly affirmativeness, the opposite of denial.

Why was this moment of transcendence not actualized, not institutionalized in an ongoing tradition, Ienaga asks himself. Others too have asked and the question has not yet by any means been fully answered. Ienaga's answer is two-fold: There were other elements within the Buddhist tradition itself that prevented the full realization of this transcendence. Here he mentions Zen, above all. Though in a sense Zen is the dialectical completion of the movement of the logic of negation, in another way it easily slips into simple affirmation. Secondly, he remarks on the rise of the dictatorial political powers who subordinated everything to themselves. He mentions that Nobunaga and Hideyoshi considered themselves to be gods, had themselves worshiped, and broke the power of the Buddhist church. There is also another point, that the power of Confucianism was enormously broadened from Kamakura, especially Muromachi times, and very much carried forward by the monks themselves, above all by the Zen monks who taught Confucian ethics and philosophy, especially the teachings of Chu Hsi. The main tendency in Confucianism is not transcendence but world-affirmation. However, besides these external factors there were important internal weaknesses in the Pure Land tradition itself.

Let me analyze the Pure Land tradition in terms of a scheme that Kiyo Takeda Cho used in her *Conflict of Views of Man,* where she discusses various thinkers with reference to their view of God and their view of man. There were structural weaknesses in the concept of the Buddha from the point of view of transcendence, at least when compared with the Western experience. What is the Buddha or what is Amida? This is a very complicated question. When we analyze too closely, transcendence is apt to disappear. There is a real question as to whether the conceptual tradition could really contain the experience of transcendence that clearly was present in the Kamakura period. Consequently the universalism deriving from the transcendence was not sharply formulated. Secondly, related to this is the view of man in this tradition, which does not provide a sociological principle for a church, at least not in the sense of the Christian church. A new form of social organization based solely on the relation to transcendence did not emerge. Instead, the Jōdo Shin sect as well as the Nichiren sect and others fell back into a traditional form of social organization, hereditary in nature and based on the *danka* ("hereditary parishioner") system, which is still alive or half-alive in Japan today. That system cannot be called a church in the Western sense. It lacks the dynamic implications of the church in Western society. It especially did not provide an institutional basis for principled individualism. Nevertheless, no serious consideration of the Japanese tradition could possibly avoid this tremendous experience of the Kamakura period, whose repercussions continue down through the centuries even until today. Ienaga himself is one example of the repercussions of that tradition.

The second case where we can see this submerged tradition of transcendence making itself felt or coming into partial realization is Confucianism. In early Confucianism the notion of Heaven (*Ten, T'ien* in Chinese) had overtones of transcendence. This is evident even in the *Analects* of Confucius and in other rather early works of pre-Ch'in Confucianism. But in later times this very incipient transcendence was almost completely lost and Heaven became almost entirely immanent, naturalistic as in "heaven and earth" (*Tenchi*), and finally in the philosophy of Chu Hsi in the Sung period the immanent side, *Tenri* (heavenly reason), becomes completely dominant. Reason (*ri*) being found in things rather than deriving from some notion of transcendence, though not lacking a universal implication, failed to provide the basis of a universalistic ethic.

However in the Tokugawa period, very interestingly, there was a rediscovery of the transcendent element, which was of course latent in early Confucian texts all the time. Very often mentioned in this respect is Yōmeigaku (the teachings of Wang Yang-ming). In the first chapter of Professor Takeda's book several interesting examples are given. And it is not only in Yōmeigaku but also in the School of Ancient Learning (Kogaku), in people like Itō Jinsai and Ogyū Sorai, we see also this notion of Heaven taking on a transcendent implication. Sorai says that the basis of the way is the reverence for Heaven, for Heaven's will. But it is not only in Yōmeigaku and Kogaku but in Shushigaku (the teachings of Chu Hsi) itself, in a rather apparent example like Kaibara Ekiken, that we see the same thing. To stress the quality of this transcendence in its implications and its limitations, a short quotation from Ekiken can be contrasted with one from Niijima Jō dealing with a similar situation.

Ekiken says,

> Thus, not only do all men at the outset come into being receiving their principle of life (*Seiri*) from heaven and earth, but from birth till the end of life they are kept in existence by the support of heaven and earth. Man surpasses all other created things in his indebtedness to the limitless bounty of heaven and earth. It will be seen, therefore, that man's duty is not only to do his best to serve his parents, which is a matter of course, but also to serve heaven and earth through his life in order to repay his immense debt. That is one thing all men should keep in mind constantly.[4]

Here is an ultimate reference point that is above the family or anything on this earth, and that is constantly involved in supporting man's life and to which man has an unrepayable obligation that he must always remember. In contrast, Niijima says, in connection with his first reading of the Bible, that he learned that Jesus Christ was

> the Son of God, bearing on his body the sins of the world, delivered

himself up to death by crucifixion. That we designate Him the Savior, I was also able to know. And when I happened to read these lines I shut the book, looked around, and asked myself who it was that created me; My parents? No! It was not my parents, but God who created me![5]

That element of negation, that "No" was not found in Kaibara Ekiken. For it is my parents and Heaven and Earth, and that is as far as he can go. There is a genuine recognition of transcendence in Ekiken, yet it does not break through the natural order. It only caps and completes it. Consequently it ends by reinforcing a particularistic morality and does not become the basis for a universalistic one.

Here again we question why this recognition of transcendence did not take a more dramatic form. First of all, let us consider the concept of *Ten* itself, which appears in the *Analects* (*Rongo*) and in other early Confucian texts. In the *Analects* it is clearly stated that Heaven does not speak. Without speaking, of course, there can be no prophet to hear what is spoken, and certainly no one would call Kaibara Ekiken a prophet. Ogyū Sorai's concept of revering Heaven is not enough to create the prophetic consciousness. Secondly, the Confucian view of man conceives of human beings only in relation to the natural *Gemeinschaft* structures. There is no basis for a church, far less even than in Buddhism, and of course there is no separate religious organization. Thus there is little basis for an individualism based on ethical universalism. Confucianism seems to have disappeared almost completely in modern Japan. Actually it has not, for it is still present in many unconscious ways in Japanese life, but as an organized movement it has survived far less successfully than the organizational structures of Buddhism and Shintō. Nevertheless the elements of transcendence that we find in Tokugawa Confucianism had a historical importance in preparing for the modernization process, as Professor Maruyama Masao has pointed out in his *Studies in the History of Japanese Political Thought*.

Finally, we must briefly consider Shintoism. Shintō, of course, remained more naive and less philosophical than either Buddhism or Confucianism, but in its ample system it contained many possibilities, one of which was transcendence of a sort. Of this there were some glimmerings earlier, but the main development occurred primarily in the Edo period in the Kokugakusha, especially in Motoori Norinaga and those who followed him. Norinaga's absolute faith has been traced to the influence of Jōdo Buddhism, of which his family were ardent members and his sisters nuns. But the influence of Jōdo

Buddhism does not dispose of the question, for there had to be some implicit possibility in Shintō itself. In Hirata Atsutane and some of his disciples this element of transcendence was reinforced by a very considerable influence from books written by Christians. Hence there is the emergence of Ama no Nakanushi no Kami as a creator god, and so on. It is extremely interesting to look at the late Kokugaku scholars in their confrontation with Christianity. They were very much influenced by it and yet made a crucial objection, namely that the Christian position would make the obligation to God absolute, thereby undercutting the obligation to ancestors and parents and the emperor and so on. We find the explicit assertion that the real Tenshi, or the real Son of God, is of course Jimmu Tennō, the grandson of Amaterasu and his descendants, and not Jesus Christ. And so finally, even more than in Buddhism and Confucianism, the element of transcendence reinforces rather then negates the traditional *Gemeinschaft* structures. It stretches Japanese particularism to the utmost but it does not attain a genuine universalism.

Having mentioned Christianity, we must say a word about it before summing up these traditions. I think that the Japanese response to Christianity belongs in this discussion both in the sixteenth century and in the Meiji period, since it is only explicable because there was a potential mutation toward transcendence in the Japanese value system. The response to Christianity is different from that in any other Asian country that I know of. The speed with which it spread in the late sixteenth century has of course often been noticed; this is only understandable in terms of its relation to the Japanese environment into which it came. There is the possibility of transmuting the loyalty to superiors, which is so stressed in the traditional value system, into loyalty to the transcendent. This happened in the Kamakura period with respect to Amida, although with the limitations mentioned above. This symbolic possibility is especially evident in the case of Christianity. After all, Jesus Christ is Lord as well as Savior, and it is possible to transpose the Japanese obligation pattern, the pattern of ideal relationships that stresses so much the relationship between lord and follower, into the pattern of Christian symbolism. The Samurai Christian, either in the sixteenth century or in the Meiji era, is in one sense a man who has simply found a new lord. But in another sense there is an absolutely different implication. Once this transposition is made a tremendously revolutionary consequence follows. For the entire system of traditional loyalties is brought into question. They no longer have absolute value but are purely conditional.

In this respect I think that the Tokugawa persecution of Christianity is not to be understood exclusively as political persecution. Certainly it went on with incredible intensity and fanaticism long after there was any objective political threat. It was, I believe, religious persecution, although this is very often denied in Japan. It was religious persecution because Christianity threatened the core of the traditional value system with its religious base. If it had only threatened Buddhism the early Tokugawa shōguns would not have cared a whit. But it threatened the basic structure on which they were ordering their society, and any society reacts with violent persecution when it finds the core of its values threatened. This threat was recognized by some of the Meiji ideologists. Inoue Tetsujiro's criticism of Christianity is a very intelligent and perceptive statement of precisely what the problem was. According to Inoue, Christianity was fatal to loyalty and filial piety as they were traditionally understood; he was quite right. So I would like to stress both sides: Transcendence was a vital possibility in the Japanese value system, a live option so to speak, but nevertheless, once having accepted its really radical Christian form the implications were very disruptive and threatening to the traditional system, which then reacted by persecuting the disruptive elements. On the other hand, modern history certainly shows us various ways in which Christian universalism has been muted and its revolutionary implications covered over.

Having discussed in a very cursory way this other tradition, the tradition of submerged transcendence if you will, nevertheless we can say that there was not an overall, cumulative trend. Elements of transcendence arose continuously but did not succeed in getting institutionalized, or in gradually penetrating the whole of society. Above all they did not effectively challenge the prevailing particularistic ethic. Consequently there was no fundamental tendency toward modernization in Tokugawa Japan. Again this is a very controversial point. Many people argue from various kinds of evidence that in fact, Tokugawa Japan was moving toward modernization. The evidence has been drawn largely from the economic field, but it is still a big question whether the degree of economic development reached in late Tokugawa times was unique and different from that reached centuries earlier in other countries where it did not lead to modernization. The same could be said about the very considerable degree of literacy, urbanization, bureaucracy, and so on, which undoubtedly existed. I think if there had been no Western challenge there would have been no modernization in Japan. Japan did not have the cultural resources to begin the process of modernization herself. Nevertheless, I think that the nature of Tokugawa society in certain ways was more readily adaptable to the acceptance of modernization than any other non-Western society. But there is a fundamental difference between accepting modernization once it actually comes into existence and creating it for the first time.

In *Tokugawa Religion* I asserted that the strength of the polity was very important in Japan's rapid modernization. There was a definite tendency in the Tokugawa period to strengthen the political values, what you might call the politicization of Japanese values. And it is interesting that the several tendencies toward transcendence in the Tokugawa period often ended up not in breaking through the traditional pattern of values but in rationalizing it, codifying it, and creating the ideological basis for the famous Meiji absolutism. Certainly Ogyū Sorai, who is a very remarkable thinker as Maruyama points out in several extremely illuminating studies, ends up with the view of society in which everyone becomes an official, everyone is politicized, everyone is a member of the bureaucracy, if you will. The Kogugaku people, too, for example Satō Nobuhiro, developed a concept of state structure that foreshadows the one of late Meiji times. He preached a version of the family state involving a complete politicization of Japan under the imperial rule. Further, if Ebisawa Arimichi is right, even Christianity in the sixteenth century made its contribution to the ethics of Bushidō, just as later it contributed to Kokugaku thought. Thus through a peculiar kind of dialectic, Christianity may have actually contributed to the strengthening of the political ideology that would become dominant in the Meiji era, even though it also provided one of its chief challenges.

The politicization of life in the Tokugawa period was not just a phenomenon found among a few intellectuals. Rather, this politicization was actually penetrating Japanese society in general. Ishida Baigan, whom I study in *Tokugawa Religion,* was certainly not an intellectual in the sense of Sorai or Motoori. He was just a peasant who became a townsman (*chōnin*), and then founded the *chōnin* ethical movement called Shingaku. Baigan, too, comes out with the conclusion that the merchant is the "vassal" in the city and the peasant is the "vassal" in the field. He says that the peasants and the townsmen have to take the samurai as a model and emulate their complete loyalty. In the last analysis they work for the whole political society.

More important even than these conscious ideological movements were developments within the collectivity structure of Japanese society in the Tokugawa period. The so-called feudal values, which are much more accurately described as Japanese values since they are certainly quite different from the values of European feudalism, were very strong in the *chōnin* class. Research by sociologists and anthropologists on the village in Japan shows that this structure of values penetrated very deeply into the villages. That is, Japanese collectivity structure was characterized by a strong stress on vertical loyalties (leader-follower, *oyabun-kobun*) through which it was possible to exercise intensive discipline and motivate a high labor output. This pattern was not limited to samurai but was found at all social levels in the Tokugawa period. There was a concerted attempt in the Meiji era to strengthen and amplify that tradition and to make it provide the energy for modernization. This, I suggest, was not the Western way, but it was, from a certain point of view and with certain limitations, a very effective way. This leads directly to the problem of Meiji absolutism, which is not at all adequately understood in terms of Tudor England or the Prussia of Frederick the Great, but only in terms of specific Japanese traditions and problems. Absolutism, if the term is adequate at all, is not to be understood in terms of a third force balanced above surviving feudal elements and the rising bourgeoisie. It has to do much more deeply with the structure of Japanese values and social relations. But I want to postpone the discussion of the Meiji period, and only to provide here the background for that treatment.

I would like to close by suggesting a little schema that, because it is a schema, cannot be pushed very far but may be suggestive with respect to our present concern. In the set of traditions that I have been treating very summarily we see a ground bass of rather naive communal religion: functional, affirmative, this-worldly. It has survived from earliest times until today with many changes, but still with remarkable continuity. In the past, in early Japanese history, there was a great wave of cultural influences which came from China—ultimately partly also from India—but directly from China and in the Chinese language. In this wave two great traditions entered Japan. One, of course, was Buddhism, and the other Confucianism.

Buddhism was, in Ienaga's words, negative (*hitei-teki*), transcendental, and religious. It tried to break through the ground bass. At one moment (Kamakura Buddhism) it did break through, but it ultimately failed to crack the old tradition, although in thousands of ways Japanese culture was never the same after Buddhism. The second tradition, Confucianism, is the opposite of Buddhism in that it is affirmative, this-worldly, ethical, and even political. The role of Confucianism, on the whole, was not to break the traditional pattern but to rationalize and reinforce it.

In the modern period there has been another great wave of culture, this time from the West. In contains many systems, but two of the most influential ones have been Christianity and socialism. I think we can say that, given proper qualification, Christianity is negative (in Ienaga's sense), transcendental, and religious, though certainly not in the Buddhist way and with greatly different ethical and political implications. Socialism, on the other hand, is fundamentally affirmative, this-worldly, and political. Of course, in the context of Japan today it is in a sense negative, but once institutionalized in a social system it tends to become absolutely affirmative. Unlike Confucianism it does not reinforce the traditional community structure, but its essence is the promise of a society in which all the "virtues" of the traditional community structure can be retained without the defects. I do not put any particular faith in this schema, but I think it has some interesting implications for the problem of Japanese modernization.

II

I have been concerned not only with Japan's modernization in the context of her traditional culture, but also with problems of approach and perspective. Everybody comes to a problem with a "*mondai ishiki*," a sense of problem, which is dictated not by objective reality but in part at least by his own situation. This is very evident in present-day Japanese treatments of the modernization problem. In the preface to a recent symposium on the history of modern Japanese thought, we were told that the whole symposium would deal with the problem of modern Japanese thought by treating history from the point of view of the question, "What are we today?" This is the standpoint of a Japanese intellectual trying to think about this modern, last hundred years. More specifically, in this preface it becomes clear that for these people at least—and they are a rather representative group—the problem of modern Japanese history takes its focus around the event of August, 1945. Any attempt to understand the last hundred years has to be able to cope with that fact. The Japanese intellectual today on the whole does not find that his nation's modern history gives him a deep sense of reassurance. It is not something about which he can unambiguously congratulate himself. Rather, he asks the question, "What went wrong?" and he hopes partly in asking that question to help make sure that whatever did go wrong will not go wrong again. It is generally agreed that this question is not entirely answered. From this same preface there is the following remark referring to the situation since the war, over the last fifteen years or so:

> The economy may have reached or passed the pre-war level but we have not returned to the basic value system (*komponteki kachi taikei*) which was destroyed by the war. And, even though it is natural not to return to it, another value system has not been constructed to take its place.[6]

This is the view of a group of people like Takeuchi, Maruyama, and Ienaga. They go on to say that there have been various attempts in the direction of developing a new value system, but that they have been scattered and uncoordinated; they conclude by saying that in the realm of the spirit Japan has not yet recovered from the impact of the last war, however much the material recovery has been in evidence.

I find myself much in sympathy with the approach in these terms, for I like the emphasis on the problem of the value system This preface is also interesting in that it expresses a great deal of methodological openness and a marked dissatisfaction with the simple superstructure and substructure distinction. The writers say that what they are doing is not the usual kind of *"shisōshi,"* history of thought, or *"seishin-shi"* in the traditional sense; they are concerned with *"seishin kōzō,"* which is not really translatable in English because "spiritual structure" is just not right in English. They mean the structure of consciousness (and unconscious) that includes elements of what Marxists usually refer to as substructure as well as superstructure. This is a way of thinking that cuts through the traditional distinction and really overcomes the materialism-idealism antinomy of Marxism. Though I have not yet seen a thoroughly worked out theoretical statement and I certainly do not claim to know precisely what is meant by *"seishi kōzō,"* I still think this is a very interesting and fruitful kind of development. But although there is, at least in a very important part of the Japanese academic world, no rigid, dogmatic adherence to mechanical Marxism, the fact nevertheless remains that the mood and problem consciousness and, in many respects, the approach still have strongly ideological characteristics that are heavily imbued consciously or unconsciously with Marxist assumptions.

It is obvious that any approach to history is made from a real situation in history, is partly controlled by the needs and desires of that situation, and hence inevitably involves an ideological dimension. So it is unfair and wrong to criticize the presence of such a dimension per se. It is the obligation of the serious scholar to be as explicit as possible about this ideological dimension and I think that the scholars to whom I have been referring are trying to state their assumptions before they start in a way which is admirable.

But it is very difficult to draw the line between the ideological and the purely analytic aspects. Even in the core of the analysis itself, in any really vital approach to historical problems—and certainly in the understanding of such an immensely important thing as the modern history of Japan—it is inevitable that there will be a dramatic or mythic quality. This is not a characteristic of one approach or another but of all approaches. It is perfectly obvious in the official version of Japanese history during the thirties and early forties, in which the mythical element was quite uncritically present. That version of Japanese history tended to treat it simply as an extension of the *Kojiki* and *Nihongi* and treated Japan's modernized empire in the same framework as Jimmu Tennō's pacification expedition from Kyūshū to the Yamato basin. That is a very obvious example, but the approach of Japanese intellectuals today and the approach that I have been developing also have their dramatic and mythic qualities, and it is important in order to estimate the degree of validity in the various approaches to make this mythic, dramatic structure as explicit as possible. That is why in the first lecture[7] I tried to make as clear as possible how I view the modernization process so that you will see the dramatic structure, the mythic structure which is really present in my thinking. Even though I think the structure that I developed can be defended on objective grounds and that it is supported by at least a very considerable weight of objectively verified evidence, it is also obvious that it is related deeply to the Judaeo-Christian tradition with its eschatological assumptions, and if I had failed to make that explicit I think it would have been a great error.

Actually, the dramatic, mythic structure of Japanese history as it is viewed by the mainstream of present-day Japanese intellectuals is not structurally very far from the approach that I developed, certainly far closer to that approach than to the dominant approach of the thirties and early forties in Japan, and it is obvious that this is because the approach of today's Japanese intellectuals relies ultimately on many of the basic assumptions in the same tradition that has influenced me. The Marxist and socialist movement is only one version of the more general Western tradition of religion, philosophy, and political thought. But even though most of the ultimate assumptions are common, there are important differences in middle-range assumptions.

Here I want to turn more concretely to some of the major issues of Meiji history, of the *"Meiji seishin kōzō"* if you will, so as to make explicit the differences in the way I would approach certain problems from the way they are often approached in Japan today, and so that you can see how the different assumptions involved work out in concrete instances. But before doing that there is one more thing that I ought to say in order to avoid possible misunderstanding. Although I insist that every approach is an approach from a real situation and involves an ideological dimension, a mythic or dramatic structure to some extent, I nevertheless believe that there is such a thing as objective historical truth, and that various approaches do not simply resolve into a miscellaneous set of perspectives from which no objective picture can ever emerge. Reaching that objective truth is very difficult, and of course it is never completely achieved, but I think we do approach gradually to clearer understanding and a better, more objective picture. So I do not want to imply a skepticism about the basic epistemological problem involved, even though I think we have to be very subtle and sophisticated about the kinds of distortions that affect all of our thinking.

The essential framework, then, that is operating with most of the Japanese intellectuals today is that of the class struggle, and Japan's modern history is viewed as a titanic struggle between progressive and reactionary forces. This drama has three main characters: One is almost pure villain, and that is feudalism. One is almost pure hero, and that is the people, divided sometimes into peasants and workers. And one is highly ambiguous, the bourgeoisie, at times extremely progressive and at times very reactionary. However much the theoretical assumptions of Marxism and dialectical and historical materialism are questioned, this dramatic structure of thinking is very strong today in Japan among people of various philosophical and even various political positions. This is a very powerful, dramatic structure, but it is one that I do not entirely share, as I have indicated before.

The fundamental assumptions are brought to bear on the starting point of modern Japanese history in a rather clear way. That is, the late Tokugawa period is treated, in important respects, as cognate with the period of late feudalism in Western Europe just before the bourgeois revolution. In other words, Tokugawa society is treated as essentially analyzable in terms of the concept of feudalism as it has been developed in Western history. Tokugawa society is considered to have been a relatively advanced and decayed feudalism with important revolutionary forces already developing within it.

There is some question as to whether this view is accurate or not. However, once one does accept this essential characterization of late Tokugawa society, that it is essentially explainable in terms of the categories of the late Western European feudalism, then certain conclusions follow. One's understanding of modern Japanese history is seen exclusively against the background of European history, above all against the background of the history of France, Britain, and the United States. This is, time and time again, the primary standard for comparison. When an outside reference is made to compare with what was happening in Japan, it is this example that is used because it is assumed that this is the most fruitful and illuminating example. It is assumed that since the basic socioeconomic situation was similar in these two places—Japan and Western Europe—that the Japanese historical development ought to have been similar and, if it was not, this is due to the peculiar aberrations or special features of Japan that prevented things from working out somehow as they should. And, when you accept Marxism as your basic theoretical tool, you are accepting a conceptual framework that was worked out for Western European late feudalism and early capitalism, a system that is very culture-bound in its assumptions; but if you assume that this is not a culture-bound system but a scheme of universal history, then your basis for believing this comparison to be the key one for analyzing Japanese historical development is strengthened.

I believe that this set of assumptions about Meiji development out of the Tokugawa background suppresses two questions that are of the greatest importance. First of all, from my point of view, stressing the cultural system and value system more than it is usual to do, I would think that it is important to point out the very great cultural differences beween Western Europe and Japan, differences that separate Japanese feudal society and European feudal society in their cultural and value systems. They are in important respects structurally fundamentally different. So, then the question is not, "Why was Japan so different?" but, "Why was it so similar?" "How was it possible for Japan to establish a meaningful relation with European culture when in so many respects they were fundamentally different?" The second question also emerges from what I have said: "If Japan culturally was similar to a number of other non-Western nations, then why was Japan's course of development in many ways so different from those of the other non-Western nations?"

However the Restoration (*Ishin*) itself is explained, and there is an enormously interesting range of problems here, the new Meiji government provides the touchstone for the treatment of the Meiji period. This government had taken power after the Meiji Ishin. It is variously referred to, usually in strongly negative terms, as the despotic, bureaucratic, clique government (the *"hanbatsu seifu," "sensei seifu," "kanryō seifu,"* more formally it is called *"Meiji zettai-shugi,"* Meiji absolutism). This government became a major villain in the dramatic structure of the Meiji era. Usually not too much time is spent on the Meiji government itself; its social characteristics are explained in rather simple terms. That is, the Meiji government represented the seizure of power by one section of the feudal ruling class, namely the Satsuma-Chōshū samurai clique, and its power rested on the balance of feudal and bourgeois elements, above which it maintained a certain independence.

There are, of course, rather serious problems about this characterization. For one thing, a government that was in the hands of one section of the feudal class proceeded to destroy the institutional structure of Tokugawa feudalism, and this has to be explained in terms of class interests and so forth. And secondly, this group of feudal ruling class people created industrial capitalism almost *ex nihilo*. There is a considerable amount of debate about this factor as to how developed the economy was in the late Tokugawa period, but if you take a cautious view of that development, as I think the evidence indicates, you find that in the initial period the two class elements on which the Meiji absolutism was supposedly based were of a rather peculiar kind. I believe that the whole Meiji absolutism theory is a convenient theory developed to explain the government, which, once explained, can then be accepted as a main reference point for further analysis; however, it is not the primary interest of the approach in question to explain that government.

The extremely negative evaluation of the "*han clique*" government is explicable in terms of the kind of motivation that is attributed to it. That is, it is said to have brought modernization and enlightenment to Japan from above and that means for the sake of the upper groups. It is a modernization and enlightenment not for the sake of the people; it is only insofar as, and only as much as will maintain and strengthen the power of the ruling clique and of the classes they represented, and so any good they did is vitiated by their motive. In the last analysis, furthermore, any possible value in what they did is vitiated by the fact that for them modernization was a means of militaristic, imperialistic expansion, and consequently any consideration of this group as a positive force in Japanese history is almost excluded by definition.

This again, I suggest, is because of the comparison with Western development. The Meiji government is compared with British constitutional government or the French revolutionary government, or the American government, and so on. Hence it is judged very negatively in terms of the standard of comparison. If instead one's standard of comparison is the government in countries like Ottoman Turkey or Iran or China, one may be forced to a somewhat different assessment of this Meiji government, but this is usually not undertaken.

In connection with the extremely negative evaluation of the Meiji government, there emerges a rather ambiguous evaluation of the early enlightenment thinkers, the people in the Meiroku-sha and so on, Fukuzawa Yukichi, and others. Of course the analysis varies considerably from the extreme of contempt, referring to these people as official scholars, bureaucrat scholars, who were simply minions of the government and only supported enlightenment insofar as it was in the interests of the despotic government, to a very positive appreciation of their significance. But even those who really appreciate the enlightenment thinkers always do so with a certain reserve.

The positive element with which the present-day intellectual really begins to identify does not emerge in modern Japanese history until the Movement for Liberty and People's Rights, the popular movement around the tenth year of Meiji. Here we have a relatively unambiguous enthusiasm, a relatively clear affirmation. This is really something very positive in Japanese history. Now, of course, there are very considerable doubts even about this movement, especially in connection with its opening phase. That is, everyone recognizes that the Movement had a somewhat inauspicious beginning: it was started by discontended samurai, people who had been forced out of the bureaucracy, and one of the things they wanted to do was to invade Korea. Both in terms of its class origin and its goal the Movement was somewhat suspect in its opening stage.

However the Movement is considered to have been a thoroughly admirable and positive force in Japanese history on two grounds. First of all, in certain instances, in Chichibu and Fukushima and so on, the mass of the peasantry joined in various kinds of riots and demonstrations. No one doubted the motivation of the peasantry, since it was the most oppressed group in this society. So the doubts in connection with the samurai are not applicable here, and hence we have that form of the Movement that represents really progressive forces. And secondly, the Movement is validated because it produced some thoroughly revolutionary thinkers, such as Ueki Emori. These thinkers are believed to have supported radical democracy. They were not guilty of supporting democracy merely as a utilitarian cover for *Fukoku kyōhei,* the rich country strong army position. This was really a committed democratic movement.

I do not want to disparage the Movement for Liberty and People's Rights. It was a very important movement and the beginning of important developments in Japanese history, but nevertheless, its significance is somewhat distorted in the version that one usually hears. If we analyze more closely we may find reasons for questioning some of the assumptions on which that estimate is based. Above all, there is an element of nostalgia around the Movement for Liberty and People's Rights, a feeling that somehow here was a really revolutionary, democratic movement that almost succeeded; that if it had not been suppressed by a reactionary government Japan's modern history would have been like that of Britain, France, or the United States; that 1875 might have been the Japanese 1776 or 1789. This quality of nostalgia is not really justified by close analysis, and a more objective, sober, and realistic consideration would not contain that quality. The mistake comes from a number of sources: from the military metaphors of Marxism, and more deeply from the set of assumptions about class relations that have already been discussed. If you assume that the situation was similar to that just before the bourgeois revolutions in Europe, then it is easy to believe that a bourgeois revolution of that kind might have occurred. But essentially overlooked is the fact that the American and the French and the English revolutions had centuries of preparation that was entirely impossible in the first ten or fifteen years of Meiji. The military analogy is badly misleading. Revolutions are not just battles of class forces; revolutions are the recognition of deep cultural and institutional changes that have been going on in society for a very long time indeed. The People's Rights movement could not really have carried out a democratic revolution. To argue that it could have, one would have to show that very deep-going democratic organizations, ideals, and values had been building up over a very long time in Japanese history, and I just do not think that was the case.

Now let us examine the People's Rights movement internally. First of all, there is a point that is generally agreed upon: The leaders'—almost all the leaders'—devotion to democracy was of a somewhat questionable nature. They were eager to return to office and, even if that narrow motive was not present, there was a strong tendency to feel that a liberal democracy was the best means to a strong state and an expansive nation. Devotion to democratic life was not really a deep principle but a utilitarian commitment, and certainly the fact that so many of the leaders later did cooperate with or join the government or become spokesmen for a very extreme form of imperialism will indicate that their commitment was not very deep. That is something about which there is little argument.

The second question is one that is a more difficult point, the question of the peasants' support. Does this make the Movement genuinely democratic? I believe it does only if you accept the Marxist class scheme. In my opinion a democratic group is one deeply committed to democratic values and ways of organizing and phrasing human relations. I cannot believe that just because this was the most exploited group in Meiji society it was necessarily democratic, since I believe it lacked that commitment that is an essential characteristic of a group that would carry out a democratic revolution. I think in fact the commitment to such an ideal was even weaker among the peasantry than it was among the leadership, primarily because I doubt whether the peasantry understood what Liberty and People's Rights were.

It does not seem to be a valid comparison to hold these groups in the same framework as the farmers of Lexington and Concord. In doing so one forgets that those North American farmers had behind them two centuries of experience in democratic self-government, church autonomy, and voluntaristic organization. They had a democratic value system as well as the concrete experience of democratic life, and that should be taken into consideration as much or more than the fact of their class relations in society. The peasants in the second decade of Meiji were only scarcely out of the Tokugawa period, and there seems no reason to assume that they did not still carry the values and modes of social organization of Tokugawa society. There are many excellent studies on the values and social organization in Japanese villages, which, though most of them are much more recent than the period we are talking about, do not indicate that the village even today is permeated with democratic institutions and values.

On the basis of all that we know about the Japanese village I think that there is very little comfort in the notion that the village was a fertile seedbed of ideas of Liberty and People's Rights in the first two decades of Meiji. Rather, it seems fairly evident that the peasants were involved in this movement because they were terribly overtaxed and burdened in many obviously unfair ways. They were reacting as they had from time immemorial with riots and uprisings and protests against the treatment that they received. I think it is their actual situation that explains their activity; the ideology mattered very little. A few years before they had been rioting against haircuts and compulsory education. Now the Liberal party was present to provide a structure of organization and ideology, and they were as ready to take to that as the next thing if it would offer hope in a hopeless situation. But this does not guarantee the democratic nature of the Movement to which they became committed, and above all there is no reason to think that had the Movement succeeded such people would have been in any position to make democracy work.

What about the rich peasant (*gōnō*)? There are examples of people from this group who were imbued with democratic ideas, but in this group, too, the mere assumption that their class position—that is, as a group of actual or potential bourgeoisie—made them necessarily antifeudal and democratic is dubious. In Tokugawa society there was no group closer in ethos and sympathy to the samurai than the rich peasants, and there is no reason why there is to be an a priori assumption that the rich peasants in the Meiji period were automatically democratic and antifeudal.

Finally we have to analyze the thought of the Movement itself. Here, too, there is grave room for doubt. The basic external stimuli are Mill and Rousseau and similar thinkers in the West. They represent a relatively secularized and utilitarian version of democracy in which a large part of the implicit assumptions, the religious assumptions of modern Western democracy, have been suppressed because these people were reacting against earlier tendencies in Western development. But taking people like Rousseau and Mill entirely out of their Western context, where they are balanced by a great many other factors, one gets a rather dubious picture of democracy.

If we consider the concrete example of Ueki Emori, whom Ienaga feels was the most thorough and complete theorist of the Movement, we have considerable room for question. He is certainly excitingly progressive with respect to a whole host of issues, one of the first to really offer a radical criticism of the family system from the democratic point of view and so on, and all that is very important. But when we move to the central issue of the whole People's Rights movement, the issue of sovereignty, the issue on which the movement ultimately foundered, then I think we have to say that what Ueki comes out with, representing the left wing of the Liberal party, was an unvarnished populism. Sovereignty is left ultimately with the people, and that, in a sense, really ends up in deifying the people. This process of deification was actually made explicit in Ueki's philosophy, as Ienaga in his Iwanami Shinsho book on Ueki points out. In breaking with Christianity Ueki adopts a position that is an explicit statement of the deification of man. Ienaga quite rightly criticizes this philosophy on the philosophical level, I think, but Ienaga does not carry his criticism through to the political plane. But I would suggest that there is a problem about democracy that is based on an absolute populism.[8]

I have argued that democracy has a transcendent dimension, that it cannot be identified with the deification of the people, and that, in fact, the deification of the people has led to crimes in the twentieth century that rival those caused by the deification of the emperor or the state. Consequently a political philosophy that ends with an absolute, unqualified populism is a dubious basis for democracy.

Taking all these objections together, I have serious doubts whether a genuine democracy would have resulted if the People's Rights movement had overthrown the Meiji oligarchs. The result would probably not have been markedly better than the Revolution of 1906 in Iran or even than the recent student revolution in Korea. The forms of democracy might have been established, but lacking substance, they would have lasted only a very short while indeed. I seriously doubt that the final result would have been anything more democratic than the Meiji government, and possibly considerably less.

If one accepts my rather pessimistic view of the People's Rights movement, which again I offer not because I do not respect the genuine contributions that the Movement made, but as a sober assessment of the potentialities that the Movement in fact had; if one does not attribute its failure exclusively or primarily, as I do not, to government suppression but rather to internal weaknesses; then one must take a somewhat different view of the "despotic" government. Because of the nature of Japanese values and the structure of social relations in the society through which those values were expressed, some rather despotic and authoritarian government was inevitable, at any rate the cards were very much stacked in that direction. The real choice was not between the Meiji government and a democratic revolution as the means for modernization but between modernization brought by this kind of government or no modernization at all. Again, in comparison not with the history of Western Europe but with a great many other countries, that government was an enlightened despotism that does not stand up badly. This is not to say that I subscribe to the values behind that despotism but simply to indicate that I believe, in terms of the structures of society at that time, that this was in important respects the way it had to be, and that the beginnings that were laid down then were not entirely unsound. From this position the dramatism of the contemporary Japanese view is very greatly muted. The government was not so much of a villain or the People's Rights movement so much of a hero as it is usual to consider, but obviously my approach has its own dramatism and has its own implication as to who the heroes were in that picture.

To me the real heroes of this early Meiji period, the real beginning of the whole modernization of Japan and of real democracy, are those who questioned the basic value system of Tokugawa society and who sought to reform the fabric of social relations inherited from that society. In this context the enlightenment thinkers should be valued quite highly, probably more so than any thinkers of the People's Rights movement. I would also include the Christians who played such an important role in many aspects of life in the Meiji period by questioning the old assumptions and by working for reforms at all levels. My list of heroes would include Ueki in his role of reformer of society more than in his role of political ideologist of the People's Rights movement, and Fukuzawa Yukichi is especially worthy of very serious attention. He is guilty of an explicit utilitarianism with respect to *Fukoku Kyōhei,* and yet his position goes much deeper than any such surface expression, for he was expressing a really revolutionary way of thinking about human relations in a nonpolitical way. He is thus not to be evaluated primarily as a political thinker but in terms of his role as a representative of a whole new way of thinking about action in society. We find that when very many of the leaders of the People's Rights movement had become imperialist that a band of committed Christians and others devoted to some principle transcending society remained loyal to democratic ideas.

Christians, too, were among those who defected to imperialism in this period of the last years of the nineteenth century. But Uchimura Kanzō and Kinoshita Naoe, though they were somewhat maverick Christians, were nevertheless representatives of a real sea change in Japanese history, and these are the kind of people that I would tend to evaluate most highly in this early period. I evaluate them so highly because they are the people who, explicitly or implicitly, stood for the dimension of transcendence, questioned the assumptions of the traditional value system, and worked through many different kinds of movements—movements for women's equality, for a democratic family, for the reform of morals, and so on—to realize a new way of phrasing human relations. These people did not deify a new social structure, the people as such, or any class or party in place of the old deified social structure characteristic of traditional Japanese society, and it is from these people that the seeds of a healthier, more truly modern value system came.

However in the middle of Meiji it is clear that the seeds were very few and the sprouts were yet very young and weak. In one sense Japanese society was becoming modernized—in its economy and many other more immediately tangible ways—very rapidly. Society was being penetrated by compulsory education, literacy, mass communication, and so on. At the same time, the developing economy was disrupting traditional forms and leading to a questioning of traditional values. All this was happening, especially in the decade of the 1890s, in the great industrial revolution in Japan. But at the same time a true modern value system had not been fully developed, and even insofar as it was developed it yet had little meaning to the great majority of the Japanese people. We must remember what a relatively small group the enlightenment thinkers were compared to the vast mass of the people who were still in the village or, if they were in the cities, were still encased almost entirely in village mentality. We thus have a situation in which the people, though increasingly separated from traditional structures of family and village and undergoing changes consonant with the modern economy, were nevertheless not really ready for a modern value system. It is in this framework that we have to explain the rise of the emperor system (*tennō sei*) and the nationalism of the Meiji twenties and thirties.

The question arises: If the emperor was not to be the basis of the new constitution, that is the source of ultimate sovereignty, then what was? If one honestly thinks about the alternatives in terms of Japan's real situation, alternatives that would have any hope of meaning to the mass of the people, one will see that they were not very numerous. The society was, in fact, committed to the traditional value system. That value system could without great difficulty be put into forms of mass culture in terms of the emperor system. This new ideology served the dual function of integrating Japanese society, which had been shaken by the industrial revolution, and unifying Japan against external danger, which was still great at the end of the nineteenth century. Unfortunately it also unified Japan for external expansion. It was basically unmodern and antidemocratic in spirit, but it left room for a certain degree of healthy development. I do not think it was the same thing as fascism. There were many diverse modes of thought, especially in areas not directly associated with politics, and contributions to Japan's modern thought continued to be made by such people as Natsume Sōseki and Nishida Kitarō. Of course the Meiji solution was not ideal, but it is difficult to imagine that a much more radical solution would have worked.

The emperor system had the virtue of maintaining social solidarity while modernization proceeded more or less rapidly in various areas.

Under the aegis of a basically unmodern value system, modernization yet continued. The balance was very delicate and easily influenced by outside forces. During the First World War, with extremely favorable economic conditions from outside as well as the political alignment with Western democracy, the circumstances were positive and shifted the balance in the direction of democratic development. In the late twenties, the world situation, economically and politically, became very unfavorable and the balance was tipped strongly the other way. The outcome was not inevitable from the point of view of Japanese development alone. That is, the Meiji emperor system did not make fascism inevitable in the thirties and early forties. It certainly raised few barriers against that development. Because it was not a democratic system it left the ground open, given certain kinds of circumstances for that outcome, but it is at least conceivable that had general world circumstances been different, healthy developments could have been achieved out of Taishō democracy without the tragic events of the thirties.

The Meiji thirties and forties saw the emergence of something new, namely the socialist movement, and this became the second great positive force for present-day Japanese intellectuals. But just as I cannot see in the emperor system (*tennō sei*) an absolutely negative picture, so I am not convinced that there are grounds for evaluating the socialist movement in absolutely positive terms, although I certainly sympathize much more closely with the values and ideals of that movement than with those of the conservative government. Though many important programs were proposed by the socialists and many contributions made to the development of democracy in Japan, again I have a basic doubt that is essentially the same as in the case of Ueki. For example, I cannot but feel that Kōtoku Shūsui's position was potentially as dangerous as that of the government that killed him. An unbroken commitment to the political process such as he had, no matter how progessive the aim, always contains the seeds of demonic fanaticism.

A really democratic value system must have a transcendental reference in terms of which the political process itself can be judged. Lacking that, and there are several examples in this century, the progressive socialist movement can become the mirror image of its enemy. This is the basis of my schematism comparing Buddhism and

Confucianism with Christianity and socialism. The transcendent, critical, religious element in the kind of Buddhism that Shinran was speaking for, relative to the affirmation of the social system in Confucianism, is somewhat comparable to the transcendent reference of Christianity relative to the socialist belief that makes the social system absolute. Of course, this comparsion was far from exact because there were Christian socialists, and actually, the early Japanese socialists were mainly Christians. And there are principled socialists who do not make an absolute commitment to a party or a class. Nevertheless, I think Kōtoku and others are examples that indicate that a danger to Japanese democracy existed and still exists from the fanatical left as well as from the conservative right.

This analysis has certain implications for the present. They are rather obvious, but let me just mention two in particular. In the present situation, granted that one is committed to modernization, there are two areas above all that need attention: the cultural area, especially the problem of values, and the structural reform of Japanese society.

In the cultural area, the reconstruction of the Japanese value system is a long, slow process, which has been going on since early Meiji and is still in progress. It cannot be accomplished without some sort of healthy union of elements from the traditional Japanese past and the Western tradition. Very deep study needs to be made of both sides. Japan today cannot be considered an Asiatic or East Asian culture. Deep now, in Japanese culture, after a hundred years, are ideas, values, and ways of handling human relations that ultimately, historically go back to the Western traditions, to Greece and to Israel. In many ways the lines that separate people living in America from those in the Eastern Mediterranean are also rather tenuous. Japan now participates in the tradition of Western culture, and therefore she must, as must America and Europe, constantly reevaluate those sources to become aware of the meaning of those traditions in which we now all participate. Deep study should also to be made of the East Asian tradition, both in Japan and in America. The kind of activity that Kiyo Takeda Cho is undertaking at Tokyo's International Christian University is part of this enterprise. In particular, the Japanese tradition must be studied in order to discover those elements that can provide fruitful soil for the development of democratic institutions in Japan. In somewhat different ways men like Ienaga Saburo and Kōsaka Masaaki are engaged in this task.

The structural reform of Japanese society is necessary, but in a somewhat different sense from that of the Japanese Socialist party. The effort to make democratic the various groups that actually exist—the family, various kinds of work groups, and so on—is a primary task that the intellectuals have to engage in right at home, in a literal sense, and also in the university, where so-called feudal attitudes in human relations remain very strong. This problem is not, of course, limited to the intellectuals, but the labor unions and the Socialist party itself are in need of a good deal of structural reform. The effort to develop voluntary organizations to meet the needs of everyday life needs to be pressed very much more than it has been, and is an important obligation of all democratic and progressive people. Tenant councils, neighborhood councils, organizations to meet the many needs of everyday life—which are constantly bearing down on people and about which they complain so much—are needed because through organizations and through democratic forms of voluntary association those many problems can begin to be handled. Politicization, in the sense of concern with the national political struggle in Japan, is partly a danger. An exclusive concentration on national and international issues can hinder the development of a local structure of democratic, voluntary organizations. The real framework of a modern, democratic society is a complex, intricate structure of voluntary associations; and here much needs to be done. If true structural reform at this level were achieved, then Diet politics would almost automatically take a healthier form. It should be emphasized that there is a danger in the polarized image of the absolutely good and absolutely bad forces in Japan today. The enemy is at home and within as well as in the "reactionary forces"; this is as true in America as in Japan. There is no democratic society that does not need to be remaking and reforming itself constantly.

Finally I want to suggest two means towards these ends. One way is through social theory. Analytical theory is important because its use is one of the best means for avoiding the possible danger of mistakes from ideological distortion. In this area much is being done in Japan that is very exciting. Secondly, the essence of modernization from the personal point of view is courage. The courage to oppose the government in mass demonstrations is important, but more important and hardest of all is the courage to stand utterly alone if necessary. In this sense Uchimura Kanzo is the real symbol of what is needed, even though I differ from him on both theological and political grounds. His kind of courage always has a transcendental reference; it can make its affirmation only through what Ienaga calls the logic of denial and not because it attributes ultimate righteousness to any group or system.

NOTES

1 *Seishinshi* translates best in German as *Geistesgeschichte,* in English as History of spirit.

2 Butsudan and Kamidana are literally "Buddha shelf" and "God shelf," the family altars for home worship.

3 Robert N. Bellah, *Tokugawa Religion* (Glencoe, Ill.: Free Press, 1957).

4 Ekiken Zenshu, *Shogaku-Kun,* vol. 3 (Tokyo, 1901–11), pp. 2–3.

5 Niijima Jo, in Kōsaka Masaaki, *Meiji Thought History,* Eng. trans., pp. 168–69.

6 Takeuchi Yoshimi, *Kindai Nihon Shisōshi Kōzo,* vol. 1 (Tokyo, 1959), pref., p. 2.

7 The first lecture in the series is omitted here, but see chap. 4 in this volume.

8 See chap. 9 in this volume.

8 Islamic Tradition and the Problems of Modernization

RELIGION is a way of making sense of the world, but ours is a world it is increasingly difficult to make sense of. Joseph Conrad describes the modern age as one "in which we are camped like bewildered travellers in a garish, unrestful hotel." But the great religious systems were not designed to deliver us from this particular hotel. Their plans and instructions are for another set of rooms. They are not wholly irrelevant, because not only in the modern age but in time and history man is camped and bewildered. The puzzlements, anxieties, and confusions of our age are not unique. Yet the religion of a millennium ago is no more lucid and compelling than the language of a millennium ago. Language can be translated; it can find new words and forms so that it is again lucid and compelling. But there precisely is the problem.

Religious symbolism in any actual human situation interacts with, or at least is juxtaposed to, a variety of other personal and social symbolisms. Its exact bearing on human decision emerges from its place in a complex web of motives. Besides religion, which I would define as a way of thinking and feeling about reality in general, there are conceptualizations of political authority, the family, and the individual, and these four levels form a kind of macrocosmic-microscosmic continuum. These are not the only relevant contexts of

This chapter was written for the Harvard Middle Eastern Seminar that I attended in January 1968. The papers by Brown, Anderson, Kerr, and Brugman referred to in the text were prepared for other meetings of the same seminar and will be published in a book edited by Nadav Safran together with this essay. I spent two years at the Institute of Islamic Studies at McGill University, 1955–57, and subsequently taught Islamic Institutions and Social Structure of the Islamic Middle East at Harvard. This paper and the article "Religious Aspects of Modernization in Turkey and Japan," not included in the present volume, are the only publications in which I have concentrated heavily on Islamic materials.

human action. Many social scientists would stress the importance of economic roles, social class and status, urban and rural patterns, and so forth. But to get at the operation of religion in human action, which is our subject, one must consider the "dramatistic" (to borrow a term from Kenneth Burke) aspect of human life. I would argue that the chief dramatistic contexts are the religious, the political, the familial, and the personal. It is in these contexts that one defines himself in relation to others, accepts (or rejects) value and authority, and determines what sort of action (or inaction) makes sense in the world. That is to put it from the point of view of the deciding actor. For most of mankind a world, a polity, a family, and a self are simply given. The element of personal choice is never wholly absent, but it is a variable, perhaps the most important variable in this entire sphere.

In order to set the stage for the subsequent argument, let me define a dramatistic universe that is at the extreme end of fusion, undifferentiation, and lack of personal choice, and one at the other extreme that is open, highly differentiated, and has the maximum element of personal choice. Needless to say these are ideal types, heuristic devices.

A state of dreaming innocence in which the world is taken as it is with no other possibilities envisioned would be one in which political and familial structures are seen as wholly "natural," of a piece with the entire cosmos, and the question of the individual would scarcely be raised at all. Such a perfect cosmic continuum has been held as an ideal by a number of the great literate traditions, perhaps nowhere more clearly than in Confucianism. But even Confucians did not believe that such a perfect pattern actually existed, except in the time of the Ancient Kings, a time out of time. Even in primitive societies where the pattern is closer to being actually descriptive, perfect fusion only exists in "the Dreaming." Nostalgia for such a state, the opposite of all garish, unrestful hotels, may be a major human motive, but on this earth it has not been realized. Nevertheless, as Max Weber pointed out, in many societies that continue to live in a "garden of magic," a fictive web of symbols exists that half convince—until the next famine, civil war, or plague—that all is as it should be, or if not, that some local holy man can quickly put it right.

The opposite state is perhaps closely approximated in Harvey Cox's *Secular City*. Here all myth, magic, and ritual are gone. God, if not dead, is merely a symbol for man's highest aspirations. Political and even familial structures are seen not as given in the nature of the universe but as changeable human constructions. Individual responsibility, which scarcely exists in dreaming innocence, is almost overwhelming in the secular city. Man makes not only his religion, his polity, and his family, but himself. Since association is voluntary and meaning individual this is an entirely pluralistic world. Every level is being simultaneously overhauled, changed, and improved, and the widest possible variety is contained within the whole. Virtually the only integrating principle is convenience or utility, the maximization of the interests of individuals and the progress of the whole. Again, no society comes very close to this ideal, though some are closer than others. In any personal experience there are "not balances that we achieve but balances that happen." We do not make ourselves up as we go along. Much is irretrievably given. Nevertheless the doubt that anything given is as it must be, once raised, will never be stilled.

All actual societies exist in some kind of uneasy compromise between these extremes. For all of them something is sacred, something stands outside and above the actual, even if it is the demonic nightmare of the Nazi dream of race. Nor in any society is the sacred entirely confined to the sphere of "religion." Fundamental social commitments are seen as partaking in the sacred. Even those who entirely deny the legitimacy of existing structures tend to commit themselves religiously to countergroups and organizations, revolutionary parties, or intense personal relations. Almost everywhere the compromise is seen as more or less unsatisfactory, the world is viewed as awry. Yet in only a few societies do very many people see the situation as one of desperate and intolerable breakdown. Most people manage, as they always have. Still, we can very roughly discriminate in the modern world between those societies that do a little better than cope, that somehow meet an increasing range of human needs, and consequently keep a majority of the citizenry not merely acquiescent, but positively committed to the legitimacy and improvement of society; those societies that are just barely hanging on, not developing much faster than the population increases but not declining either; and those that slip slowly or rapidly into chaos. There are, in S. N. Eisenstadt's terms, societies that are developing, stagnating, and in the process of breakdown. The ease with which any society can move from one of these categories to another must remove us from any complacency, especially when American society, not perhaps for the first time but in some kind of new way, is developing limited but unmistakable signs of virulent distress. The rest of this essay will consider some of the ways in which Islam, as a way of making sense of the world and structuring the relation between God, society, and man, contributes to the more and less satisfactory compromises that contemporary Muslim societies are making between the real and the ideal, the religious and the secular, the coherent and the autonomous, in a word, to the problems of this world in the modern era.

Early Islam

We must begin with early Islam because that is what Muslims do. The early community under the prophet and the rightly guided caliphs is a paradigm to which they return again and again and from which they draw an understanding of their own times. *Qur'an* and Sunna are the glasses through which many Muslims view the world, and it is essential that we discern the shapes they see. Early Islam can by no means be equated with the state of dreaming innocence depicted above. It was by no means a "natural" continuum of cosmos, society, and self. The act and word of God stand outside the natural world and break or threaten to break every natural structure. Here an individual, first of all Muhammad but after him, (at least in principle) every Muslim, is called upon to stand out from every tie of kinship and polity if need be. A higher obligation to God makes every man not in the first place a member of a given clan or tribe or town, but a self in direct relation to an eternal deity.

This particular conception of the world did not begin with Muhammad. The *Qur'an* itself traces it back to the Old Testament prophets, to biblical religion. It is the paradigm of Moses at Sinai, perhaps more than any other, which helps us understand the initial message of Islam. It is at Sinai that Israel makes a covenant with God, establishing its nationhood on a basis that entirely transcends ancient Near Eastern conceptions of kingship. For, the Bible insists, Moses is no divine king but merely a man, an instrument of the divine will. It is at the moment of Sinai that Israel breaks with the whole ancient Near Eastern pattern of cosmic social fusion and makes possible, not only Christianity, but Islam itself.

Another Old Testament paradigm that is of almost equal significance is the story of Abraham and Isaac. Here kinship is brought under the sign of divine transcendence. Kinship is removed from the cosmic round of ritual and sacrifice and divested of any sacredness except that which God decrees. As a result of the innovations of biblical religion relative to its ancient background, all social structures lose their intrinsic sacredness and the individual self stands face to face with God, not as a hieratic actor following a predetermined script but as a man responsible for his action in history. These innovations have the greatest significance for all subsequent religious history and certainly for Islam.

We cannot trace here the history of these innovations in the two millennia before the birth of Muhammad. We can only mention that Christianity developed the inherent split between sacred and secular that biblical religion had opened up much more extensively than did ancient Israel. On the one hand it developed a monastic ideal of radical withdrawal from the world, particularly its familal and political contexts, which was quite alien to Old Testament ways of thought. On the other it granted a degree of independent legitimacy to the secular society and its political structure, partly on principle and partly as a response to the political conditions of its origin, which was equally alien to Israelitic conceptions. It is important to remember that for the *Qur'an* the Old Testament is far more central than the New. The experience of ancient Israel, not that of the Christian church, can help us to understand Islam.

This is partly because the social structure that faced Muhammad had far more in common with that which faced Moses than with that of Jesus or Paul. Muhammad did not begin his preaching in a great and closely organized world empire but rather in a tribal society, which had not yet attained a political structure that could be called a state. He had not so much to work out a relationship to an existing political order as to create a new one. Further, in a society where almost every important relationship was phrased in terms of kinship he had to develop a political organization that would transcend kinship. There is no question but that under Muhammad, Arabian society made a remarkable leap forward in social complexity and political capacity. When the structure that took shape under the prophet was extended by the early caliphs to provide the organizing principle for a world empire, the result is something that for its time and place is remarkably modern. It is modern in the high degree of commitment, involvement, and participation expected from the rank-and-file members of the community. It is modern in the openness of its leadership positions to ability judged on universalistic grounds and symbolized in the attempt to institutionalize a nonhereditary top leadership. Even in the earliest times certain restraints operated to keep the community from wholly exemplifying these principles, but it did so closely enough to provide a better model for modern national community building than might be imagined. The effort of modern Muslims to depict the early community as a very type of equalitarian participant nationalism is by no means entirely an unhistorical ideological fabrication.

In a way the failure of the early community, the relapse into pre-Islamic principles of social organization, is an added proof of the modernity of the early experiment. It was too modern to succeed. The necessary social infrastructure did not yet exist to sustain it. When dissatisfactions and demands from important parts of the community built up under the third caliph, the institutional structure was too fragile to contain and meet them. Instead a chain of political disturbances was set off that resulted in the establishment of hereditary kingship, *mulk,* under the Ummayyads. Whatever the justification of modern scholarship in rehabilitating the Ummayads, an enterprise begun by Ibn Khaldun, the traditional Muslim suspicion of them must be taken seriously as a social fact. It is another indication that something precious was lost with the collapse of the early experiment, something that would continue to exercise the pressure of an ideal through subsequent centuries.

Let us consider the strucural elements of early Islam that are relevant to our argument. First was a conception of a transcendent monotheistic God standing outside the natural universe and related to it as creator and judge. Second was the call to selfhood and decision from such a God through the preaching of his prophet to every individual human being. Third was the radical devaluation, one might legitimately say secularization, of all existing social structures in the face of this central God-man relationship. This meant above all the removal of kinship, which had been the chief locus of the sacred in pre-Islamic Arabia, from its central significance. And finally, there was a new conception of political order based on the participation of all those who accepted the divine revelation and thus constituted themselves a new community, *umma.* The dominant ethos of this community was this-worldly, activist, social, and political, in these ways also closer to ancient Israel than to early Christianity, and also relatively accessible to the dominant ethos of the twentieth century.

Yet not only did early Islam not precipitate the Muslim community into an untimely modernity, the militant return to the ideal of the early community has had only an ambiguous relation to the struggle for modernity in recent times. In considering the relation of traditional Islam to the problems of modernization we must deal with some of the constraints and limitations both inherent in the early community and arising from its situation.

The political system worked out by Muhammad at Medina and developed by the early caliphs, especially Umar, was an advance over earlier Arab political organization. It was indeed the emergence of a state out of a previously tribal society. By the very nature of the case, however, it was a state in which the religious and the political were inextricably intermixed. A "church" was not possible in seventh-century Arabia. Any organization that in principle transcended kinship necessarily had political implications. The rise of religious movements in the marginal lands and tribal areas of the Middle East has continued to have political implications down through the centuries. Carl Brown in his paper earlier in this series mentioned the Abbasids, Fatimids, Almoravids, Almohades, Wahhabis, and the Sudanese Mahdiyya in this connection. Sufi movements in such areas have also tended to have such implications, the Sanusiya being only a recent example. But the fusion of the religious and the political, which is structurally appropriate and indeed unavoidable in the marginal areas, creates severe problems when transferred to the urban, agricultural centers. The tensions generated by this transformation are already evident in the history of Israel, when a loose religious-tribal federation became an urban-based kingdom.

The solution to these problems worked out in the early Christian era by both Byzantines and Sassanids was some sort of differentiation of religious and political spheres. This did not eliminate the tensions between them but it did create somewhat more complex mechanisms for handling them. As already noted, similar tensions developed early in Islamic history and led to the incipient split between religious and secular under the Ummayyads. Since this development was seen, to some extent rightly, as a lapse not only from the precedent of the prophet but also from the ideal of a just and equalitarian society, it was not accepted as legitimate. But, as Gibb has shown in his articles on early Muslim political development, the religious community failed to develop any workable alternative to the Ummayad solution. Instead the growing religious opposition simply reasserted the original prophetic model. The Abbasid Caliphate was in part the result of this movement of religious dissatisfaction with the Ummayads, and can be seen as the classic effort to put the Islamic ideal of religious-political fusion into effect in a large-scale empire.

The basic flaw in this effort and the fundamental reason for its failure is that it relied on public relations promotion rather than structural innovation. When the increasingly self-conscious religious community saw that the Abbasids were merely cloaking an all too familiar Near Eastern autocracy in claims of religious legitimacy, it rapidly became disillusioned and turned either to some brand of Shi'i utopianism (which in time would suffer similar disillusionment) or to the relatively apolitical effort of Sunni community building. The post-Abbasid period, then, saw a *de facto* differentiation of religion and politics punctuated by an occasional outburst of religious-political utopianism emerging from the hinterlands in disruptive but largely ephemeral military conquests. (There is no need here to trace the development of Muslim political theory from Mawardi through al-Ghazzālī to Ibn Taimiyya, with its increasing tendency to legitimate any political regime that would guarantee a modicum of protection to Muslim institutions.)

The *de facto* situation, however, was never accepted as fully legitimate. Political power remained suspect not only to rural utopians but to urban *ulama,* who viewed it as a necessary evil. In this situation the state and the political realm in the Islamic world failed to develop an inner coherence and integrity. The state as a legitimate realm of thought and action with its indispensable role of the citizen failed to emerge. The Muslim community itself, even though without any effective means to exercise power, continued to express the only legitimate political self-consciousness in the society, and the role of adult Muslim believer, not that of citizen, was the only inclusive political role. The Machiavelli of the *Prince* could emerge in the Muslim world (Nizam al-Mulk and other writers of mirrors for princes), but not the Machiavelli of the *Discourses.*

To the extent that there was any non-Muslim political thought it came from the Greek political philosophers and was the property of a small philosophically educated elite. The enormous influence of Plutarch, Livy, and Cicero on European political thought and action from the sixteenth and seventeenth centuries on was completely missing in Islam. It was the revival of the classical notion of citizenship that played so important a role in early modern European political development. This whole avenue of independent political development was virtually absent in the Islamic world. Thus the political resources of the Islamic tradition in the modern world have been limited to the powerful but necessarily utopian—in advanced traditional societies not to speak of industrial society—image of the fusion of religion and politics in the first decades of Islam.

The history of the family in Islam shows a similar picture of development and arrest. The main burden of the Quranic family legislation, it seems clear today, was to stabilize the nuclear family, limit polygamy and divorce, and to protect the interests of wives and children. The Islamic family as it took shape under the prophet's guidance was to reflect the reduced significance of extended kinship in the new Muslim community and to express the enhanced dignity of the individual, including women and children, as persons standing in direct relation to God. Once again, as in certain aspects of early Muslim political experience, this is a strikingly modern series of developments.

The main tendencies of Quranic thinking about the family, however, were not only not developed in the early centuries of Islam, but they suffered a serious retrogression. As Gibb showed in careful detail in his lectures on Islamic institutions, the situation of the conquest in which the family law was worked out led to provisions that violated the intent of Quranic family legislation. In particular, the legitimation of concubinage and the effective removal of the restraints on divorce with which the *Qur'an* had specifically been concerned reflect a military situation in which women had come to be treated as booty. Unfortunately, in accordance with the way Islamic law developed, it was the post-Quranic and not the Quranic provisions that became the effective precedents in Sharia family law. While a family ideal of mutual respect and obligation between all family members continued to be enjoined as exemplary, in fact practices tending to undermine inner family equality and solidarity and elevate patriarchal arbitrariness were pronounced legitimate. Traditional Islam thus presented a mixed heritage to the modern family reformers.

So far we have been concerned with the structural resources of the

Islamic tradition for the problems of modernization. Even though the subject is difficult and vast perhaps a word should be added about symbolic resources. Without intending any disrespect one can speak of a certain poverty of symbolic reference to God in the *Qur'an*. Ancient Israel, according to George Mendenhall and other contemporary scholars, first built up its conception of a transcendent God on the model of the ancient Near Eastern great king. God was above all King, Lord, Ruler. Christianity continued this line of analogical thought, but added to it a stress on God as Father, which was much less central in Israelite thought. In the *Qur'an* God is understood first of all neither as king nor as father but simply as God. The only analogy for God is God. This is an accurate reflection of the fact that the key reference point in Muhammad's thought was not king or father but the God of Israel. Biblical thought is far more determining than any current social model.

One consequence of this situation, perhaps, was to emphasize the gulf between divine and worldly authority. God was not primarily understood as a perfect expression of legitimate political or parental power. Rather, political and parental power were understood as perhaps faintly illegitimate shadows of God's power, the only true reality. The combination of arbitrariness and illegitimacy in all worldly power creates a kind of uneasy absolutism which is hardly favorable political soil for the institutional innovations required by modernization.

As part of the polemic with Christianity, parental symbolism for God was decisively rejected by Islam. The *Qur'an* is also striking in the extent to which the feminine dimension of experience is excluded. Of course Muhammad's struggle against the goddesses, the so-called "daughters of Allah," is part of a long tradition of the struggle of biblical religion against the great mother deities of the Mediterranean world. The Old Testament God is uncompromisingly masculine, and Christianity included no female in its trinity. In Christianity, however, in a variety of ways and especially through the person of Mary, the feminine dimension of religious experience found expression. Even in Christianity it remained problematic, and Protestants vigorously rejected what they called Mariolatry. Nevertheless, partly through the humanization of Mary in Renaissance art and partly through more purely secular means, the symbolic valence of the feminine shifted in a positive direction in Europe from late medieval times on. In the Islamic world the modern cultural significance of women, with its implications for family and personality, has had less traditional preparation.

The unadorned majesty of the Islamic conception of God, which has stood aloof from the variety of cultural expressions to be found in many other religions, has found its chief expression in the realm of right action: ethics and law. Here again the Islamic impulse toward a just society that has expressed itself in every Islamic century is powerfully resonant with the needs of modern society. But the formalization of that ethical imperative in the vast body of the Sharia, though it has succeeded in providing a critical rallying point for the unity of the *umma* down through the ages, has rendered it singularly inflexible in the face of the major contemporary problems of the Muslim peoples.

This section has tried to indicate cursorily some of the ways in which early Islam, as a central reference point for all Muslims, is on the one hand highly contemporaneous and relevant and on the other problematic and constrictive. Such a situation cries out for a rethinking of the tradition, a process which has been only very uncertainly begun. But before turning to modern Muslim thought we must consider that part of the heritage of the past that is not traceable to the *Qur'an* and the early community.

Medieval Islam

Though the ethical view of man was never lost in Islam and the community continued to produce an Ibn Hanbal or an Ibn Taimiyya down through the centuries, it can be argued very generally that from Abbasid times until the nineteenth century Islam moved away from the "secular city" end of our continuum in the direction of "dreaming innocence." (It should be noted that in this understanding, biblical and Quranic religion—as well as Buddhism, Confucianism, and a number of other religious developments—are seen as among the great *secularizing* forces in human history.) This great religious regression might be characterized under the rubric of "the rise of Sufism" if one remembers, as Clifford Geertz has recently pointed out, that Sufism is not to be defined in any simple terms but stands for a wide variety of practices that reflect the pre-Islamic local religious traditions. The rise of Sufism was a great accommodation of Islam to the religious needs and consciousness of the masses. It was a great compromise formation, but one that allowed Islam to spread halfway around the globe and to penetrate social strata to which the original austere faith had never appealed. In many ways it was a complementary opposite of Quranic religion: warm, emotional, ecstatic, and more concerned with inner states than outer acts. Above all it was comfortable and local, with its local shrines, local cults, and local saints. It represented the return of Islam to the garden of magic where divinity is inherent rather than transcendent and where the social order is part of the nature of things and semidivine itself.

From the Maraboutic kings of Morocco to the exemplary sultans of Java (both brilliantly described in Geertz's recent Terry Lectures), the rise of Sufism was accompanied by a tendency to sacralize political rule. Even in the Arab heartland rulers were immodestly compared to the deity. The attempt by rulers to identify their regimes with the nature of reality never went unchallenged, but to the extent that the rulers were successful this tendency contributed to political and social stagnation.

It was not only the political order but the entire range of customary practices that the medieval mind wished to absorb into Islam. The struggle against the introduction of new techniques and practices in the Ottoman Empire from the late eighteenth century on was always carried on in the name of Islam. As an absurd example, we might cite the opposition to Mahmud II's introduction of the fez as an "innovation in Islam," and the opposition to Ataturk's abolition of it on the same ground. Local kinship customs and practices tended to receive the same kind of absolute religious legitimation.

The late medieval Muslim world was capable of some remarkable feats of political organization in the Ottoman, Safavid, and Mughal empires. But the tensions of the first Islamic centuries had largely gone out of Muslim culture. Classical philosophy had been extruded or encapsulated. It did not survive as a nucleus for a nonreligious cultural tradition as in the West any more than the classical political ideal contributed to a secular political tradition in Islam. The only challenge to the all-embracing Sufi synthesis came from men like Abd al-Wahhab, raising the banner of Quranic austerity.

This late medieval Islamic society is not here of interest in itself. Its only relevance is that it was into this world, enraptured in its Sufi dreams, that the modern West abruptly and loudly entered. Today Islam in most of the Muslim world means the prophet, Abu Bakr, and Umar or the high culture of the Abbasid period. But it should not be forgotten that no Muslim country is more than decades away from this very different Islam. Nor even now is it entirely dead. It still suffuses the unconscious ways of thinking and habits of action of the masses of the people and to some extent of even the intellectuals. It helps to account, as Geertz has shown, for the very different responses to modernization which have developed in various Muslim countries. For everywhere the late medieval patterns are local and diverse.

The Breakdown of Traditional Society and the Reform Efforts

The process of modernization is enormously complex and by no means well understood. Some things are relatively clear. Structurally it involves increases in complexity, efficiency, adaptability, and productivity. Ideologically it involves an increased sense of the dignity of the individual and his right to be included as a full and equal participant in a society with some minimal guarantee of material and personal security. However, the disturbances touched off by the modernization process have often led, at least temporarily, to declining complexity, efficiency, adaptability, and productivity and to the most massive violations of human dignity in all history.

"Traditional society," which means something different in each particular instance, while always profoundly disturbed, is never simply obliterated. Traditional societies themselves are complex entities, full of inner tensions that the initial impact of modernization simply exacerbates. With increased technical and organizational tools, despotic government may simply become more arbitrary, parasitic landlords more oppressive. On the other hand, the latent alienation that is always widespread in traditional societies finds new forms of organization and new means to effect violent change. Traditional society is no paradise. The relative stagnation of peasant society may help men to accept their suffering as part of the nature of things, but it is no absolute good.

The pressures of modernization, then, do not undermine idyllic societies of happy farmers whose lives would be perfectly happy if they were only left alone. It provides the concepts to express doubts and demands that were already just below the surface of consciousness. It provides an atmosphere of hope, often unrealistic, that things will soon be better. It unleashes powerful forces of destruction and rebellion as well as of innovation and construction. But it does not create these forces. Rather, they emerge from the patterns of motivation and relationship already existing in the traditional society. That is why modernization cannot be treated as a simple unitary process. Everywhere it takes effect only in relation to the tensions and forces, the historical bent, of particular societies. Let us now try to discern how Islam has helped to shape the modernization process in Muslim societies.

We may begin by spelling out what is involved in the modernization process as it applies to the four dramatistic levels of primary interest here. Modernization carries with it a conception of a relatively autonomous individual with a considerable capacity for adaptation to new situations and for innovation. Such an individual has a relatively high degree of self-consciousness and requires a family structure in which his independence and personal dignity will be recognized and where he can relate to others not so much in terms of authority and obedience as in terms of companionship and emotional participation. Such an individual also requires a society in which he feels like a full participating member, whose goals he shares and can meaningfully contribute to. Finally he requires a worldview that is open to the future, gives a positive value to amelioration of conditions in this world, and can help to make sense of the disruptions and disturbances of the historical process.

Where Islam has simply been identified with the specificities of an existing traditional society it has been little more than an obstruction to modernization at the personal, familial, political, and religious levels. Every institutional or ideological change in education, family, or law has simply been blindly opposed. Such blind reaction has almost everywhere precipitated its dialectical opposite: the importation of Western secular ideologies as the real guiding forces of life. This need not necessitate the outright rejection of Islam in some form of atheism or agnosticism, though this too has occurred. It may involve simply the relegation of Islam to the realm of purely private concern so that it is without relevance to most of life. Whether such an Islam has much relation to what has historically been known as such is of course a question. The Ottoman Empire and the Republic of Turkey give perhaps the best examples both of intransigent opposition and radical secularism. These developments are of great importance in their own right, but here it seems more useful to concentrate on tendencies that fall between these extremes, efforts to make Islam relevant today without either rejecting or wholly embracing the modern secular world.

The terminology in this field is bewildering—conservative, liberal, reformist, fundamentalist, modernist, neo-orthodox—and by most accounts misleading. Two basic tendencies in the thought of Muhammad Abduh and his many disciples of various hue stand out. One is the assertion that Islam is a religion and an ideology wholly appropriate to the needs of the modern world. The other is the claim that whatever good in the modern world is not already included in Islam is not in conflict with it. The conservative-liberal distinction seems really to apply to whether the first or the second of these assertions is emphasized. As Malcolm Kerr, in his paper in this series, has emphasized, neither of these assertions involves a radical rethinking of Islam. Muhammad Abduh and his followers do not make any real break in content or in method with previous Muslim thought. It is true that they come out of and emphasize one strand of that tradition, what Clifford Geertz has very usefully called "scripturalism." But in this they are the true descendants of Ibn Hanbal, Ibn Taimiyya, and Abd al-Wahhab. This does not mean, however, that their influence has been necessarily reactionary or even conservative. From what has been said earlier it should be clear how a scripturalist position could be a profoundly modernizing one.

Muhammad Abduh and his scripturalist descendents from Morocco to Indonesia for nearly three-quarters of a century now have been arguing that Islam is a religion that gives profound diginity to the individual, that is oriented to a better social order in this world, that demands the full inclusion of every Muslim in a functioning community, and that grants high status and protection to women within the family. And of course they are right. The reassertion of the basic message of the *Qur'an* in the face of the overgrown garden of magic of late medieval Islam has had a profoundly modernizing consequence. Awakening to membership in the universal community of Islam has often been the first mode of consciousness to break through stagnant localisms, as Geertz has pointed out. Anticolonialist and nationalist impulses as well as all kinds of social reform efforts have originated at this source. There could be no clearer tribute to the universalistic, progressive, and indeed, revolutionary potential of Quranic religion.

There are, however, problems. We have already noted that there were constraints and limitations in early Islam, as well as progressive tendencies. The scripturalists, however, have not been able to see, or if they saw to discuss those limitations. The Islam of *Qur'an* and Sunna was seen as a perfect entity, immaculate from the hands of God, and as such utterly removed from any possible criticism. As has often been pointed out, this kind of attitude, which has earned for the scripturalists the soubriquet "fundamentalist," is understandable as a defensive reaction to the arrogant self-confidence of Western culture, though its roots go much deeper than that. We need not so much explain it as understand its consequences in several spheres of modernization.

The problems in the political sphere need not detain us at length, as Malcolm Kerr has already given them a masterly treatment. I want to emphasize that the problems have arisen not from any basic antipathy between Islam and nationalism but because of their deep interpenetration. Everywhere nationalism has been more or less closely associated with Islam. Indonesian nationalism began under the aegis of Islamic reformism. Pakistan would not exist except for the national consciousness of the Muslim peoples of British India. Arab nationalism may or may not have originated with Christians but it soon took on a strong Islamic cast. The movement for Moroccan national independence was originally led by scripturalist Muslims.

This association was inevitable because in traditional Muslim society the only political community that could transcend the local ties to village, quarter, or tribe was the Islamic *umma.* Nationalist leaders could appeal not to "citizens," a meaningless concept, but only to "believers." The conflict between Islamic universalism and nationalist particularism was not as severe as it perhaps logically ought to have been. The Muslim peoples had been politically divided for too long for this to appear wholly anomalous. The various efforts to revive the caliphate were widely recognized as chimerical. Even the efforts of the ultraconservative to implement the classical Sharia as the law of the land were only marginally disruptive. The real problem has been in the development of a secular poltical consciousness that may derive moral guidance from Islam but faces political problems in political terms. The scripturalists have not been able to establish their own political regimes anywhere, and except for their radical right wing, it is doubtful if they have really tried. But the near identity of national and religious consciousness together with the continual assertion that Islam is an all-sufficient ideology places real limits on the flexibility of political thought and action, as Kerr has demonstrated with respect to Arab (Muslim) socialism.

The crux of the political problem is simply this: The resurgence of Quranic Islam in the last century has contributed greatly to the emergence of the collective consciousness of the Muslim peoples, to what Karl Deutsch would call their "social mobilization." The limitations inherent in this process do not derive chiefly from the problem of converting Muslim consciousness into national loyalty, or from unrealistic attempts to implement detailed prescriptions of the Sharia. The limitation comes, rather, from the veto power that Islamic consciousness continues to exercise over the whole realm of political ideology and action. Of course this may not be entirely a bad thing. It perhaps exercises restraint over totalitarian tendencies. But it is also related to the tendency in many Muslim lands to rely on what Soedjatmoko calls "virtual images," rhetorical devices as a substitiute for any serious and thorough program of political reform.

Given the weakness of the *ulama* and the apparent spread of secularism, this veto power might be thought to be insignificant. But in the context of the history of Muslim societies it is serious. The shadow of illegitimacy that has for centuries accompanied political power is still not absent, even where personal charisma has been intense. The loss of the Muslim consensus undoubtedly helped to bring down Sukarno. The very social mobilization to which Islamic consciousness has contributed is jeopardized by any government that too flagrantly violates that consciousness. This places consideable restraints on the range of political choice. It will be interesting to see whether the present Syrian regime survives the casualness with which it has taken Islamic sentiment. Its superheated opposition to Israel may be in part a cover for its own loss of Islamic legitimacy.

The problems with respect to the family are even clearer. Scripturalist Islam has never thrown itself into the struggle for family reform and the emancipation of women the way it has into efforts for national liberation. Indeed, the very considerable reforms that have been achieved in these areas have often been gained in the face of scripturalist opposition. The problem has been not so much substantive—we have seen that there is Quranic warrant for family reform—as formal. In spite of the talk about opening the gates of *ijtihad,* any thoroughgoing criticism of the hadith literature and the historical formation of the Sharia has been avoided. The fear, perhaps justified, has been that any such criticism might lead to a critical examination of the *Qur'an* itself, and so undermine the entire scripturalist position. Consequently the very considerable changes in family law, admirably summarized by J. N. D. Anderson in his paper in this series, have been accepted grudgingly and without enthusiasm by most representatives of Islamic thought.

In spite of tortured textual interpretations, such as the one which makes Islam "really" enjoin monogamy, Islam remains a religion in which women are second-class citizens, largely barred from public participation in their religion and still suffering from the kind of disability symbolized by the fact that the Sharia accepted the testimony of a woman as having only half the weight of the testimony of a man. As William Goode in his *World Revolution and Family Patterns* has shown, the movement for the full inclusion of women in society and their acceptance as partners within the family is one of the most general features of change in developing societies. In China the drive for the emancipation of women generated almost as much energy as the struggle against landlords, and women have been among the most stalwart supporters of the Communist regime. This movement and its potential energy remain largely unrelated to Islamic thought in contemporary Muslim countries. The drive of youth for greater influence in society, another general feature of modernizing societies, has, on the other hand, been more easily linked to Islamic movements as was evident earlier in the Muslim Brotherhood and more recently in Indonesia. Whether Islamic movements will continue to appeal to youth or will be limited only to certain categories of the culturally disoriented remains to be seen. It is by no means clear that the enormous energies involved in the demand for fuller social participation on the part of women and youth and the rise of the ideal of the small equalitarian family can be accommodated, much less advanced, under the banner of present Islamic thought.

Indeed, it might be argued that just as Islam has not fully legitimated the political sphere, it remains deeply suspicious of the realm of kinship and family relations. Islam never sacramentalized marriage the way Christianity did. The realm of sexual relations has been viewed as one to be regulated and controlled rather than given positive religious meaning. Associated with this attitude has been a deep suspicion of women. Without external restraint, it was felt, their sexual passions would run wild. This may be more folk belief than religious teaching, but the latter has on the whole reinforced the former. This is not to say that the family has not been important in the Muslim world, but that the family, like politics, has been only partially legitimized. This has operated to prevent the strong pattern of familistic loyalty and aggrandizement from being socialized for transfamilial ends. Deep family commitments have tended to undermine, rather than to reinforce as in the Japanese case, modernizing reforms.

The consequence of the continuation of traditional family patterns has also had implications for individual personality. The second-class position of women has been reflected in an inability by men to accept the feminine aspects of their own personalities, resulting, at least in the Arab world, in a kind of rhetorical masculinity which is not wholly different from Latin American *machismo*. The brittle narcissism of the Arab male personality is related to certain inflexibilities in political behavior that come out most noticeably in international relations. On the other hand the deep dependency feelings that flamboyant masculinity scarcely succeeds in hiding lead to easy submission to authoritarian leadership and the building up of leader-client relationships in many spheres of life only partially legitimate in the larger society. Success in the effort to improve the position of women and strengthen the independent small family would undoubtedly contribute to a stronger and more flexible organization of the personality.

I have emphasized the relation between rigorist Islam and personal selfhood. Perhaps the "fundamentalist" rigidity of the religious commitment is related to the relative weakness of other supports for an independent self. Consequently any threat to the received purity of religion is viewed as entailing personal chaos. Greater familial and institutional support for an independent personality would undoubtedly allow increased flexibility with respect to religious symbols. Thus in the realm of individual personality, too, we see that Quranic religion makes a contribution, but by itself not a sufficient contribution, to the modernization process.

Finally we must consider the problem of the modernization of Islam as a symbol system. It has become clear from Kerr's *Islamic Reform,* Safran's *Egypt in Search of Political Community,* and other recent work that neither Muhammad Abduh nor his various disciples have produced anything that warrants the name "modernism" or anything which can be called "reform" except in the restricted sense of return to the past, as the term "Salafiya" indeed implies. I have tried to show that in spite of this fact a great contribution by this trend of thought has been made, thanks to the modernizing potential of Quranic religion itself. The very success of the scripturalist movement, however, may have limited its further evolution. Greater justification in the charges of "backwardness" and "irrelevance" or more complete failure in competition with other trends of thought might have forced a deeper revaluation. But relative success does not preclude present and growing problems.

The main criticism of contemporary Muslim thought and its impact on society is that it fails to distinguish adequately between the realms of reason and faith, and that explicitly or implicitly it binds and restrains the use of reason in the solution of social problems. This is undoubtedly correct, but its implications extend not only to the problem of the effective use of reason in society but to the effective capacity of Islam to act as a religion. The gambit of proclaiming that Islam is perfectly "reasonable" and could never conflict with science and reason, without any serious attempt to face the theological issues involved in such an assertion, has been justly criticized. It has been pointed out that this assertion serves to obscure the fact that Islam in fact severely limits certain possibilities of social thought. But the continual harping on the reasonableness of Islam has other consequences.

Man is by no means simply a rational animal. A perfectly reasonable religion and a perfectly rational man would conform to the ideal type of the secular city. But we have already asserted that as an empirical fact such an idea is an anthropological impossibility. Man is not only a secular-critical being, but also a mythical, nonrational being. A profoundly nonrational order and form is the necessary precondition for the emergence of rationality at all. Mythical and critical thought exist in eternal tension, but mythical thought has a certain psychological priority. For myth gives a sense of the whole; it is, in Suzanne Langer's terms, presentational in its symbolism. Critical thought is analytical and discursive. It rests on an assumption of order that it cannot prove. In the eighteenth century the gambits of "reasonable religion" and "reason alone" were tried and failed. The nineteenth and twentieth centuries have seen an enormous revival in the influence of Christianity in a variety of new forms, and of other master myths in competition with them.

The Islamic world in its own way must inevitably face the same set of problems. The survival of popular religion and Sufism in the face of scripturalist attack indicates that scripturalism has not met all religious needs, however successful it is as an ideology. It is difficult to imagine that an intransigent literalism can cope with the profound problems of meaning raised by modern experience in the minds of men, even those best educated in the Islamic tradition. Of course there are great resources in the Islamic past to meet such needs. Brugman's mention of the efforts of a few Islamic existentialists to draw on the Sufi tradition may be a forestaste of things to come. That the efforts are not very sophisticated may simply indicate how early is the day in such rethinking. The Muslim world comes relatively late to these issues and can begin to discern them only after certain of the absorbing political and social issues have begun to settle. But if Islam out of its own resources cannot provide an encompassing myth for the Muslim peoples—and of course it must be a new kind of myth, more self-conscious, flexible, and expressive than the traditional ones—then other kinds of thought will.

Perhaps the greatest problem of modernization of all for Islam is not whether it can contribute to political, familial, or personal modernization, but whether it can effectively meet the specifically religious needs of the modern Muslim peoples.

Bibliography

Bellah, Robert N., ed. *Religion and Progress in Modern Asia.* Glencoe, Ill.: Free Press, 1965. Note especially the chapters by Coulson, Geertz, and Bellah.

Berkes, Niyazi. *The Rise of Secularism in Turkey.* Toronto: McGill Univ. Press, 1965.

Cox, Harvey. *The Secular City.* New York: Macmillan Co., 1965.

Geertz, Clifford. *Islam Observed: Religious Development in Morocco and Indonesia.* The Terry Lectures. New Haven: Yale Univ. Press, 1968.

Gibb, Hamilton A. R. *Studies on the Civilization of Islam.* Boston: Beacon Press.

Goode, William. *World Revolution and Family Patterns.* Glencoe, Ill.: Free Press, 1963.

Kerr, Malcolm H. *Islamic Reform.* Berkeley: Univ. of Calif. Press, 1966.

Lapidus, Ira. *Muslim Cities in the Late Middle Ages.* Cambridge, Mass.: Harvard University Press, 1967.

Rosenthal, E. I. J. *Islam in the Modern National State.* Cambridge: Cambridge University Press, 1965.

Safran, Nadav. *Egypt in Search of Political Community.* Cambridge, Mass.: Harvard University Press, 1961.

9 Civil Religion in America

While some have argued that Christianity is the national faith, and others that church and synagogue celebrate only the generalized religion of "the American Way of Life," few have realized that there actually exists alongside of and rather clearly differentiated from the churches an elaborate and well-institutionaliezed civil religion in America. This article argues not only that there is such a thing, but also that this religion—or perhaps better, this religious dimension—has its own seriousness and integrity and requires the same care in understanding that any other religion does.[1]

The Kennedy Inaugural

John F. Kennedy's inaugural address of January 20, 1961, serves as an example and a clue with which to introduce this complex subject. That address began:

We observe today not a victory of party but a celebration of freedom—symbolizing an end as well as a beginning—signifying renewal as well as change. For I have sworn before you and Almighty God the same solemn oath our forebears prescribed nearly a century and three quarters ago.

This chapter was written for a Daedalus *conference on American Religion in May 1966. It was reprinted with comments and a rejoinder in* The Religious Situation: 1968, *where I defend myself against the accusation of supporting an idolatrous worship of the American nation. I think it should be clear from the text that I conceive of the central tradition of the American civil religion not as a form of national self-worship but as the subordination of the nation to ethical principles that transcend it and in terms of which it should be judged. I am convinced that every nation and every people come to some form of religious self-understanding whether the critics like it or not. Rather than simply denounce what seems in any case inevitable, it seems more responsible to seek within the civil religious tradition for those critical principles which undercut the everpresent danger of national self-idolization.*

The world is very different now. For man holds in his mortal hands the power to abolish all forms of human poverty and to abolish all forms of human life. And yet the same revolutionary beliefs for which our forebears fought are still at issue around the globe—the belief that the rights of man come not from the generosity of the state but from the hand of God.

And it concluded:

Finally, whether you are citizens of America or of the world, ask of us the same high standards of strength and sacrifice that we shall ask of you. With a good conscience ou[illegible] sure reward, with history the final judge of our deeds, let us go f[illegible] the land we love, asking His blessing and His help, but kn[illegible] th God's work must truly be our own.

These are the three places [illegible] s in which Kennedy mentioned the name of G[illegible] erstand why he mentioned God, the way in [illegible] what he meant to say in those three reference[illegible] nd much about American civil religion. But [illegible] e or obvious task, and American students of [illegible] bly differ widely in their interpretation of these [illegible]

Let us consider f[illegible] he three references. They occur in the two op[illegible] d in the closing paragraph, thus providing a s[illegible] more concrete remarks that form the middle [illegible] ooking beyond this particular speech, we woul[illegible] eferences to God are almost invariably to be f[illegible] tements of American presidents on solemn occa[illegible] not in the working messages that the Presi[illegible] ess on various concrete issues. How, then, ar[illegible] placing of references to God?

It might b[illegible] sages quoted reveal the essentially irrelevant ro[illegible] ery secular society that is America. The placing [illegible] this speech as well as in public life generally i[illegible] has "only a ceremonial significance"; it gets on[illegible] hat serves largely to placate the more unenligh[illegible] community before a discussion of the really se[illegible] which religion has nothing whatever to do. A [illegible] t even say that an American President has to [illegible] k losing votes. A semblance of piety is merely one o[illegible] n qualifications for the office, a bit more traditional than but not essentially different from the present-day requirement of a pleasing television personality.

But we know enough about the function of ceremonial and ritual in various societies to make us suspicious of dismissing something as unimportant because it is "only a ritual." What people say on solemn occasions need not be taken at face value, but it is often indicative of deep-seated values and commitments that are not made explicit in the course of everyday life. Following this line of argument, it is worth considering whether the very special placing of the references to God in Kennedy's address may not reveal something rather important and serious about religion in American life.

It might be countered that the very way in which Kennedy made his references reveals the essentially vestigial place of religion today. He did not refer to any religion in particular. He did not refer to Jesus Christ, or to Moses, or to the Christian church; certainly he did not refer to the Catholic church. In fact, his only reference was to the concept of God, a word that almost all Americans can accept but that means so many different things to so many different people that it is almost an empty sign. Is this not just another indication that in America religion is considered vaguely to be a good thing, but that people care so little about it that it has lost any content whatever? Isn't Dwight Eisenhower reported to have said "Our government makes no sense unless it is founded in a deeply felt religious faith—and I don't care what it is,"[2] and isn't that a complete negation of any real religion?

These questions are worth pursuing because they raise the issue of how civil religion relates to the political society on the one hand and to private religious organization on the other. President Kennedy was a Christian, more specifically a Catholic Christian. Thus his general references to God do not mean that he lacked a specific religious commitment. But why, then, did he not include some remark to the effect that Christ is the Lord of the world or some indication of respect for the Catholic church? He did not because these are matters of his own private religious belief and of his relation to his own particular church; they are not matters relevant in any direct way to the conduct of his public office. Others with different religious views and commitments to different churches or denominations are equally qualified participants in the political process. The principle of separation of church and state guarantees the freedom of religious belief and association, but at the same time clearly segregates the religious sphere, which is considered to be essentially private, from the political one.

Considering the separation of church and state, how is a president justified in using the word "God" at all? The answer is that the separation of church and state has not denied the political realm a religious dimension. Although matters of personal religious belief, worship, and association are considered to be strictly private affairs, there are, at the same time, certain common elements of religious orientation that the great majority of Americans share. These have played a crucial role in the development of American institutions and still provide a religious dimension for the whole fabric of American life, including the political sphere. This public religious dimension is expressed in a set of beliefs, symbols, and rituals that I am calling the American civil religion. The inauguration of a president is an important ceremonial event in this religion. It reaffirms, among other things, the religious legitimation of the highest political authority.

Let us look more closely at what Kennedy actually said. First he said, "I have sworn before you and Almighty God the same solemn oath our forebears prescribed nearly a century and three quarters ago." The oath is the oath of office, including the acceptance of the obligation to uphold the Constitution. He swears it before the people (you) and God. Beyond the Constitution, then, the president's obligation extends not only to the people but to God. In American political theory, sovereignty rests, of course, with the people, but implicitly, and often explicitly, the ultimate sovereignty has been attributed to God. This is the meaning of the motto, "In God we trust," as well as the inclusion of the phrase "under God" in the pledge to the flag. What difference does it make that sovereignty belongs to God? Though the will of the people as expressed in majority vote is carefully institutionalized as the operative source of political authority, it is deprived of an ultimate significance. The will of the people is not itself the criterion of right and wrong. There is a higher criterion in terms of which this will can be judged; it is possible that the people may be wrong. The president's obligation extends to the higher criterion.

When Kennedy says that "the rights of man come not from the generosity of the state but from the hand of God," he is stressing this point again. It does not matter whether the state is the expression of the will of an autocratic monarch or of the "people"; the rights of man are more basic than any political structure and provide a point of revolutionary leverage from which any state structure may be radically altered. That is the basis for his reassertion of the revolutionary significance of America.

But the religious dimension in political life as recognized by Kennedy not only provides a grounding for the rights of man that makes any form of political absolutism illegitimate, it also provides a transcendent goal for the political process. This is implied in his final words that "here on earth God's work must truly be our own." What he means here is, I think, more clearly spelled out in a previous paragraph, the wording of which, incidentally, has a distinctly biblical ring:

> Now the trumpet summons us again—not as a call to bear arms, though arms we need—not as a call to battle, though embattled we are—but a call to bear the burden of a long twilight struggle, year in and year out, "rejoicing in hope, patient in tribulation"—a struggle against the common enemies of man: tyranny, poverty, disease and war itself.

The whole address can be understood as only the most recent statement of a theme that lies very deep in the American tradition, namely the obligation, both collective and individual, to carry out God's will on earth. This was the motivating spirit of those who founded America, and it has been present in every generation since. Just below the surface throughout Kennedy's inaugural address, it becomes explicit in the closing statement that God's work must be our own. That this very activist and noncontemplative conception of the fundamental religious obligation, which has been historically associated with the Protestant position, should be enunciated so clearly in the first major statement of the first Catholic president seems to underline how deeply established it is in the American outlook. Let us now consider the form and history of the civil religious tradition in which Kennedy was speaking.

The Idea of a Civil Religion

The phrase "civil religion" is, of course, Rousseau's. In chapter 8, book 4 of *The Social Contract,* he outlines the simple dogmas of the civil religion: the existence of God, the life to come, the reward of virtue and the punishment of vice, and the exclusion of religious intolerance. All other religious opinions are outside the cognizance of the state and may be freely held by citizens. While the phrase "civil religion" was not used, to the best of my knowledge, by the founding fathers, and I am certainly not arguing for the particular influence of Rousseau, it is clear that similar ideas, as part of the cultural climate of the late eighteenth century, were to be found among the Americans. For example, Benjamin Franklin writes in his autobiography,

> I never was without some religious principles. I never doubted, for instance, the existence of the Deity; that he made the world and govern'd it by his Providence; that the most acceptable service of God was the doing of good to men; that our souls are immortal; and that all crime will be punished, and virtue rewarded either here or hereafter. These I esteemed the essentials of every religion; and, being to be found in all the religions we had in our country, I respected them all, tho' with different degrees of respect, as I found them more or less mix'd with other articles, which, without any tendency to inspire, promote or confirm morality, serv'd principally to divide us, and make us unfriendly to one another.

It is easy to dispose of this sort of position as essentially utilitarian in relation to religion. In Washington's Farewell Address (though the words may be Hamilton's) the utilitarian aspect is quite explicit:

> Of all the dispositions and habits which lead to political prosperity, Religion and Morality are indispensable supports. In vain would that man claim the tribute of Patriotism, who should labour to subvert these great Pillars of human happiness, these firmest props of the duties of men and citizens. The mere politician, equally with the pious man ought to respect and cherish them. A volume could not trace all their connections with private and public felicity. Let it simply be asked where is the security for property, for reputation, for life, if the sense of religious obligation *desert* the oaths, which are the instruments of investigation in Courts of Justice? And let us with caution indulge the supposition, that morality can be maintained without religion. Whatever may be conceded to the influence of refined education on minds of peculiar structure, reason and experience both forbid us to expect that National morality can prevail in exclusion of religious principle.

But there is every reason to believe that religion, particularly the idea of God, played a constitutive role in the thought of the early American statesmen.

Kennedy's inaugural pointed to the religious aspect of the Declaration of Independence, and it might be well to look at that document a bit more closely. There are four references to God. The first speaks of the "Laws of Nature and of Nature's God" that entitle any people to be independent. The second is the famous statement that all men "are endowed by their Creator with certain inalienable Rights." Here Jefferson is locating the fundamental legitimacy of the new nation in a conception of "higher law" that is itself based on both classical natural law and biblical religion. The third is an appeal to "the Supreme Judge of the world for the rectitude of our intentions," and the last indicates "a firm reliance on the protection of divine Providence." In these last two references, a biblical God of history who stands in judgment over the world is indicated.

The intimate relation of these religious notions with the self-conception of the new republic is indicated by the frequency of their appearance in early official documents. For example, we find in Washington's first inaugural address of April 30, 1789:

> It would be peculiarly improper to omit in this first official act my fervent supplications to that Almighty Being who rules over the universe, who presides in the councils of nations, and whose providential aids can supply every defect, that His benediction may consecrate to the liberties and happiness of the people of the United States a Government instituted by themselves for these essential purposes, and may enable every instrument employed in its administration to execute with success the functions allotted to his charge.
>
> No people can be bound to acknowledge and adore the Invisible Hand which conducts the affairs of man more than those of the United States. Every step by which we have advanced to the character of an independent nation seems to have been distinguished by some token of providential agency. . . .
>
> The propitious smiles of Heaven can never be expected on a nation that disregards the eternal rules of order and right which Heaven itself has ordained. . . . The preservation of the sacred fire of liberty and the destiny of the republican model of government are justly considered, perhaps, as *deeply*, as *finally*, staked on the experiment intrusted to the hands of the American people.

Nor did these religious sentiments remain merely the personal expression of the President. At the request of both Houses of Congress, Washington proclaimed on October 3 of that same first year as President that November 26 should be "a day of public thanksgiving and prayer," the first Thanksgiving Day under the Constitution.

The words and acts of the founding fathers, especially the first few presidents, shaped the form and tone of the civil religion as it has been maintained ever since. Though much is selectively derived from Christianity, this religion is clearly not itself Christianity. For one thing, neither Washington nor Adams nor Jefferson mentions Christ in his inaugural address; nor do any of the subsequent presidents, although not one of them fails to mention God.[3] The God of the civil religion is not only rather "unitarian," he is also on the austere side, much more related to order, law, and right than to salvation and love. Even though he is somewhat deist in cast, he is by no means simply a watchmaker God. He is actively interested and involved in history, with a special concern for America. Here the analogy has much less to do with natural law than with ancient Israel; the equation of America with Israel in the idea of the "American Israel" is not infrequent.[4] What was implicit in the words of Washington already quoted becomes explicit in Jefferson's second inaugural when he said: "I shall need, too, the favor of that Being in whose hands we are, who led our fathers, as Israel of old, from their native land and planted them in a country flowing with all the necessaries and comforts of life." Europe is Egypt; America, the promised land. God has led his people to establish a new sort of social order that shall be a light unto all the nations.[5]

This theme, too, has been a continuous one in the civil religion. We have already alluded to it in the case of the Kennedy inaugural. We find it again in President Johnson's inaugural address:

> They came here—the exile and the stranger, brave but frightened—to find a place where a man could be his own man. They made a covenant with this land. Conceived in justice, written in liberty, bound in union, it was meant one day to inspire the hopes of all mankind; and it binds us still. If we keep its terms, we shall flourish.

What we have, then, from the earliest years of the republic is a collection of beliefs, symbols, and rituals with respect to sacred things and institutionalized in a collectivity. This religion—there seems no other word for it—while not antithetical to and indeed sharing much in common with Christianity, was neither sectarian nor in any specific sense Christian. At a time when the society was overwhelmingly Christian, it seems unlikely that this lack of Christian reference was meant to spare the feelings of the tiny non-Christian minority. Rather, the civil religion expressed what those who set the precedents felt was appropriate under the circumstances. It reflected their private as well as public views. Nor was the civil religion simply "religion in general." While generality was undoubtedly seen as a virtue by some, as in the quotation from Franklin above, the civil religion was specific enough when it came to the topic of America. Precisely because of this specificity, the civil religion was saved from empty formalism and several as a genuine vehicle of national religious self-understanding.

But the civil religion was not, in the minds of Franklin, Washington, Jefferson, or other leaders, with the exception of a few radicals like Tom Paine, ever felt to be a substitute for Christianity. There was an implicit but quite clear division of function between the civil religion and Christianity. Under the doctrine of religious liberty, an exceptionally wide sphere of personal piety and voluntary social action was left to the churches. But the churches were neither to control the state nor to be controlled by it. The national magistrate, whatever his private religious views, operates under the rubrics of the civil religion as long as he is in his official capacity, as we have already seen in the case of Kennedy. This accommodation was undoubtedly the product of a particular historical moment and of a cultural background dominated by Protestantism of several varieties and by the Enlightenment, but it has survived despite subsequent changes in the cultural and religious climate.

Civil War and Civil Religion

Until the Civil War, the American civil religion focused above all on the event of the Revolution, which was seen as the final act of the Exodus from the old lands across the waters. The Declaration of Independence and the Constitution were the sacred scriptures and Washington the divinely appointed Moses who led his people out of the hands of tyranny. The Civil War, which Sidney Mead calls "the center of American history,"[6] was the second great event that involved the national self-understanding so deeply as to require expression in the civil religion. In 1835, Alexis de Tocqueville wrote that the American republic had never really been tried and that victory in the Revolutionary War was more the result of British preoccupation elsewhere and the presence of a powerful ally than of any great military success of the Americans. But in 1861 the time of testing had indeed come. Not only did the Civil War have the tragic intensity of fratricidal strife, but it was one of the bloodiest wars of the nineteenth century; the loss of life was far greater than any previously suffered by Americans.

The Civil War raised the deepest questions of national meaning. The man who not only formulated but in his own person embodied its meaning for Americans was Abraham Lincoln. For him the issue was not in the first instance slavery but "whether that nation, or any nation so conceived, and so dedicated, can long endure." He had said in Independence Hall in Philadelphia on February 22, 1861:

> All the political sentiments I entertain have been drawn, so far as I have been able to draw them, from the sentiments which originated in and were given to the world from this Hall. I have never had a feeling, politically, that did not spring from the sentiments embodied in the Declaration of Independence.[7]

The phrases of Jefferson constantly echo in Lincoln's speeches. His task was, first of all, to save the Union—not for America alone but for the meaning of America to the whole world so unforgettably etched in the last phrase of the Gettysburg Address.

But inevitably the issue of slavery as the deeper cause of the conflict had to be faced. In his second inaugural, Lincoln related slavery and the war in an ultimate perspective:

> If we shall suppose that American slavery is one of those offenses which, in the providence of God, must needs come, but which, having continued through His appointed time, He now wills to remove, and that He gives to both North and South this terrible war as the woe due to those by whom the offense came, shall we discern therein any departure from those divine attributes which the believers in a living God always ascribe to Him? Fondly do we hope, fervently do we pray, that this mighty scourge of war may speedily pass away. Yet, if God wills that it continue until all the wealth piled by the bondsman's two hundred and fifty years of unrequited toil shall be sunk, and until every drop of blood drawn with the lash shall be paid by another drawn with the sword, as was said three thousand years ago, so still it must be said "the judgements of the Lord are true and righteous altogether."

But he closes on a note if not of redemption then of reconciliation—"With malice toward none, with charity for all."

With the Civil War, a new theme of death, sacrifice, and rebirth enters the civil religion. It is symbolized in the life and death of Lincoln. Nowhere is it stated more vividly than in the Gettysburg Address, itself part of the Lincolnian "New Testament" among the civil scriptures. Robert Lowell has recently pointed out the "insistent use of birth images" in this speech explicitly devoted to "these honored dead": "brought forth," "conceived," "created," "a new birth of freedom." He goes on to say:

The Gettysburg Address is a symbolic and sacramental act. Its verbal quality is resonance combined with a logical, matter of fact, prosaic brevity. . . . In his words, Lincoln symbolically died, just as the Union soldiers really died—and as he himself was soon really to die. By his words, he gave the field of battle a symbolic significance that it had lacked. For us and our country, he left Jefferson's ideals of freedom and equality joined to the Christian sacrificial act of death and rebirth. I believe this is a meaning that goes beyond sect or religion and beyond peace and war, and is now part of our lives as a challenge, obstacle and hope.[8]

Lowell is certainly right in pointing out the Christian quality of the symbolism here, but he is also right in quickly disavowing any sectarian implication. The earlier symbolism of the civil religion had been Hebraic without in any specific sense being Jewish. The Gettysburg symbolism (". . . those who here gave their lives, that that nation might live") is Christian without having anything to do with the Christian church.

The symbolic equation of Lincoln with Jesus was made relatively early. W. H. Herndon, who had been Lincoln's law partner, wrote:

For fifty years God rolled Abraham Lincoln through his fiery furnace. He did it to try Abraham and to purify him for his purposes. This made Mr. Lincoln humble, tender, forbearing, sympathetic to suffering, kind, sensitive, tolerant; broadening, deepening and widening his whole nature; making him the noblest and loveliest character since Jesus Christ. . . . I believe that Lincoln was God's chosen one.[9]

With the Christian archetype in the background, Lincoln, "our martyred president," was linked to the war dead, those who "gave the last full measure of devotion." The theme of sacrifice was indelibly written into the civil religion.

The new symbolism soon found both physical and ritualistic expression. The great number of the war dead required the establishment of a number of national cemeteries. Of these, the Gettysburg National Cemetery, which Lincoln's famous address served to dedicate, has been overshadowed only by the Arlington National Cemetery. Begun somewhat vindictively on the Lee estate across the river from Washington, partly with the end that the Lee family could never reclaim it,[10] it has subsequently become the most hallowed monument of the civil religion. Not only was a section set aside for the Confederate dead, but it has received the dead of each succeeding American war. It is the site of the one important new symbol to come out of World War I, the Tomb of the Unknown Soldier; more recently it has become the site of the tomb of another martyred President and its symbolic eternal flame.

Memorial Day, which grew out of the Civil War, gave ritual expression to the themes we have been discussing. As Lloyd Warner has so brilliantly analyzed it, the Memorial Day observance, especially in the towns and smaller cities of America, is a major event for the whole community involving a rededication to the martyred dead, to the spirit of sacrifice, and to the American vision.[11] Just as Thanksgiving Day, which incidentally was securely institutionalized as an annual national holiday only under the presidency of Lincoln, serves to integrate the family into the civil religion, so Memorial Day has acted to integrate the local community into the national cult. Together with the less overtly religious Fourth of July and the more minor celebrations of Veterans Day and the birthdays of Washington and Lincoln, these two holidays provide an annual ritual calendar for the civil religion. The public school system serves as a particularly important context for the cultic celebration of the civil rituals.

The Civil Religion Today

In reifying and giving a name to something that, though pervasive enough when you look at it, has gone on only semiconsciously, there is risk of severely distorting the data. But the reification and the naming have already begun. The religious critics of "religion in general," or of the "religion of the 'American Way of Life,' " or of "American Shinto" have really been talking about the civil religion. As usual in religious polemic, they take as criteria the best in their own religious tradition and as typical the worst in the tradition of the civil religion. Against these critics, I would argue that the civil religion at its best is a genuine apprehension of universal and transcendent religious reality as seen in or, one could almost say, as revealed through the experience of the American people. Like all religions, it has suffered various deformations and demonic distortions. At its best, it has neither been so general that it has lacked incisive relevance to the American scene nor so particular that it has placed American society above universal human values. I am not at all convinced that the leaders of the churches have consistently represented a higher level of religious insight than the spokesmen of the civil religion. Reinhold Niebuhr has this to say of Lincoln, who never joined a church and who certainly represents civil religion at its best:

> An analysis of the religion of Abraham Lincoln in the context of the traditional religion of his time and place and of its polemical use on the slavery issue, which corrupted religious life in the days before and during the Civil War, must lead to the conclusion that Lincoln's religious convictions were superior in depth and purity to those, not only of the political leaders of his day, but of the religious leaders of the era.[12]

Perhaps the real animus of the religious critics has been not so much against the civil religion in itself but against its pervasive and dominating influence within the sphere of church religion. As S. M. Lipset has recently shown, American religion at least since the early nineteenth century has been predominantly activist, moralistic, and social rather than contemplative, theological, or innerly spiritual.[13] De Tocqueville spoke of American church religion as "a political institution which powerfully contributes to the maintenance of a democratic republic among the Americans"[14] by supplying a strong moral consensus amidst continuous political change. Henry Bargy in 1902 spoke of American church religion as "la poésie du civisme."[15]

It is certainly true that the relation between religion and politics in America has been singularly smooth. This is in large part due to the dominant tradition. As de Tocqueville wrote:

> The greatest part of British America was peopled by men who, after having shaken off the authority of the Pope, acknowledged no other religious supremacy: they brought with them into the New World a form of Christianity which I cannot better describe than by styling it a democratic and republican religion.[16]

The churches opposed neither the Revolution nor the establishment of democratic institutions. Even when some of them opposed the full institutionalization of religious liberty, they accepted the final outcome with good grace and without nostalgia for an *ancien régime*. The American civil religion was never anticlerical or militantly secular. On the contrary, it borrowed selectively from the religious tradition in such a way that the average American saw no conflict between the two. In this way, the civil religion was able to build up without any bitter struggle with the church powerful symbols of national solidarity and to mobilize deep levels of personal motivation for the attainment of national goals.

Such an achievement is by no means to be taken for granted. It would seem that the problem of a civil religion is quite general in modern societies and that the way it is solved or not solved will have repercussions in many spheres. One need only to think of France to see how differently things can go. The French Revolution was anticlerical to the core and attempted to set up an anti-Christian civil religion. Throughout modern French history, the chasm between traditional Catholic symbols and the symbolism of 1789 has been immense.

American civil religion is still very much alive. Just three years ago we participated in a vivid reenactment of the sacrifice theme in connection with the funeral of our assassinated President. The American Israel theme is clearly behind both Kennedy's New Frontier and Johnson's Great Society. Let me give just one recent illustration of how the civil religion serves to mobilize support for the attainment of national goals. On March 15, 1965, President Johnson went before Congress to ask for a strong voting-rights bill. Early in the speech he said:

> Rarely are we met with the challenge, not to our growth or abundance, or our welfare or our security—but rather to the values and the purposes and the meaning of our beloved nation.
>
> The issue of equal rights for American Negroes is such an issue. And should we defeat every enemy, and should we double our wealth and conquer the stars and still be unequal to this issue, then we will have failed as a people and as a nation.
>
> For with a country as with a person, "What is a man profited, if he shall gain the whole world, and lose his own soul?"

And in conclusion he said:

> Above the pyramid on the great seal of the United States it says in Latin, "God has favored our undertaking."
>
> God will not favor everything that we do. It is rather our duty to divine his will. I cannot help but believe that He truly understands and that He really favors the undertaking that we begin here tonight.[17]

The civil religion has not always been invoked in favor of worthy causes. On the domestic scene, an American-Legion type of ideology that fuses God, country, and flag has been used to attack nonconformist and liberal ideas and groups of all kinds. Still, it has been difficult to use the words of Jefferson and Lincoln to support special interests and undermine personal freedom. The defenders of slavery before the Civil War came to reject the thinking of the Declaration of Independence. Some of the most consistent of them turned against not only Jeffersonian democracy but Reformation religion; they dreamed of a South dominated by medieval chivalry and divine-right monarchy.[18] For all the overt religiosity of the radical right today, their relation to the civil religious consensus is tenuous, as when the John Birch Society attacks the central American symbol of Democracy itself.

With respect to America's role in the world, the dangers of distortion are greater and the built-in safeguards of the tradition weaker. The theme of the American Israel was used, almost from the beginning, as a justification for the shameful treatment of the Indians so characteristic of our history. It can be overtly or implicitly linked to the idea of manifest destiny that has been used to legitimate several adventures in imperialism since the early nineteenth century. Never has the danger been greater than today. The issue is not so much one of imperial expansion, of which we are accused, as of the tendency to assimilate all governments or parties in the world that support our immediate policies or call upon our help by invoking the notion of free institutions and democratic values. Those nations that are for the moment "on our side" become "the free world." A repressive and unstable military dictatorship in South Vietnam becomes "the free people of South Vietnam and their government." It is then part of the role of America as the New Jerusalem and "the last best hope of earth" to defend such governments with treasure and eventually with blood. When our soldiers are actually dying, it becomes possible to consecrate the struggle further by invoking the great theme of sacrifice. For the majority of the American people who are unable to judge whether the people in South Vietnam (or wherever) are "free like us," such arguments are convincing. Fortunately President Johnson has been less ready to assert that "God has favored our undertaking" in the case of Vietnam than with respect to civil rights. But others are not so hesitant. The civil religion has exercised long-term pressure for the humane solution of our greatest domestic problem, the treatment of the Negro American.

It remains to be seen how relevant it can become for our role in the world at large, and whether we can effectually stand for "the revolutionary beliefs for which our forebears fought," in John F. Kennedy's words.

The civil religion is obviously involved in the most pressing moral and political issues of the day. But it is also caught in another kind of crisis, theoretical and theological, of which it is at the moment largely unaware. "God" has clearly been a central symbol in the civil religion from the beginning and remains so today. This symbol is just as central to the civil religion as it is to Judaism or Christianity. In the late eighteenth century this posed no problem; even Tom Paine, contrary to his detractors, was not an atheist. From left to right and regardless of church or sect, all could accept the idea of God. But today, as even *Time* has recognized, the meaning of "God" is by no means so clear or so obvious. There is no formal creed in the civil religion. We have had a Catholic president; it is conceivable that we could have a Jewish one. But could we have an agnostic president? Could a man with conscientious scruples about using the word "God" the way Kennedy and Johnson have used it be elected chief magistrate of our country? If the whole God symbolism requires reformulation, there will be obvious consequences for the civil religion, consequences perhaps of liberal alienation and of fundamentalist ossification that have not so far been prominent in this realm. The civil religion has been a point of articulation between the profoundest commitments of the Western religious and philosophical tradition and the common beliefs of ordinary Americans. It is not too soon to consider how the deepening theological crisis may affect the future of this articulation.

The Third Time of Trial

In conclusion it may be worthwhile to relate the civil religion to the most serious situation that we as Americans now face, what I call the third time of trial. The first time of trial had to do with the question of independence, whether we should or could run our own affairs in our own way. The second time of trial was over the issue of slavery, which in turn was only the most salient aspect of the more general problem of the full institutionalization of democracy within our country. This second problem we are still far from solving though we have some notable successes to our credit. But we have been overtaken by a third great problem that has led to a third great crisis, in the midst of which we stand. This is the problem of responsible action in a revolutionary world, a world seeking to attain many of the things, material and spiritual, that we have already attained. Americans have, from the beginning, been aware of the responsibility and the significance our republican experiment has for the whole world. The first internal political polarization in the new nation had to do with our attitude toward the French Revolution. But we were small and weak then, and "foreign entanglements" seemed to threaten our very survival. During the last century, our relevance for the world was not forgotten, but our role was seen as purely exemplary. Our democratic republic rebuked tyranny by merely existing. Just after World War I we were on the brink of taking a different role in the world, but once again we turned our backs.

Since World War II the old pattern has become impossible. Every president since Franklin Roosevelt has been groping toward a new pattern of action in the world, one that would be consonant with our power and our responsibilities. For Truman and for the period dominated by John Foster Dulles that pattern was seen to be the great Manichaean confrontation of East and West, the confrontation of democracy and "the false philosophy of Communism" that provided the structure of Truman's inaugural address. But with the last years of Eisenhower and with the successive two presidents, the pattern began to shift. The great problems came to be seen as caused not solely by the evil intent of any one group of men, but as stemming from much more complex and multiple sources. For Kennedy it was not so much a struggle against particular men as against "the common enemies of man: tyranny, poverty, disease and war itself."

But in the midst of this trend toward a less primitive conception of ourselves and our world, we have somehow, without anyone really intending it, stumbled into a military confrontation where we have come to feel that our honor is at stake. We have in a moment of uncertainty been tempted to rely on our overwhelming physical power rather than on our intelligence, and we have, in part, succumbed to this temptation. Bewildered and unnerved when our terrible power fails to bring immediate success, we are at the edge of a chasm the depth of which no man knows.

I cannot help but think of Robinson Jeffers, whose poetry seems more apt now that when it was written, when he said:

Unhappy country, what wings you have! . . .
Weep (it is frequent in human affairs), weep for
  the terrible magnificence of the means,
The ridiculous incompetence of the reasons, the
  bloody and shabby
Pathos of the result.

But as so often before in similar times, we have a man of prophetic stature, without the bitterness or misanthropy of Jeffers, who, as Lincoln before him, calls this nation to its judgment:

> When a nation is very powerful but lacking in self-confidence, it is likely to behave in a manner that is dangerous both to itself and to others.
>
> Gradually but unmistakably, America is succumbing to that arrogance of power which has afflicted, weakened and in some cases destroyed great nations in the past.
>
> If the war goes on and expands, if that fatal process continues to accelerate until America becomes what it is not now and never has been, a seeker after unlimited power and empire, then Vietnam will have had a mighty and tragic fallout indeed.
>
> I do not believe that will happen. I am very apprehensive but I still remain hopeful, and even confident, that America, with its humane and democratic traditions, will find the wisdom to match its power.[19]

Without an awareness that our nation stands under higher judgment, the tradition of the civil religion would be dangerous indeed. Fortunately, the prophetic voices have never been lacking. Our present situation brings to mind the Mexican-American war that Lincoln, among so many others, opposed. The spirit of civil disobedience that is alive today in the civil rights movement and the opposition to the Vietnam War was already clearly outlined by Henry David Thoreau when he wrote, "If the law is of such a nature that it requires you to be an agent of injustice to another, then I say, break the law." Thoreau's words, "I would remind my countrymen that they are men first, and Americans at a late and convenient hour,"[20] provide an essential standard for any adequate thought and action in our third time of trial. As Americans, we have been well favored in the world, but it is as men that we will be judged.

Out of the first and second times of trial have come, as we have seen, the major symbols of the American civil religion. There seems little doubt that a successful negotiation of this third time of trial—the attainment of some kind of viable and coherent world order—would precipitate a major new set of symbolic forms. So far the flickering flame of the United Nations burns too low to be the focus of a cult, but the emergence of a genuine transnational sovereignty would certainly change this. It would necessitate the incorporation of vital international symbolism into our civil religion, or, perhaps a better way of putting it, it would result in American civil religion becoming simply one part of a new civil religion of the world. It is useless to speculate on the form such a civil religion might take, though it obviously would draw on religious traditions beyond the sphere of biblical religion alone. Fortunately, since the American civil religion is not the worship of the American nation but an understanding of the American experience in the light of ultimate and universal reality, the reorganization entailed by such a new situation need not disrupt the American civil religion's continuity. A world civil religion could be accepted as a fulfillment and not as a denial of American civil religion. Indeed, such an outcome has been the eschatological hope of American civil religion from the beginning. To deny such an outcome would be to deny the meaning of America itself.

Behind the civil religion at every point lie biblical archetypes: Exodus, Chosen People, Promised Land, New Jerusalem, and Sacrificial Death and Rebirth. But it is also genuinely American and genuinely new. It has its own prophets and its own martyrs, its own sacred events and sacred places, its own solemn rituals and symbols. It is concerned that America be a society as perfectly in accord with the will of God as men can make it, and a light to all the nations.

It has often been used and is being used today as a cloak for petty interests and ugly passions. It is in need—as is any living faith—of continual reformation, of being measured by universal standards. But it is not evident that it is incapable of growth and new insight.

It does not make any decision for us. It does not remove us from moral ambiguity, from being, in Lincoln's fine phrase, an "almost chosen people." But it is a heritage of moral and religious experience from which we still have much to learn as we formulate the decisions that lie ahead.

NOTES

1 Why something so obvious should have escaped serious analytical attention is in itself an interesting problem. Part of the reason is probably the controversial nature of the subject. From the earliest years of the nineteenth century, conservative religious and political groups have argued that Christianity is, in fact, the national religion. Some of them have from time to time and as recently as the 1950s proposed constitutional amendments that would explicitly recognize the sovereignty of Christ. In defending the doctrine of separation of church and state, opponents of such groups have denied that the national polity has, intrinsically, anything to do with religion at all. The moderates on this issue have insisted that the American state has taken a permissive and indeed supportive attitude toward religious groups (tax exemption, et cetera), thus favoring religion but still missing the positive institutionalization with which I am concerned. But part of the reason this issue has been left in obscurity is certainly due to the peculiarly Western concept of "religion" as denoting a single type of collectivity of which an individual can be a member of one and only one at a time. The Durkheimian notion that every group has a religious dimension, which would be seen as obvious in southern or eastern Asia, is foreign to us. This obscures the recognition of such dimensions in our society.

2 Dwight D. Eisenhower, in Will Herberg, *Protestant-Catholic-Jew* (Garden City, N.Y.: Doubleday & Co., 1955), p. 97.

3 God is mentioned or referred to in all inaugural addresses but Washington's second, which is a very brief (two paragraphs) and perfunctory acknowledgment. It is not without interest that the actual word "God" does not appear until Monroe's second inaugural, March 5, 1821. In his first inaugural, Washington refers to God as "that Almighty Being who rules the universe," "Great Author of every public and private good," "Invisible Hand," and "benign Parent of the Human Race." John Adams refers to God as "Providence," "Being who is supreme over all," "Patron of Order," "Fountain of Justice," and "Protector in all ages of the world of virtuous liberty." Jefferson speaks of "that Infinite Power which rules the destinies of the universe," and "that Being in whose

hands we are." Madison speaks of "that Almighty Being whose power regulates the destiny of nations," and "Heaven." Monroe uses "Providence" and "the Almighty" in his first inaugural and finally "Almighty God" in his second. See *Inaugural Addresses of the Presidents of the United States from George Washington 1789 to Harry S. Truman 1949,* 82d Congress, 2d Session, House Document No. 540, 1952.

4 For example, Abiel Abbot, pastor of the First Church in Haverhill, Massachusetts, delivered a Thanksgiving sermon in 1799, *Traits of Resemblance in the People of the United States of America to Ancient Israel,* in which he said, "It has been often remarked that the people of the United States come nearer to a parallel with Ancient Israel, than any other nation upon the globe. Hence 'Our American Israel' is a term frequently used; and common consent allows it apt and proper." In Hans Kohn, *The Idea of Nationalism* (New York: Macmillan Co., 1961), p. 665.

5 That the Mosaic analogy was present in the minds of leaders at the very moment of the birth of the republic is indicated in the designs proposed by Franklin and Jefferson for a seal of the United States of America. Together with Adams, they formed a committee of three delegated by the Continental Congress on July 4, 1776, to draw up the new device. "Franklin proposed as the device Moses lifting up his wand and dividing the Red Sea while Pharaoh was overwhelmed by its waters, with the motto 'Rebellion to tyrants is obedience to God.' Jefferson proposed the children of Israel in the wilderness 'led by a cloud by day and a pillar of fire at night.' " Anson Phelps Stokes, *Church and State in the United States,* vol. 1 (New York: Harper & Co., 1950), pp. 467–68.

6 Sidney E. Mead, *The Lively Experiment* (New York: Harper & Row, 1963), p. 12.

7 Abraham Lincoln, in Allan Nevins, ed., *Lincoln and the Gettysburg Address* (Urbana, Ill.: Univ. of Ill. Press, 1964), p. 39.

8 Robert Lowell, in *ibid.,* "On the Gettysburg Address," pp. 88–89.

9 William Henry Herndon, in Sherwood Eddy, *The Kingdom of God and the American Dream* (New York: Harper & Row, 1941), p. 162.

10 Karl Decker and Angus McSween, *Historic Arlington* (Washington, D.C., 1892), pp. 60–67.

11 How extensive the activity associated with Memorial Day can be is indicated by Warner: "The sacred symbolic behavior of Memorial Day, in which scores of the town's organizations are involved, is ordinarily divided into four periods. During the year separate rituals are held by many of the associations for their dead, and many of these activities are connected with later Memorial Day events. In the second phase, preparations are made during the last three or four weeks for the ceremony itself, and some of the associations perform public rituals. The

third phase consists of scores of rituals held in all the cemeteries, churches, and halls of the associations. These rituals consist of speeches and highly ritualized behavior. They last for two days and are climaxed by the fourth and last phase, in which all the separate celebrants gather in the center of the business district on the afternoon of Memorial Day. The separate organizations, with their members in uniform or with fitting insignia, march through the town, visit the shrines and monuments of the hero dead, and, finally, enter the cemetery. Here dozens of ceremonies are held, most of them highly symbolic and formalized." During these various ceremonies Lincoln is continually referred to and the Gettysburg Address recited many times. W. Lloyd Warner, *American Life* (Chicago: Univ. of Chicago Press, 1962), pp. 8–9.

12 Reinhold Niebuhr, "The Religion of Abraham Lincoln," in Nevins, ed., *op. cit.*, p. 72. William J. Wolfe of the Episcopal Theological School in Cambridge, Massachusetts, has written: "Lincoln is one of the greatest theologians of America—not in the technical meaning of producing a system of doctrine, certainly not as the defender of some one denomination, but in the sense of seeing the hand of God intimately in the affairs of nations. Just so the prophets of Israel criticized the events of their day from the perspective of the God who is concerned for history and who reveals His will within it. Lincoln now stands among God's latter-day prophets." *The Religion of Abraham Lincoln* (New York, 1963), p. 24.

13 Seymour Martin Lipset, "Religion and American Values" in *The First New Nation* (New York: Basic Books, 1964), chap. 4.

14 Alexis de Tocqueville, *Democracy in America,* vol. 1 (Garden City, N.Y.: Doubleday & Co., Anchor Books, 1954), p. 310.

15 Henry Bargy, *La Religion dans la Société aux États-Unis* (Paris, 1902), p. 31.

16 De Tocqueville, *op. cit.,* p. 311. Later he says, "In the United States even the religion of most of the citizens is republican, since it submits the truths of the other world to private judgment, as in politics the care of their temporal interests is abandoned to the good sense of the people. Thus every man is allowed freely to take that road which he thinks will lead him to heaven, just as the law permits every citizen to have the right of choosing his own government" (p. 436).

17 Lyndon B. Johnson, in U.S., *Congressional Record,* House, March 15, 1965, pp. 4924, 4926.

18 See Louis Hartz, "The Feudal Dream of the South," pt. 4, *The Liberal Tradition in America* (New York: Harcourt, Brace & Co., 1955).

19 Senator J. William Fulbright, speech of April 28, 1966, as reported in *The New York Times,* April 29, 1966.

20 Henry David Thoreau, In Yehoshua Arieli, *Individualism and Nationalism in American Ideology* (Cambridge, Mass.: Harvard Univ. Press, 1964), p. 274.

PART THREE

Religion in Modern Society

THE ARTICLES in Part III deal with "Modern Religion," the fifth stage of religious evolution put forth in Part I. The major social problems of this stage are no longer those of the takeoff from an agricultural society into an industrial one but the many new problems that arise once that departure has occurred. One problem that seems to characterize the most advanced contemporary societies is a major crisis of meaning. Not only are there severe problems of meaning with respect to the traditional culture, which now seems remote in manys ways, but there is also the profound question, "So What?," once technological proliferation has begun. Such a historical period raises starkly what Paul Tillich called the question of meaninglessness. Rather than dwelling on the more depressing side of this picture, the following chapters emphasize the resources for new solutions, including the new possibilities for reappropriating the culture and religion of the past. Chapter 9 in Part II serves as a kind of transition to Part III, and Chapter 13 below picks up some of the themes of civil religion and its possible transnational successors. In general the following essays are more tentative and more engaged than most of the earlier ones. They deal with the situation that we are currently in the midst of. The presence of two book reviews indicates an effort to define a position in dialogue with other writers. Throughout this section there is expressed my deepening conviction that the relations between religion and social science will be ever closer in the coming years, that, indeed, social science may soon play the role that traditionally philosophy filled: that is, to provide the intellectual tools for religious self-reflection.

10 "It Doesn't Go Far Enough"

AS A social scientist, I find the real significance of *Honest to God* in the fact that it is a direct attack on classical theism not from some liberal fringe point of view but from the core of the Christian tradition itself. Bishop Robinson is in the most involved sense a churchman. I think we must accept his remark on page 27: "I have never really doubted the fundamental truth of the Christian faith. . . ." But, he continues, "I have constantly found myself questioning its expression." His quarrel is not with the Christian faith but with the way in which that faith is symbolized.

He cannot accept a symbolization of God as "up there" or "out there" because such symbolization simply has no meaning in the light of the tremendous intellectual advances of the last two centuries. With the emergence of the conception of an infinitely multiplex universe, there is no longer any room for the old duplex conception whether of cosmology or metaphysics. So far so good.

Robinson is saying plainly what the theologians he quotes have been saying involvedly. That is why I think the book has such resonance. A lot of people, including many theologians, know that Robinson's insight is basically true. The church has managed to avoid saying so quite so plainly, but the issue once opened is not likely to be easily closed.

Liberalism could be rejected because of its obvious superficiality. It was willing to renounce anything in the Christian tradition that did not conform to a very culture-bound notion of "reason." But Robinson and the major figures he quotes are not in that sense

This review was requested by Christianity and Crisis *in 1963 as one of three brief comments on Bishop Robinson's best-selling book. The other reviews were by Paul Lehmann and John C. Bennett.* Christianity and Crisis *gave to my comments the title "It Doesn't Go Far Enough." It illustrates my growing interest in the dialogue between social science and religion.*

liberals. They do not want to jettison great chunks of the tradition that they at the moment do not understand. They want to reinterpret what has become meaningless so that its message can communicate again. They are seeking for another way between liberalism and Barthianism.

But the question is how far have they succeeded, more specifically, how far has Robinson succeeded? I believe he has one great insight that is on the right track, but the structure of his position as a whole does not provide the basis for the reinterpretation he desires. The insight is to see that it is more meaningful to speak of God in terms of within than without.

Essentially since Kant the attempt to anchor theism in metaphysics, in any kind of cognitive statement about the structure of the cosmos, has been exposed as hopelessly delusory. Kant turned to the structure of man as a moral being as the basis for his notion of God. Though later philosophy and theology greatly expanded his rather limited conception of man, it has only been in terms of the structure of the human situation—of a centered self trying to make sense out of an encompassing world—that theology has made any sense.

But the tendency has been very strong, once one has grounded religious symbolism firmly in the human situation, to assume that one has "proved God" once again. We can heave a sigh of relief. Once again God is in his heaven and all is right with the world. But Robinson won't buy it. He knows that you can't have it both ways. You can't both understand God in terms of the human situation and have him safely "out there." Or can you?

My main criticism of the book is that it doesn't really go far enough. Robinson himself seems to know it. He indicates at several points that it will not be long before his book is itself considered conservative. I believe this is true, for I think Robinson via Tillichian ontology really brings back in the God "out there." He says, "To assert that '*God* is love' is to believe that in love one comes in touch with the most fundamental reality in the universe, that Being itself ultimately has this character" (p. 53). I know that Tillich wants to assert this only in the most paradoxical way. With Robinson the paradoxicality is pretty well lost. We are safe again. God is still there.

The problem for Robinson and for those he represents is that they are trapped in their own theological language. They know something is wrong, but they have no means to get outside and see what it is. They talk about taking the world seriously but do not do so. They don't, at least not seriously enough, ask what the world has found out about man, society, symbolism, and religion. They don't ask how this might help the present urgent need for reinterpretation of symbols.

Here is the sort of answer I would give if I were asked: We have not begun to understand the full implications of religious language and symbolism. Social science has not begun to fathom the deep insights into human motives and human action that the religious tradition contains. But we do know that religious symbols are the way man has related himself, from the beginning of his existence as a cultural being, to the conditions of his existence. Through religious symbols man has symbolized to himself his own identity and the order of existence in terms of which his identity makes sense.

These symbols are not "made up" by the human ego or deduced by rational reflection. They are born out of the tragedy and the suffering, the joy and the victory of men struggling to make sense out of their world. They tell us nothing at all about the universe except insofar as the universe is involved in human experience. The symbols, though they come to each one of us as individuals from outside, are nevertheless always the product of specifically human experience. We cannot choose the symbols that will direct our life, at least not until we are already grown up and even then only within certain limits. But nonetheless we must accept responsibility for our own symbols.

And so in reinterpretation I would prefer not to say that Christ is a window into the universe, except insofar as man is a part of the universe. But Christ may be a window into the depths of man, revealing what we have only barely begun to understand.

11 Transcendence in Contemporary Piety

We believe without belief, beyond belief.[1]
—Wallace Stevens

IN TRADITIONAL THEOLOGY transcendence is an attribute of God that indicates that he is outside and independent of the world. A number of metaphysical arguments have been developed over the centuries to prove this point. Both biblical and Quranic religions have also asserted the existence of God outside the world on the basis of revelation. Today arguments based on metaphysical proofs or revelation are not very compelling. These approaches may be viewed as interesting "perspectives," which can be illuminating if properly interpreted in some contemporary frame of reference. It is not now so much the substance of that which it is claimed is transcendent as the function of the claim itself that is of interest. There is a parallel here with the present state of the discussion of original sin, for example. "Original sin" may be accepted as an essential perspective on human nature without at all believing Augustine's involved biotheological argument.

What, then, is the central function of the idea of transcendence that may make it worth retaining even though traditional arguments for it must be abandoned? If, in terms of twentieth-century cosmology, the idea of anything being "outside the world," at least in a physicospatial sense, is no longer meaningful, it still seems essential

This chapter was written for a conference on transcendence in contemporary culture sponsored by the Church Society for College Work in May 1968. It represents an effort to discern how social science treats the kinds of experience that traditionally gave rise to religious notions of transcendence and to see whether such experiences are still viable today. The use of a major poet as a central reference point for the discussion is based on the assumption that a poet may be especially sensitive to the kinds of experience of interest here.

to appreciate that there is a reality independent of ourselves, our societies, or our cultures:

> From this the poem springs: that we live in a place
> That is not our own and, much more, not ourselves
> And hard it is in spite of blazoned days.[2]

In fact "reality" has become a highly charged word with a definite overtone of transcendence, especially in the thinking of Freud, whose famous contrast between reality principle and pleasure principle emphasizes the "over-againstness" of reality. But it is to Wallace Stevens that I wish to turn repeatedly in this essay. As the greatest American "theological poet" of the twentieth century he may be particularly useful in helping us discern the structure of contemporary religious consciousness. In the following passages we can see Stevens giving his own interpretation to certain theological perspectives:

> The theologians whose thought is most astir today do make articulate a supreme need, and one that has now become also imperative, as their urgency shows, the need to infuse into the ages of enlightenment an awareness of reality adequate to their achievements and such as will not be attenuated by them. There is one most welcome and authentic note; it is the insistence on a reality that forces itself upon our consciousness and refuses to be managed and mastered. It is here that the affinity of art and religion is most evident today. Both have to mediate for us a reality not ourselves. This is what the poet does. The supreme virtue here is humility, for the humble are they that move about the world with the love of the real in their hearts.[3]

> And the wonder and mystery of art, as indeed of religion in the last resort, is the revelation of something "wholly other" by which the inexpressible loneliness of thinking is broken and enriched.[4]

It is worth noting the element of piety in Stevens' words. (I am using "piety" not in its pejorative sense but to indicate an element of action that "religion" does not convey and for which "religious behavior" or "religious action" or even Wilfred Smith's helpful suggestion, "religiousness," seems a bit too clumsy.) For "reality" as an ultimate term has its own religious pathology. With respect to it, too, can occur what Tillich called "the sin of religion," namely the identification of God's will with one's own. This is usually what the "realist" does when he seeks to justify himself: "I was only being realistic." But such a realist lacks humility; he does not love the real in his heart. He lacks a Stevensian piety. But if the notion of reality is the first thing to be said in connection with the contemporary sense of transcendence it is certainly not the last. The concept alone is too crude and undifferentiated. Stevens himself offers some further considerations about it to which we shall return later. First we need to develop a series of levels in terms of which the idea of reality may have various meanings.

Reality may be encountered in the self as well as in the "external" world. Augustine said, "Men go to gape at mountain peaks, at the boundless tides of the sea, the broad sweep of rivers, the encircling ocean and the motions of the stars: and yet they leave themselves unnoticed; they do not marvel at themselves."[5] He further argued that it is precisely "within" that we should begin our search for God. But in those vast inner regions that we can never know completely Augustine recognized that there are other realities besides the divine: "For no one is known to another so intimately as he is known to himself, and yet no one is so well known even to himself that he can be sure as to his conduct on the morrow."[6] The heights and depths of the inner life have been among the central realities of religious men in many times and cultures. The overwhelming reality of the inner life precludes any simple use of the word "subjective," as though the inner life were less "real" that external things. Above all the inner life is not a matter of personal whim or simple control of the ego. It is precisely its "constraining" nature, its "objectivity," which makes it a vehicle for transcendence.

It is with respect to unsatisfied desires and longings that overwhelm all men at certain times and largely dominate the existence of many that the "externality" of the inner life is most pronounced. These "deficiency needs," to use Abraham Maslow's terms,[7] have by and large been viewed negatively by the great religious traditions, though they exist in partly disguised form in the central myths and theologies of many religions. We have learned today not simply to flee from these desires, like St. Anthony in the desert, but to take them seriously, indeed to view them as revelatory. An existence that is so deeply unsatisfying that one's very biological organism cries out against it is revealed by that fact alone as needing change. This is not to say that deficiency needs are the only reality or that satisfying them willy-nilly is the only morally legitimate course of action. Deficiency needs must be considered in terms of a whole that must include many other structures and processes. But deficiency needs cannot just be dismissed or denied; they must be taken as one indication of the structure of reality.

The inner experience not of need but of fulfillment has always been the chief "inner" dimension of transcendent reality. Herbert Richardson has recently argued that the chief aspects of such a religious experience are the feelings of wholeness, rightness, and well-being.[8] Unlike the experience of deficiency, the experience of fulfillment tends to overcome all opposition, to be as much immanent as transcendent. Yet it is viewed subsequently as a revelation about reality, not simply as an aesthetic or emotional experience of a purely "subjective" sort. Such experiences are as basic in Western spirituality as in Asian religions. In Christianity one needs to think only, for example, of Paul on the road to Damascus, of Augustine in the garden in Milan, or of Martin Luther, Blaise Pascal, Jonathan Edwards, or Paul Tillich to see that in different periods and with different theologies the experience itself has remained central. This is not to say that the categories of interpretation do not differ significantly between various religions.

Recently Maslow,[9] in his analysis of what he calls "peak experiences," has pointed out that this sort of experience is not confined to the conventionally religious sphere. Rather, individuals appear to have experiences analogous with the classical religious ones in the realms of love, art, sports, child rearing, and so on. To the extent that they are later interpreted as genuinely revelatory they are indeed parallel to religious experiences more narrowly defined. Let me turn to a particularly beautiful account in Stevens for an example of such "secular" revelation:

> Perhaps
> The truth depends on a walk around a lake,
>
> A composing as the body tires, a stop
> To see hepatica, a stop to watch
> A definition growing certain and
>
> A wait within that certainty, a rest
> In the swags of pine-trees bordering the lake.
> Perhaps there are times of inherent excellence,
>
> As when the cock crows on the left and all
> Is well, incalculable balances,
> At which a kind of Swiss perfection comes

And a familiar music of the machine
Sets up its Schwärmerei, not balances
That we achieve but balances that happen,

As a man and woman meet and love forthwith.
Perhaps there are moments of awakening,
Extreme, fortuitous, personal, in which

We more than awaken, sit on the edge of sleep,
As on an elevation, and behold
The academies like structures in a mist.[10].

Elsewhere Stevens speaks of a moment when one experiences "A self that touches all edges."[11] It is curious how the notion that such experiences are the exclusive property of religious virtuosi ever got started, since they are probably as old and as widespread as the human race itself. The present student generation seems to be particularly open to them and deeply affected by them.

Without some such experience of transcendence consideration of it must probably remain abstract, verbal, and theoretical. Yet individual experience alone is an inadequate basis for knowledge of reality. Science proceeds on the assumption that experiments must be replicable, and indeed, scientific evidence is treated skeptically if it rests on the work of only one investigator and has not been duplicated by others. Traditionally religious men have acted on a parallel assumption. Individual religious experience must be checked against the experience of others. A religious tradition is in fact a community of religious experience. This is not to say that the religious experience of a community always takes precedence over that of an individual when there is a conflict between them. But if an innovator fails to arouse any response from others and if others cannot participate in his new modes of experience, then his religious innovation dies with himself and has no meaning for human religious history.

Religious experience is almost impossible without some form of group support. Maslow has indicated the necessity of adequate social arrangements for dealing with deficiency needs as a prerequisite for personal growth toward self-realization. Religious institutions are social settings for the encouragement of the spiritual life. When they seem no longer capable of fulfilling their function for significant numbers of people then revolutionary or reformist action to improve the situation also takes group form. Every great innovator has required his band of disciples and his lay sympathizers.

In a word, society, too, is a locus for the confrontation with reality. In the work of Emile Durkheim, society becomes almost the representative of a reality principle much like Freud's. It is society, according to Durkheim, that disciplines the individual, raises him above his petty desires and interests, and supports his rational capacity to deal objectively with the structures of reality. Durkheim sees society not only as a hard taskmaster but as the source of the best in man, for it is only in and through society that he can be fully human. In this perhaps Durkheim betrays his rabbinic heritage in that he holds not only that we should obey the law, but that it is worthy of our love.

It is also through society that man encounters history. There is a historical dimension at the level of personality. But it is in society that one's individual life history and history as collective experience intersect. History is the proving ground for both personal and social values. Given structures, personal and social, may prove inadequate in the face of the contingencies and catastrophes of history. In history reality is encountered as judgment, and no finite structure is ever entirely adequate to that encounter. Since history reveals the inadequacy of every empirical society, it becomes clear that society no more than the individual is a final repository of transcendence. Rather every society is itself forced to appeal to some higher jurisdiction, to justify itself not entirely on its actual performance but through its commitment to unrealized goals or values. The kind of symbolism that societies develop to indicate their commitment to higher values and define their legitimacy itself varies in historical perspective. But there is no society that can avoid such symbolism. Even in the most complex modern societies it is necessary. Indeed, Richardson argues it is especially necessary there:

> The total cybernetic system must be fortified by an eschatological symbolism which can provide it with general goals and assist men to make the continual transitions an increasingly complex system requires. A cybernetic system determines a rate and form of change, but it does not determine the ultimate end of change. Rather it is guided by some encompassing social vision of the good society. This vision cannot be conceptually precise—for then it would be static rather than dynamic. But it must be symbolically precise if it is to give real direction to the social process.

The American philosopher Charles Peirce has helped us to understand the guiding power of a myth or symbol which must be conceptually "vague" if it is to guide rational development. Such a "vague" symbol is open to continual conceptual specification; hence it is capable of providing direction to a total cybernetic society. It is conceptually imprecise, but symbolically precise. Such symbolism must be religious, i.e., it must portray a transcendent kingdom of God. The very transcendent character of religious eschatology is the condition of its adequacy for guiding a cybernetic society; for trans-historical symbolism always retains the "vagueness" and conceptual openness that prevent man from expecting any absolute fulfillment in time. Only transcendent religious symbolism can undergird an infinite development of society at a controlled pace. Only "other-worldly" religious symbolism can preserve the system from falling into an intra-historical stasis.[12]

Our analysis, then, forces us to consider the symbols that transcend individual and society, symbols that attempt to grasp reality as a whole, symbols like God, Being, Nothingness, and Life, which individuals and societies have used to make sense of themselves and give direction to their actions. These symbols may emerge out of individual, social, and historical experiences but they are not identical with them. They are not symbols for empirical realities in any scientifically verifiable sense. In some respects they are systems of pure terminology, displaying what Kenneth Burke[13] has called the principle of perfection that he finds inherent in language itself. But these great summary symbols that refer to the totality of being, to the transcendent dimension of reality, and to the differentiated terminologies which have grown up around them, cannot be dismissed as "subjective" just because they are not in a simple sense "objective" in their reference. They are neither objective nor subjective, neither cosmological nor psychological. Rather, they are relational symbols that are intended to overcome precisely such dichotomies of ordinary conceptualization and bring together the coherence of the whole of experience.

It seems clear that we cannot distinguish reality as such from our symbolizations of it. Being human we can only think in symbols, only make sense of any experience in symbols. But these considerations reopen the issue of our confrontation with reality conceived of as standing over-against us. For that formulation seems to imply somehow that we stand outside of reality, that there is a split between ourselves and reality. But that is not the case. We participate in reality and not passively but actively. Thus in another mood Stevens can emphasize not the otherness of reality but its openness:

"Reality is not what it is. It consists of the many realities which it can be made into."[14] And nowhere else is the creativity and openness of reality more apparent than in the realm of the highest most comprehensive symbol systems themselves: "The world is the world through its theorists. Their function is to conceive of the whole and, from the center of their immense perspectives, to tell us about it."[15] This is the function of

> The impossible possible philosopher's man,
> The man who has had the time to think enough,
> The central man, the human globe, responsive
> As a mirror with a voice, the man of glass,
> Who in a million diamonds sums us up.[16]

The conclusion that Stevens drives toward is determined by his recognition of the nature of symbolism and of the kind of symbols that ultimate symbols are: "The final belief is to believe in a fiction, which you know to be a fiction, there being nothing else. The exquisite truth is to know that it is a fiction and that you believe in it willingly."[17]

It would be a mistake to think that this last quotation of Stevens cancels out all the others. For if he is the poet of the "Supreme Fiction" he remains also the poet of reality. Perhaps his position is best summed up in the line that stands at the head of this essay: "We believe without belief, beyond belief." Had he stopped with "We believe without belief" we might have understood him simply as some stoic existentialist trying to make the best of a world he never made. But "beyond belief" shows that the symbolism, unavoidable though it is, is not final but only provisional. Our "central men" will go on giving us ever new conceptions of the whole, which, though fictional and provisional, will take us ever deeper into the mystery of being.

Again let me emphasize that this is not a reductionistic theory of religious symbolism. It does not claim to explain religious symbolism as a simple function of biology, psychology, sociology, or history, though it involves all of them. Religious symbolism is necessitated precisely by the inadequacy of all partial symbolisms. It has its irreducible *sui generis* nature. Without it man would not be human. We believe in it seriously, we believe in it willingly, we believe in it, if we follow Stevens, knowing it to be a fiction.

To press the issue one step further, it is the idiom of "belief" that forces us to the term "fiction." But religious symbolism operates in important respects differently from what we usually call belief. Stevens tells us that "The poem is the cry of its occasion,/Part of the res itself and not about it."[18] Religious symbolization, too, is part of the religious experience itself, and the experience would not be complete without its symbolization. Only when the symbol has been torn from its experiential context and taken literally as a belief "about" something must we assert its fictional nature. As part of the experience itself it is perfectly and supremely real.

What may seem to be a very "modern" theory of religious symbolism may be a necessary prerequisite for the adequate understanding of any religious symbolism, especially in the exacting task of understanding a symbol that is not one's own. In a recent book Wilfred Smith argues that to understand a religious symbol one

> . . . must ask oneself how much transcendence it can be made to carry for those who have chosen its particular shape to represent the pattern of their religiousness. The sacred must always be not only ambiguous but unlimited: it is a mystery, so that no specific significance can exhaust it—there is always more waiting to be explored. A religious symbol is successful if men can express in terms of it the highest and deepest vision of which they are capable, and if in terms of it that vision can be nourished and can be conveyed to others within one's group. . . . Admittedly, some progress towards understanding symbols can be made if one asks not what does the symbol mean, simply; but rather, what does it mean for the particular men who use it religiously. Fundamentally, however, even this must be transcended; one must think of the symbol in terms not of its meaning something, but of its focusing or crystallizing what *life* means, what the universe means, to those who through this symbol find that life and the universe can be seen (or felt) to *have* coherent meaning.[19]

One feature of this understanding of religious symbols that derives from the fact that it views them as only provisionally final, as ultimate not substantively but regulatively, is that it is non-authoritarian. The traditional view has tended to make God an absolute or a benevolent despot. This postrevolutionary conception tends to make the idea of God into a democratic president who can be replaced at a later date by a more suitable candidate. This is by no means to deprive the highest term of all seriousness and authority. A democratic president must have authority and respect if he is to fulfill his function. But he is not immune to criticism. He exists in a reflective, reticular relation to his electorate. Communication is two-way, not one-way as in despotism. In considering the adequacy of any particular conceptualization of the whole all the levels of consideration that I have developed above, and more, must be taken into account. For instance, if there is a conception of God that mainly succeeds in producing abject anxiety in those who hold it and that exacerbates frustrated deficiency needs, then one may legitimately question the conception. Upon further consideration it may be that the social and historical situation is such that this conception of God is an adequate expression of its reality, in which case what needs to be changed is not the conception of God but the social historical situation. But in principle no particular symbolization is itself above criticism.

One feature of the modern situation that is largely new is the extent to which it has become possible to appropriate religious symbol systems from many times and cultures. They have been made available to us through the achievements of historical and comparative research. They can be appropriated if one views them as capable of "focusing or crystallizing what *life* means, what the universe means, to those who through this symbol find that life and the universe can be seen (or felt) to *have* coherent meaning." One can bracket one's other symbolic commitments and see how this perspective would make life feel to *us*. This is what we do in a minor way any time we look at a Chinese painting or listen to an Indian raga. It is only a step further to try to understand with Nagarjuna the absolute emptiness of the world or with Chu Hsi the organic network of its interdependencies. And it is only a step beyond that to recognize with Ernst Troeltsch that our own religion is our historical fate, but that it has no more claim to absoluteness or finality than any other. This is not to say that all religious symbol systems are of equal value and meaning, for clearly they are not, but rather that their relative meaning and value must be derived from their involvement in human existence, not from some transphysical fiat.

It might be asked whether once religious symbolism is revealed as a supreme fiction it might not be abandoned altogether. After all, the history of culture is the history of the growth of consciousness. Traditionally religious symbolism has always been redolent of the unknown and the unconscious. As consciousness grows and ego more and more takes the place of id, cannot we expect the gradual disappearance of religious symbols altogether? The answer partly depends on one's definition of religion. It is true that a theory of religious symbolism that recognizes its fictional quality can no longer differentiate between religion and the highest and most serious forms of art. (Though it might be doubted whether in any definition of religion such forms of art can be entirely excluded.)

But the most serious issue has to do with whether the growth of consciousness itself can be expected to eliminate the need for religious symbols, the functions of transcendence. It seems worth arguing that the relation between consciousness and unconsciouness, between science and religion, is not of the nature of a zero sum, so that the more of one automatically produces the less of the other. May it not be, as Philip Slater has suggested, that as the islands of consciouness grow broader the surrounding seas of the unconscious grow deeper? In any case the need to integrate the whole, known and unknown, conscious and unconscious, grows stronger. Somehow or other men must have a sense of the whole if they are to live; they must have something to believe in and to commit themselves to. Life in its immediacy will not yield to objective analysis, will not wait till all the research results are in. Men must act in the face of uncertainty and unpredictability and consequently they must have faith; they must be willing to take the gamble, the risk of faith. In this sense some symbolization of transcendent reality seems inescapable, whether religious in a traditional sense or not. Only such symbolism can overcome the splits in consciousness between public and private, individual and collective, conscious and unconscious, experience and concept, and surrender and control, and so render personality, society, and culture capable of healthy activity.

Science itself posits an unknown, a mystery. If everything were grasped in terms of clear and distinct ideas, if everything were accurately predicted, there could be no *science,* for inquiry would be unnecessary. There would be no need of hypothesis, experiment, and verification. Instead there would be a kind of "paradise" in which "the boughs/Hang always heavy in that perfect sky,/Unchanging."[20] In such a paradise there would be need for neither science nor religion. Until that time, since both answer to the structure of human existence, both will continue.

This essay has been based on the assumption that the absolute separation of social science and theology is impossible. Every theology implies a sociology (and a psychology, and so on) and every sociology implies a theology. Or at least any definite theological position limits the variety of sociological positions compatible with it and vice versa. To say that they are separate enterprises is not to deny that there is any relation between them, as some have done, or to argue that they operate at levels so different that there is no necessity to integrate them. On the contrary, I would argue that theology and social science are parts of a single intellectual universe. To refuse to relate them is to admit intellectual bankruptcy; it is to admit an inability to confront the totality of human experience. I have much less confidence in the particular integration I have attempted than in the necessity of the task. If I have communicated a sense of urgency in the task I will have succeeded. With Stevens,

> We feel the obscurity of an order, a whole,
> A knowledge, that which arranged the rendezvous,
>
> Within its vital boundary, in the mind.
> We say God and the imagination are one . . .
> How high that highest candle lights the dark.
>
> Out of this same light, out of the central mind,
> We make a dwelling in the evening air,
> In which being there together is enough.[21]

NOTES

1 Wallace Stevens, *Collected Poems* (New York: Alfred A. Knopf, 1954), p. 336.

2 *Ibid.*, p. 383.

3 Stevens, *Opus Posthumous* (New York: Alfred A. Knopf, 1957), p. 238.

4 *Ibid.*, p. 237.

5 Augustine, *Confessions,* X.

6 Augustine, quoted in Peter Brown, *Augustine of Hippo* (Berkeley: Univ. of Calif. Press, 1967), p. 405.

7 Abraham H. Maslow, *Toward a Psychology of Being* (New York: Van Nostrand, 1962), chap. 3.

8 Herbert W. Richardson, *Toward an American Theology* (New York: Harper & Row, 1967), chap. 3.

9 Maslow, *op. cit.*

10 Stevens, *Collected Poems, op. cit.*, p. 386.

11 *Ibid.*, p. 209.

12 Richardson, *op. cit.*, p. 24.

13 Kenneth Burke, *The Rhetoric of Religion* (Boston: Beacon Press, 1961).

14 Stevens, *Opus Posthumous, op. cit.*, p. 178.

15 *Ibid.*, p. 232.

16 Stevens, *Collected Poems, op. cit.*, p. 250.

17 Stevens, *Opus Posthumous, op. cit.*, p. 163.

18 Stevens, *Collected Poems, op. cit.*, p. 473.

19 Wilfred Cantwell Smith, *Problems of Religious Truth* (New York: Scribner's, 1967), pp. 16–17.

20 Stevens, *Collected Poems, op. cit.*, p. 69.

21 *Ibid.*, p. 524.

12 The Dynamics of Worship

For everything that lives is Holy.
—William Blake

I

BLAKE'S WORDS do not really deny the contrast between sacred and profane. For the sacred is not simply a property of external objects any more than it is purely a subjective feeling. It is a quality of experience, of relation between subject and object. The apprehension that everything that lives is holy does not arise from sense perception; it does not have in Blake's words a "Philosophic and Experimental" character. Rather, it arises from a different kind of perception that Blake called "Poetic or Prophetic." The first thing about worship, if we define it as a human activity that attempts to relate to the sacred or holy, is that it tries to break through the straight or profane world of everyday pragmatic common sense.

Evidence that worship attempts to break the hold of the ordinary and the usual is the frequent conception of worship as a symbolic "trip," an identification with the travels of a hero or the journey to Golgotha, a "descent" into the depths, the caves of mystery, or an "ascent" to the realms of light "above." At any rate there is a

This chapter was also written for a Church Society for College Work conference. The subject of the conference was worship and it involved participant observation in a worship service at Canterbury House in Ann Arbor, Michigan, on October 20, 1968. In spite of its name, Canterbury House is a student coffeehouse in what was once a printing plant. On Sunday mornings the coffeehouse doubles as a place of worship under the leadership of Episcopal Chaplain Daniel Burke. Much in the service, including the appearance of the San Francisco Mime Troupe, was continuous with the normal activities of the coffeehouse and with student culture generally. A complete transcript of the service including many photographs, together with comments by several other writers, some of whom were less ambivalent then I, can be found in Myron B. Bloy, ed., Multi-Media Worship.

departure from the plane of the mundane, a departure which often rouses a sense of the uncanny, of the presence of the *mysterium tremendum.* A wide variety of techniques have been developed to break up the ordinary patterns of perception and to allow the emergence of other dimensions of experience: rhythmic chanting, ecstatic dancing, or, more familiarly, the silence and simplicity of the Quaker meeting or the solemn orderliness of Episcopal morning prayer. It is one of the chief problems of contemporary worship that the traditional types of aesthetic manipulation do not work, do not precipitate the worshipers into a state of altered consciousness. Remaining in the state of everyday common sense, they see nothing in the service but the literal, which may be instructive or not, but which is very seldom religiously transformative.

There must, of course, be links between the worship service and the immediate personal and social reality of the worshipers. But even when attained, the element of "relevance," so highly regarded today, is only a shaky first step. Unless there is a link between the religious symbols making up the worship ceremony and the particular past and present of the worshipers, then the worship process cannot begin. Indeed, the more deeply the symbols do grasp the real problems and conflicts of the worshipers the more powerful the subsequent experience can be. But what happens in worship is the transformation of the personal into the transpersonal, the immediate into the transtemporal. Through this transformation the immediate problems and conflicts can be seen in a new light, insight can be achieved, and postworship changes in behavior can ensue. How we evaluate these changes, which may range from fleeing to the desert to starting a social revolution, depends on our values and is not the issue here. But the point is that the mythical, archetypal, timeless character of religious symbols provides a perspective relative to everyday reality without which, in Blake's words, the latter would "stand still unable to do other than repeat the same dull round over again."

Worship, to be maximally effective, must provide not only a symbolic reordering of experience but an element of consummation and fulfillment. The experience of worship should produce an influx of life and power, a feeling of wholeness, of the grace of God, of being at the still center of the turning wheel. If this happens there may occur a shift in the definition of the boundary of the self, perhaps, as with Blake, an identification with everything that lives, but at any rate a transformation of motivation, commitment, and value that may galvanize not only individuals but the collectivity of worshipers.

If worship doesn't "work" it may not be because it is "irrelevant." It almost certainly is not because modern man is capable of living a purely secular existence without it. A modern straight type is apt to be in the grip of powerful unconscious fantasies that repeat themselves endlessly but get nowhere. He is on a very bad trip but he doesn't know it, or he knows it only when he becomes conscious of his incipient alcoholism, his bad marriage, and his unsatisfying job. It is just because he is on such a bad trip, not because he is so "mature," that he cannot let down his defenses enough to participate meaningfully in an act of worship. Worship involves a partial regression from normal defensive ego-functioning so that there is a greater openness to both inner and outer reality. But it is precisely this regression and this openness that may be seen as dangerous and threatening to the ego. Traditionally, religious ritual has often solved this problem by itself being taken up into a compromise formation as a compulsive defense mechanism.

Worship, then, whose essential function we have argued is to facilitate the experience of the holy, can actually become a defense against that experience. If the traditional rituals often attempted to bind the power of the sacred into a compulsive pattern that acted like a neurotic symptom, the modern debasement of worship into moral edification devoid of the power of the holy is not adequate either. I would not want to exaggerate the extent to which worship is ineffective today. I recall a Catholic student of mine, who after many years of routine attendance at mass one Sunday completely identified with the mass, understood for the first time what it meant, and was deeply changed by the experience. Many less dramatic examples come to mind. But the situation is sufficiently troublesome to justify the wide range of experimentation and innovation that is currently going on in this area.

II

I wrote the above before attending the worship service at Canterbury House on October 20, 1968. I now must consider that service in the light of my previous views, and my views in light of the service. Anything I might say about the service is extremely personal. Extensive interviews with a cross section of those present would be necessary before one could begin to speak of what happened in a totally unbiased way.

The first thing that strikes me is the contrast in atmosphere with most services I have attended, services mainly in urban and suburban Protestant churches. Perhaps the closest approximation in my experience to the general informality and relaxation which prevailed was the Mormon meeting that I went to during several months of field work in rural New Mexico some fourteen years ago. But whereas the casual dress and crying babies reminded me of the Mormons, the sitting on the floor in a room utterly devoid of any of the qualities of a church pushed the atmosphere of official religion even more into the background. What seemed to be going on was not merely a relaxation of some of the stringencies of middle-class decorum, but a conscious opposition to the accepted symbolizations of what is religious. Bob Dylan's "Like a Rolling Stone," for example, which was sung quietly, almost tenderly (in contrast to Dylan's own defiant rendition), before the service began, would not normally be considered "religious" by anyone in American society.

Indeed, in a number of respects—the use of music with sexual and aggressive overtones, the coffeehouse atmosphere, the movies, the political activism of the San Francisco Mime Troupe—what was being included was not merely the religiously neutral but the consciously profane. The symbolic context of the worship was not the world of everyday—of business, domesticity, or academia—but the worlds of teenage recreation (with its overtone of "sin") and of activist politics, two worlds as set apart from daily life as is the more usual conception of the religious. The elements of danger and excitement that are partially associated with these worlds helped to heighten the atmosphere of the nonordinary, to give the worship the quality of a "trip." While this venture into the outskirts of the forbidden may seem daring in contrast to the conventionalities of middle-class religiosity, it is of course quite mild compared with the frequent appearance of orgiastic behavior in religious contexts throughout the world. Durkheim, among others, has pointed out the ambivalence of the sacred and how the sacrilegious can be easily, much more easily than the religiously neutral, transformed into its opposite.

Of course I do not mean to exaggerate the use of profane themes. The basic structure and much of the language of the service was provided by the Episcopal Liturgy of the Lord's Supper with its thoroughly traditional symbolism. However, the continuous switching between the words of the prayer book and such things as "The Fool on the Hill" or "Hey Jude" was itself a central device of the service. Presumably it served to heighten the meaning both of the biblical language and symbols and of the consciously secular cultural allusions, including them in some kind of greater whole. The form was a kaleidoscopic series of juxtaposed interludes without any central argument to tie them together. The sermon was conspicuously absent and the Mime Troupe performance in no way took its place. It was one fragment alongside others, with no attempt at intellectual integration. The atmosphere of spontaneous disorganization was so complete as to be almost contrived. Indeed Dan Burke seemed deliberately bent on shattering any possible element of solemnity by following almost every heavily formal statement in the liturgy with an ad lib remark in ordinary language. Whether in fact an atmosphere of deliberate spontaneity rather than one of contrived solemnity helps to provide a meaningful experience of worship depends on the response of particular worshipers. But here we can perhaps say a bit more about the kind of experience that the Canterbury House group was trying to convey.

On the basis of Dan Burke's paper and also of the article in the Michigan Daily of October 25, 1968, by Jeremy Joan Hewes, we can surmise that the central idea behind the service is communion and communication. What is being asserted is that (in spite of appearances) communion is basic, all men are acceptable, and we can communicate with each other. We need not preclude the issue of meaning by restricting it to this consciously intended level; there are obviously many unconscious levels of meaning going on and the powerful symbols invoked in such a service have meanings that cannot be entirely shaped to conscious intention. But we can consider the extent to which the conscious aim may have been fulfilled, though lacking the evidence to really answer the question.

For me there was a sense of spontaneous participation, though, and this may be due to my age and worldview, it was partial and flickering. Much of what happened, as in conventional services, was a performance put on by a few people for an audience of nonparticipators. This holds for the beautiful and touching movie as well as for the (to me) somewhat less effective performances by the Mime Troupe. The music and the responsive readings might have been more effective in creating a sense of participation if they had been more familiar or, in one case, "The Telephone Pole Song," less sentimental. The moment when we were asked to touch each other and move together was somewhat artificial and strained (I consciously wanted it to work but perhaps I was too uptight). The one moment when communion became reality was the communion itself. Perhaps here for me there was just the right admixture of the familiar and the unfamiliar. The good brown bread in the round loaves and the bottles of wine being poured into the earthenware cups really were somehow transmuted into the body and the blood, and partaking of them was to become one with the body of Christ, the body of man. In that moment the self-consciousness that I carried into the service and held on to tightly throughout most of it was broken through.

III

Finally let me reconsider some of the theoretical issues first put forth in the light of the experience of this service. Certainly one of the things the service was trying to do was to break through the usual cognitive frameworks and put things in a new perspective. This it did mainly through the radical juxtaposition of things normally considered separate, so that their fundamental unity, the reality of communion, would shine through. The service attempted as much as possible to touch upon and gather up the concerns of the worshipers, very centrally the anxieties and protests about the Vietnam War. The purpose of these references, however, was not just to moralize but to show in the midst of disruption and distortion the present reality of communion as symbolized centrally in the age-old performance of the Eucharist. Presumably the disparate cultural elements brought together in the service and transmuted into some kind of form, however loose, should provide an objective framework in terms of which the inner psychic transformation of the worshiper could take place. In the recent movie "Rachel, Rachel," one was shown how a worship experience, even one where it was not clear whether the experience was a good or a bad trip for the heroine, opened up entirely new life possibilities for her. Our lack of access to the inner lives of the Canterbury House worshipers prevents us from knowing if any comparable transformation occurred. But that could have happened, and less drastic transformations of feeling almost certainly occurred.

But as in any human situation the aims of this event were only partially attained. I have already touched on the problem of the failure of the worshiper "to get with it" because of his own inner blocks. Let us now consider the possible perversion of the worship ceremony itself into a defense against the experience it is supposed to embody.

The conventional service today lacks authenticity because it has no surprises; it is not a point at which the world of everyday is broken through but only a particularly cozy corner of it. Certainly the Canterbury House service contained the possibility of opening up new ranges of experience. I could not help but feel, however, that there was an ever so slight element of exhibitionism, of deliberate shock (this is in part because the Mime Troupe clearly suffers from this problem, though not wholly from that source), in taking what is familiar in one group, namely left-wing student culture, and deliberately mixing it with traditional religion. The danger here is that the kick may come not from discovering something genuinely new oneself but from appearing avant garde to others, even to others not actually present, such as parents. The clichés of student culture are no more inherently profound than the clichés of any other group. Left-wing politics can be as much an escape from reality as compulsive moneymaking. There is the danger, then, of simply switching from one style of culture religion to another. To the extent that the traditional religious symbols operated to call into question and not simply to validate the contemporary cultural materials in the service, the danger was avoided.

13 Religion and Belief: The Historical Background of "Non-Belief"

> Some will ask if I believe all that this book contains, and I will not know how to answer. Does the word belief, used as they will use it, belong to our age, can I think of the world as there and I here judging it?
>
> —William Butler Yeats

I

"UNBELIEF," like "theology," is a product of the Greek mind, one might almost say of the mind of Plato. It is in Book X of the *Laws* that Plato argues for necessary theological beliefs: the existence of God, the immortality of the soul, and the moral government of the world. Unbelief in these propositions is a crime, punishable with five years of solitary confinement for a first offense and death for a second. Such notions are on the whole quite alien to the Bible. Where the word "belief" is used to translate biblical Hebrew and Greek it means not the "belief that" of Plato, but "belief in," a matter not of cognitive assent but of faith, trust, and obedience.

The background for Plato's thinking is, of course, the intellectual revolution in Greece associated with the Sophists and Socrates. This

This chapter was prepared for an International Symposium on the Culture of Unbelief held in Rome in March 1969. The symposium was sponsored by the Vatican Secretariat for Non-Believers with the scientific collaboration of the Department of Sociology of the University of California, Berkeley. This chapter was one of three formal papers discussed at the conference, the others being by Charles Y. Glock and Thomas Luckmann. The symposium brought together a number of theologians and social scientists from Europe and the United States. The conference was useful for the exchange of opinions and also for beginning a series of further discussions between Catholics and non-Catholics in various relevant fields.

great change, so lamented by Nietzsche and Heidegger, involved a shift from unself-conscious expression through mythical forms, even of such sophisticated thinkers as Heraclitus and Parmenides, to the highly self-conscious concern with whether myths are "really true" of the Sophists, and a search for more stable bases of orientation than myths by Socrates and Plato (though the highly artful use of myth by Plato raises a number of questions that must be left aside). The problem of "unbelief" arose with the first stratum of free intellectuals to appear in human history, and Plato was deeply concerned with coping with its corrosive effects. The Bible was not, on the whole, created by similarly self-conscious intellectual strata, but by religious and political enthusiasts much closer to the common religious conscience. Questions of where to put one's faith, in idols or in the one God, and questions as to what kind of obedience the one God demands are central to the Bible, but issues of purely cognitive validity are of very minor import. In general we can say that until the eighteenth century, or even perhaps until the nineteenth, the problem of non-belief has been limited to relatively small groups of intellectuals, cultural elites. The masses have been afflicted not with non-belief but with over-belief, at least from the point of view of religous orthodoxy, in a dismaying variety of magical notions, superstitions, and taboos.

It is important to realize that Plato's "theology" is not in fact an accurate apprehension of traditional religion. It is the self-conscious intellectual's translation of that religion into terms that he can understand. From Plato to Rousseau the intellectual in the West, including the Islamic world, has been in a very difficult situation relative to whether or not he "believes" that theology. Almost inevitably he cannot believe the version of the religion that is current among the (largely illiterate) common people. He requires either a highly complex intellectual structure of "proof" to underpin religious belief (Thomas), direct mystical illumination (Suhrawardi), or a combination of both (Augustine, al-Ghazzālī). But intellectuals have been highly conscious of the social utility of popular belief. Avicenna argued that the masses required vivid images, not philosophic demonstration, and only such a religion would be of any use in controlling them.[1] Spinoza's *Tractatus Theologico-Politicus* emphasizes the moral-political control function of biblical religion. As late as Rousseau we find a reassertion of Plato's position in Book X of the *Laws*. Book IV, chapter VIII of the *Social Contrast* requires subscription to the "dogmas of civil religion," which include the existence of God, the life to come, and the happiness of the just and the punishment of the wicked. Failure to subscribe to these beliefs is to be punished by banishment; falsely subscribing to them is punishable by death.

There seems to be a deep conflict in the minds of philosophers in the Christian and Islamic worlds at least through the eighteenth century between the complexity of their own beliefs and doubts and their sense of the absolute necessity of clear and simple beliefs for the preservation of social order. This led to dissimulation of what the philosophers really believed and to severe accusations against those philosophers who were thought to have said too much publicly. This was partly because of danger from the fanatical mob or over-zealous autocrats. But mainly it was a matter of a responsible assessment of the possible consequences of general consumption of esoteric views.

We may ask whether the extreme anxiety in the cultural and political elites of Christian and Muslim societies about the propagation of skeptical views was indeed justified. Certainly from the nineteenth century on it became possible to assert that there is no God, no afterlife, and no eternal reward and punishment, without, as in previous centuries, going to jail or the stake, and social order has not collapsed. Even the very grave instabilities that have arisen in the last two centuries do not seem to be mainly attributable to the decline of orthodox belief, though some might argue the point. Why in recent times has orthodox belief come to be openly challenged by large numbers of people, and why have the consequences of this challenge not been more disastrous?

II

The rise of what would classically have been considered "non-belief" in the modern world has been correlated with the enormous expansion of just those classes among whom non-belief always was a problem: the self-conscious intellectuals. The growth of an educated elite continued steadily from the seventeenth century on. The nineteenth century saw an enormous reversal of centuries-old literacy statistics as many Western nations began to approach total literacy. Educational systems were expanded and continue to expand to the point where in some parts of the United States over fifty per cent of the high school population goes on to college. Necessarily subjects that were formerly the property of tiny literate minorities are now open to the public. Traditional forms of thought control have become unworkable.

This vast increase in literacy and education in the past two centuries has been intimately related to the rise of antiauthoritarianism as a major cultural theme. The notion of the dignity of the individual and his inherent freedom from purely external authority has become widely accepted. Hierarchical modes of organization have been challenged not only in politics but in the family, education, and religion as well. In place of hierarchy the stress is on self-control, autonomous choice of values, and subsequent self-regulation. Obviously we are far from lacking external constraints in any modern society, but the trend is to leave more to the individual's discretion and control. Culture, from being conceived as an exoskeleton, is becoming an endoskeleton, something self-consciously chosen and internalized, not immutably given from without.

Both the increase of education and the rise of antiauthoritarianism are part of a vast social transformation and are closely linked to each other. Autonomous self-regulation requires a highly individuated, self-conscious, and educated person. On the other hand such an individual cannot easily accept the dictates of arbitrary external authority. Again, this linkage is not exactly new in human society, except in scale. Intellectuals have never felt easy with external systems of authority. Plato, unable to accept the traditional myths of his society, made up his own. Augustine, feeling acutely uncomfortable with the literal, fundamentalist beliefs of his mother, had to have Ambrose's intellectually convincing arguments before he could become a Christian. Pascal, losing confidence in purely intellectual statements of the faith, found meaning in it as a true apprehension of the greatness and misery of man.

The intellectual has always needed to find a religious form that genuinely expressed his own individuality. This was seldom the naive faith that he learned at his mother's knee. Often only through the greatest suffering has a coherent and authentic position been reached. Conscious of the agony of the struggle and of the dangers of doubt, intellectuals before modern times—such as Plato, Augustine, al-Ghazzālī, and even Rousseau—have been ready to impose on others what in themselves had been so personal an acquisition. But in modern times, as the intellectual classes have expanded, this has become less and less possible. Broader and broader strata of the population have demanded the freedom of conscience that the philosophers traditionally arrogated only for themselves.

This change has gone along with and has been deeply interrelated with a vast change in the fundamental presuppositions of Western thought. The ontological split between subject and object and the assumption that the most fundamental truths can be objectively demonstrated have been called into question. Convictions about the meaning and value of life have become regarded as inherently personal, and acquired through personal experience rather than objective demonstration. This has not, in the main, been accomplished through accepting the other side of the old dichotomy and collapsing into subjectivism and relativity. Rather, especially since Kant, there has been the increasing realization that, as in the words of Yeats quoted earlier,[2] the most fundamental cultural forms are neither objective nor subjective, but the very way in which the two are related. This also was by no means entirely new, but involved a rediscovery and generalization of elements deep within the mystical tradition of Western thought and religion. This way of thinking allowed the collapse of the traditional certainties without the loss of faith and commitment, an apprehension beautifully expressed by Wallace Stevens when he says, "We believe without belief, beyond belief."[3] This shivering of the objective notion of belief allows a reassessment of religion in general and provides a key to why the collapse of belief has not been followed by an end of religion.

III

It is my contention that what I would call "the objectivist fallacy," namely the confusion of belief and religion, which is found only in the religious traditions deeply influenced by Greek thought—Christianity and Islam—and is almost completely missing in China and India, involves a fundamental misapprehension of the nature of religion, both the religion of the masses and of the cultural elite. Not infrequently the educated have even admitted that such beliefs were only convenient fictions—"noble lies"—for the control of the masses while their own religion was more a matter of personal illumination. But I would contend that this was a sophisticated error in understanding the religious life of the ordinary man, which has never been primarily a matter of objectivist belief.

It is true that the intellectuals of the church long accepted objectivist assumptions. In crowning Greek reason with biblical revelation they assimilated revelation to an objectivist cognitive framework as though what was revealed were "higher" cognitive truths rather than the direct confrontation with the divine that the Bible is concerned with. But a more contemporary understanding of religious life would perhaps give us a more accurate apprehension of the real vitality of the church down through the ages. As Yeats informs us, "Man can embody truth but he cannot know it."[4] This would seem to be the case at least with the most important truths. Religion is embodied truth, not known truth, and it has in fact been transmitted far more through narrative, image, and enactment than through definitions and logical demonstrations. The church is above all the body of Christ—the embodiment of its truth—and it cannot be discerned through counting those who assent to certain dogmas. The life of the church has been its capacity to produce human beings who base their lives on the paradigm of the Gospels, the saints and martyrs, even modest and hidden ones, who have constantly renewed it and are renewing it today. If the vitality of the church has rested in its capacity to reproduce itself in the image of Christ, it is understandable that it can survive the collapse of dogmatic orthodoxies.

Of course the centuries-long concentration on orthodox belief, at least in some parts of the church, must have had some social meaning, as any sociologist would know. "Mistakes," if indeed this is one, do not perpetuate themselves for no reason. The effort to maintain orthodox belief has been primarily an effort to maintain authority rather than faith. It was part of a whole hierarchical way of thinking about social control, deeply embedded in traditional society. Functional equivalents to Christian and Islamic orthodoxy can even be discerned in the establishment of Chu Hsi Confucianism in post-Sung China and Tokugawa Japan, though, since the Greek assumptions about belief were missing, these orthodoxies were but a shadow compared to those of religions farther west, and crumbled away in modern times with much less outcry. When new, less authoritarian modes of social control become established, however, faith does not necessarily disappear. In its genuine form faith is never a matter of external coercion, of what Paul Tillich called "belief in the unbelievable." Its modes have changed along with the great shift in religious consciousness of modern times, but it has continued to live both within and without the church. Indeed the apprehension that faith is deeply embedded in man's existential situation and a part of the very structure of his experience, first powerfully expressed in modern times by Pascal and strongly reiterated in the early nineteenth century by Kierkegaard, has become an insistent note in twentieth-century religion. This understanding of religion seems to provide a more phenomenologically accurate understanding of ordinary religious experience than the assumption that it is primarily a matter of cognitive belief.

The modern shift in the understanding of religion has been greatly strengthened by the cultural revolution brought on by modern scholarship. It is now possible to move out of the cultural frame dominated by the Greek cognitive bias in both time and space in a way that was scarcely dreamed of two hundred years ago. Already in the eighteenth century a few thinkers such as Giovanni Vico and Johann Herder were beginning to discover in the poetic sagas of early European peoples ways of thinking quite different from philosophic thought. Vico, for example, came to see the world of Homer as far more dominated by symbolic words and actions than by logical argumentation. He even had the genius to discover that the street culture of Naples was in some ways more "Homeric" than was the culture of the educated salons.

The nineteenth century discovered not only scores of preliterate societies that tended to confirm Vico's and Herder's intuitions, but also great literate civilizations based on cultural premises very different from those of the West. In these highly cultivated realms the "rational beliefs" of "natural theology," those things that it was assumed would be obvious to all men in all times and places, failed to appear: such beliefs as the existence of God and the immortality of the soul, for instance, both vehemently denied by Buddhism. Here inner experience and expressive gesture were far more highly regarded than creeds and syllogistic arguments. A great and influential religion like Zen Buddhism, for example, denied the value of any beliefs at all, and Taoism showed the same tendency. Even Confucianism refused to speculate on the "existence" of spirits, and held that it was enough if one simply paid them proper respect "as if" they existed. More significant, of course, than the lack of certain views the West had virtually identified with religion was the fact that a rich, complex, and compelling religious life seemed to be possible in their absence. Further evidence that oriental religions are not on the whole based on cognitive belief is the almost total failure of the conflict between religion and science to materialize in the Eastern milieu, even though in the minds of some Western scholars it "ought" to have.

This broadening of the cultural horizon has played into and reinforced postdogmatic religiosity in the West. There seems little doubt in my mind, for example, that the modern liturgical revival has been stimulated by the recognition of the centrality of ritual and symbol in primitive and Eastern religions as well as in earlier periods in the history of the church itself. The failure of the predictions of nineteenth-century rationalists and positivists as to the impending end of religion have not only become evident in the increased vitality of many aspects of Judaism and Christianity, but also in the vast array of new religious and semireligious movements that have arisen. Coming from the University of California at Berkeley, I can personally testify to the multitude of religious enthusiasms sweeping the American campus today. Few of these tendencies evince any concern with the dread conflict between religion and science, mainly because it is assumed that religion is not a matter of objective cognitive assertion that might conflict with science, but a symbolic form within which one comes to terms with one's fate.

When to these examples is added the fact that those most vociferous in their denunciation of "religion," the Marxists for example, are discovered to live in the grip of a great archetypal myth, the whole idea that religion can be ended by cognitive argument or disproof becomes even less tenable. Instead the conclusion grows ever stronger that religion is a part of the species life of man, as central to his self-definition as speech. But the very plethora of religious phenomena in the contemporary scene, the lack of an apparent consensus, raises another serious question. Has religion retreated from the public sphere? Has it become totally privatized? Is it a purely personal escape from social and political urgencies that serves only to divert and titillate while the world slips ever more deeply into chaos?

IV

We have seen that one aspect of the great modern transformation involves *the internalization of authority,* and that this has profound consequences for religion. Of course there have been major breakdowns and countertendencies. Politically, fascism represents a new quest for outer authority and communism an incomplete or arrested internalization. Religiously, new fundamentalisms of various sorts have emerged in recent times. But if internalization has been the main direction, as I think it has, this might argue in favor of the notion of increasing privatization.

The contemporary religious consciousness certainly has a strong note of innerness. There is an intense preoccupation with authentic personal experience. Anything that is merely given by authority is suspect, for it is compelling only because of the source from which it comes, not because it rouses genuine personal response. There is even an increasing turn to the exploration of "inner space" and a feeling that much of the givenness of everyday life is a sham, a put-on, something suffocatingly constricting. Perhaps the contemporary equivalent to traditional non-believers would be those who do not experience this dimension of innerness, who accept the literalness of everyday as the sole reality. This contemporary turn within is intensely preoccupied with the self, as mystical religion has always been. And yet this quest for personal experience, personal choice, and personal authenticity is only partly identical with what is usually meant by privatization. The crux of the issue, as it has always been in mystical religion, is the relation of this self, myself, and other selves, the universe itself. Only when the definition of self remains constricted to the petty private self, to self-worship, does the concept of privatization become relevant. A religious impulse that identifies the self with others, with man, and with the universe may be inner and individual but it is not private. Far from making a purely personal sense of well-being its only goal (though by no means necessarily rejecting it), it can motivate to sacrificial involvement with others and suffering unto death for their sakes.

Indeed, the search for personal authenticity has been more often united with rather than divorced from group membership and social purpose. Nationalism, with its frequently religious overtones, is an obvious example. Consider the example of black nationalism in the United States, where a "religion of Black Power" has recently been discerned.[5] The literature of Black Power again and again reveals that it is not economic or political grievances that propel the activists, though they are acute, but rather a profound need for inner worth and authenticity, a feeling that through the movement one can overcome self-hatred and the unconscious rejection of one's own blackness. The movement is seen not only as personally redemptive but also as redemptive for the black community, and perhaps universally redemptive as well. The great themes are love, sacrifice, and communion. Black nationalism, like any nationalism, runs the risk of becoming socially "private," of refusing to identify with any outside one's own community. But the controlling universalistic imagery keeps alive, at least so far, the notion of an ultimate union of humanity, even though it is seen as possible only with the prior attainment of black self-respect and autonomy and the exorcising of white racism.

As another example, what I have called elsewhere "civil religion in America"[6] has continued to produce new ways in which personal and social vision can be fused. I have in mind a rather extraordinary phenomenon, less than a decade old: the Peace Corps.[7] This movement, sometimes known symbolically as "the sons of Kennedy" (it has never liked to associate itself with the name of Johnson), though ostensibly a government agency, is actually more like a secular monastic order whose members take a voluntary vow of poverty and go out to work for the alleviation of the sufferings of the world. From the beginning it has been recognized that its significance is more (not "merely") expressive and symbolic than practical. The Peace Corps has almost consciously capitalized on the quest for personal meaning and authenticity among contemporary American college youth. The mode of operation of the Peace Corps—the lack of bureaucracy, the autonomy of the volunteer and his poverty—has from the beginning been recognized as perhaps more important than its objective achievements. The Peace Corps has been an expressive statement of the volunteers to themselves, to their own society, and to the world of certain value commitments that are basic to the American civil religion, in whose context John F. Kennedy first formulated it. But partly because of the Vietnam War and more basically because of the division of the world into affluent and poverty-stricken peoples, the Peace Corps has had to try to transcend the American civil religion. To the extent that it has been unable to do so, it has failed to achieve its full potential.

Among a large section of precisely the most affluent, best educated white American youth (and I suspect this is the case elsewhere as well), nationalism for themselves has lost any appeal, however much they may sympathize with the nationalism of others. Intensely suspicious of purely personal ambition, of merely "making it" in the affluent society, they pursue their quest for personal authenticity outside the claim of any purely communal loyalty. Many of them seem, somewhat inchoately, to have taken as their first tenet the identfication with and responsibility for the sufferings of others anywhere in the world. They seem like a sort of latter-day embodiment of Auguste Comte's "religion of humanity."[8] The recent worldwide outburst of youth in search of social justice, but motivated more by personal values than class resentments, is a kind of vivid surfacing of a vast value consensus that has been growing in the modern world and whose actualization youth impatiently demands. This great international moral movement—which already has its saints and its martyrs, its Gandhis and its Martin Luther Kings, who entirely transcend national identification—may be, though only half conscious of itself, the most significant religious movement of our times.

It is clear that this nascent religion of humanity is not simply at odds with existing moral and religious communities. Its antecedents include the Western ideological movements of socialism, liberal humanism, and Christianity, and in the East, Buddhism and Hinduism. Its chief tenets, the sanctity and dignity of the individual and the full flowering of human personality, have their roots in many traditions. But precisely because it is so intensely individual at the same time that it is social and moral it is not a new "ism," a new exclusive community either of church or state. Instead all existing churches, parties, and states are vulnerable to its criticisms. All, whether the Communist party, the Catholic church or the Government of the United States, are under intense pressure to realize human freedom and human fulfillment, and all, of course, resist to some extent, however much they give lip service. But while the practical problems of the world seem more insoluble than ever and there is little objective ground for optimism, it should not be forgotten that this great international community—a community without boundaries—continues to grow and to call forth the self-sacrifice of many. It is worth noting that Comte's rather ghastly version, still caught in the Western overestimation of belief with its syncrestisic rituals and artificial calendar of saints, has not been realized. This international moral community, which I suggest is immediately tangible when any two people feel that their mutual humanity transcends their commitment to any particular group or groups to which either of them happens to belong, is not the product of any objective creed or enforced dogma. It is the supreme contemporary example of how a stress on inner authenticity and autonomy can yet have the most profound social and moral consequences.

V

By arguing that religion and belief are not the same,[9] that their identification is found in one great but historically discrete cultural tradition and not outside it, and that even in that tradition it is no longer possible to maintain, I have made non-belief generic to contemporary consciousness, religious and nonreligious alike. What is generally called secularization and the decline of religion would in this context appear as the decline of the external control system of religion and the decline of traditional religious belief. But religion, as that symbolic form through which man comes to terms with the antinomies of his being, has not declined, indeed, cannot decline unless man's nature ceases to be problematic to him. The difference between the committed and the indifferent, those with vision and those without it, exists today as it always has, but it seems unlikely that the proportions of the two groups have changed appreciably. If anything, the twentieth century has probably produced more than its share of the committed and the visionary.

If a quantitative decline of religion must be rejected as a characteristic of modern society, at least as religion is defined here, it is clear that modern religious consciousness is different from that in previous epochs. For one thing, a great shift in the balance between elite and mass religiosity has taken place. The unexamined magical and religious conceptions of nonliterate or semiliterate strata, what used to make up the bulk of the religious life in any society, has come more and more under conscious inspection and critical evaluation as levels of literacy and education reach unprecedented peaks. This has involved the erosion of numerous beliefs and practices, some formerly considered essential to orthodoxy, but many peripheral or of doubtful orthodoxy. On the other hand the old elite notion that religion involves a personal quest for meaning, that it must express the deepest dimensions of the self and in no way violate individual conscience, has been generalized as the dominant conception of religion in modern society. Enormous expansion in our historical and comparative knowledge of religion and of its social and psychological dimensions has made a naive literalism impossible among ever larger numbers of people. And yet the ultimate questions about the meaning of life are asked as insistently, perhaps more insistently, than ever.

It might be asked where does this leave organized religion, where does this leave the Christian church? In one sense it leaves the church in the same place that it has always been; it is as necessary as ever to take up the cross and follow the one who was crucified outside the gates of the city. In another sense it relieves the church of a great burden. It no longer has to provide the social cement for an imperfect social order; it no longer has to double as the Nocturnal Council of Plato's *Laws*.[10] In a nonauthoritarian world the church can only be, as it was originally, a voluntary society. This does not mean that the church is isolated and alienated, although in today's world any morally concerned person must often feel alone and alien. But it becomes possible to recognize the operation of the holy spirit, to use Christian symbolism, in groups and individuals who would not call themselves Christian and to recognize a biblical mold in movements that proclaim their vociferous anti-Christianity. Christians can join with non-Christians in discerning the emerging value consensus, in criticizing existing values in terms of the standard of common humanity and personal integrity, and in insisting that values to which societies are already committed be actualized for all social groups. Multiplicity does not mean chaos. This, however imperfectly, has already been shown in America. Effective moral and political action, as in the antiwar movement in the United States today, can be carried out by those with widely different religious motivation.

In a word, much has been taken away but much has been given. The modern world is as alive with religious possibility as any epoch in human history. It is no longer possible to divide mankind into believers and non-believers. All believe something, and the lukewarm and those of little faith are to be found inside as well as outside the churches. The spirit bloweth where it listeth and men of passionate integrity are found in strange places. If we have outgrown the idea of mission, we have probably also to outgrow the idea of dialogue, as though separated human groups must talk across a chasm. Christians along with other men are called on to build the boundaryless community, the body of man identified with the body of Christ, though all men are free to symbolize it in their own way.

NOTES

1 Avicenna, in F. Rahman, *Prophecy in Islam: Philosophy and Orthodoxy* (London: Allen & Unwin, 1958), pp. 42–44.

2 William Butler Yeats, quoted by Richard Ellman, *Yeats, the Man and the Masks* (New York: Dutton, 1948), p. 263.

3 Wallace Stevens, *Collected Poems* (New York: Alfred A. Knopf, 1954), p. 336.

4 Yeats, in Ellman, *op. cit.*, p. 285.

5 Vincent Harding, "The Religion of Black Power," in Donald R. Cutler, ed., *The Religious Situation: 1968* (Boston: Beacon Press, 1968), pp. 3–38.

6 Bellah, Robert N., "Civil Religion in America," *Daedalus*, 1967; reprinted in *The Religious Situation: 1968, op. cit.*, and in this volume as chap. 9.

7 The analysis of the religious dimension of the Peace Corps has been developed by Ricardo B. Zuniga in *The Peace Corps as a Value-Oriented Movement* (Ph.D. diss., Harvard Univ., 1969).

8 Indeed, one could look much further back for an analogy. These young people resemble the young Roman aristocrats who chose Christianity in the latter part of the fourth century A.D.

9 This point, and indeed much of this paper, are indebted to Wilfred Smith's unpublished paper, "Believing as a Religious Category, with special reference to the Qur'ān," and other of his writings.

10 I do not intend to make Plato a villain. His own views were very complex. Books I and II of the *Laws* present one of the profoundest analyses of ritual ever written and do not suffer from cognitive bias. In making the man Socrates the very heart of his teaching, Plato seems to recognize the importance of embodied truth. And yet there is little doubt that Book X of the *Laws*, with its troublesome implications, has had an enormous influence.

14 Review of *Love's Body,* by Norman O. Brown

Love's Body is an unsettling book. When it first came out I glanced through it, read a paragraph here and there, and put it away, disturbed. It was two years later, in the spring of 1968, that I read it on the plane coming home from the East Coast. It made me dizzy, intoxicated; it made me change. I am still living with the book, teaching with it, absorbing it. This review must be a personal response to one of the most personal books of the century. It is also one of the most important books, both for what it does and for what it signals; I must try to find words to say why.

The aphoristic form has many predecessors—Marshall McLuhan, Nietzsche, Johann Hamann, Blaise Pascal—but Brown uses it for his own purposes. It allows him to combine range and concentration. In less than 300 pages he rolls through sixteen chapters: Liberty, Nature, Trinity, Unity, Person, Representative, Head, Boundary, Food, Fire, Fraction, Resurrection, Fulfillment, Judgment, Freedom, and Nothing. Each paragraph of each chapter is a monad, complete in itself yet related to every other. The book is about almost everything: politics, education, society, personality, epistemology, symbolism, religion, and time, but it proceeds in a nonlinear way, beginning everything at once and finishing nothing. It moves by endless free association—primary process—like the process of actual thinking, like life itself. Yet it is the expression of a cultured and controlled intelligence—artful, playful, witty. It is uniquely personal, yet it cites or quotes "authorities" in every paragraph. It is as far from the form of the linear academic treatise (in which *Life Against Death,* Brown's celebrated 1959 volume, was still cast) as one could get; it is an outcry against most of what passes for college teaching;

This review was written in April 1969.

and yet it could only have been written by a teacher in an American university in the later twentieth century. Among the many things it signals is the aching need to embrace the whole, to break down the walls of academic specialization, to reunite the separated. And its very form is a means to and expression of that reunion.

In this book, where so much is going on, one cannot assert the finality of any one interpretation. The book is, among other things, a protest against literalism, and the quotation from Blake with which Brown ended his famous article "Apocalypse" could almost serve as a motto for *Love's Body:*

> Twofold always. May God us keep
> From single vision and Newton's sleep.

Any prose reading of such a book is bound to be one-sided, determined as much by the reader's problems as by Brown's. With this proviso in mind let me develop a few of the themes of the book that have been especially illuminating to me.

First is the very richness of texture itself, in large part brought on by the simultaneous use of several very different vocabularies. The two most extensively used vocabularies are derived from Christianity and psychoanalysis. A variety of other vocabularies—political, religious, and poetic—emerge from time to time, of which the most important, perhaps, are the Buddhist and the Marxist. What is most important about these simultaneous vocabularies is that no one of them provides an ultimate standard to which all the others are reduced. All have a certain validity. Any one vocabulary can crosscut another, break into it, force it to yield new meanings. The constant recombination of diverse vocabularies to render unexpected meanings is one of the central devices of the book. But if all languages have a certain equivalency, it is clear that for Brown some languages are more central, more controlling, than others. I will risk oversimplification in arguing that it is Christian language that provides the most basic framework within which the book works. Creation, fall, incarnation, sacrifice, resurrection, judgment, transfiguration—these are terms that provide a kind of ground plan. The language of psychoanalysis, particularly that of Ferenczi, Roheim, and Melanie Klein, as well as Freud himself, might at first glance appear to be even more central, because if anything more frequent, than the Christian terminology. But one of the major functions of the psychoanalytic language, especially the insistent sexual language of penis, vagina, coitus, and castration, is to purge the religious language of any false spirituality. The resurrection of the body means the whole body. The draperies that Pope Paul IV had painted on Michelangelo's Last Judgement have been removed. All body parts, as in the David or the Sistine ceiling, are equally beautiful, equally worthy. The resurrection of the body means "an erotic sense of reality."

If the persistent body language renders traditional Christian terms in a new light, the Christian (and to some extent Buddhist) context yields a drastic critique of psychoanalysis. The ego is the self that one must lose if he is to be born again. The reality principle is the fallen world, the world of illusion and death. Brown finds ambiguous warrant for both readings within psychoanalysis itself, but it is clearly the religious context that heightens these conclusions. There is no reduction; every term has its own weight. But the juxtaposition has its own fused meaning, its own new implication, as in the following paragraphs:

> The unconscious, then, is not a closet full of skeletons in the private house of the individual mind; it is not even, finally, a cave full of dreams and ghosts in which, like Plato's prisoners, most of us spend most of our lives—
>
> The unconscious is rather that immortal sea which brought us hither; intimations of which are given in moments of "oceanic feeling"; one sea of energy or instinct; embracing all mankind, without distinction of race, language, or culture; and embracing all the generations of Adam, past, present, and future, in one phylogenetic heritage; in one mystical or symbolical body (pp. 88–89).

What emerges is not a syncretism, for there is no system into which the diverse components are finally forced. Rather there is a consciousness of symbolism or "symbolic consciousness," which sees through all the particular terminologies:

> Meaning is made in a meeting between the holy spirit buried in the Christian and the holy spirit buried underneath the letter of scripture; a breakthrough, from the *Abgrund,* from the unconscious of the reader past the conscious intention of the author to the unconscious meaning; breaking the barrier of the ego and the barrier of the book. *Spiritus per spiritum intellegitur* (p. 196).

Symbolic consciousness is a way of outflanking literalism, of avoiding "taking abstractions . . . as autonomous powers" (p. 222). It thus frees us from being imprisoned in particular vocabularies at the same time that it makes all existing vocabularies available to us. To use the language of Freud, Augustine, Blake, Govinda, and Pascal simultaneously, and yet take none of them "literally" but all "symbolically" in a book that is at the same time religious and an analysis of religion has, I think, great significance for anyone seriously concerned with religion today. It tells us something about the present religious temper as well as something about human religious consciousness in general and thus needs to be explored by both social scientists and historians of religion. In order to reveal some of the implications of Brown's "symbolic consciousness," let us consider what happens to Christian terminology in the book, though parallel arguments could be made for any of the terminological systems that occur prominently.

One consequence of the mass of symbolic equivalences in which the Christian language of the book is enmeshed could be called purgative or "fiery." Here everything specifically Christian seems to be washed away or burned up. If Buddhism, Marxism, and psychoanalysis are all saying "the same thing" as Christianity, then what is left of Christian particularity? God is more or less equivalent to the unconscious; the idea of the Fall is similar to the Buddhist notion of the world as illusion; the sacrament of the eucharist is "oral incorporation" or "primitive participation," and so forth. But since none of these equations is to be taken "literally," since the effort is least of all to "explain" Christianity in terms of some consistent theory that claims a higher truth value than the Christian terms themselves, what eventually is purged away is not Christian particularity but Christian parochialism. Christianity is seen finally not as "a religious tradition" or even as "a great religion" but as a way of thinking about what it means to be human, and a way which is as immediate, powerful, and contemporary as any terminology we possess to deal with that problem.

Christian terminology, then, liberated from its ghetto location in a special group, is released to play its role in the general psychic life of man. What Brown is saying is that Christianity no longer belongs to the self-styled Christians or Buddhism to the self-styled Buddhists. Neither do they belong only to their historians. They are to be released from their idolaters, those who take them literally, and from their embalmers, those who think of them only as historical but not as present realities.

In the face of this challenge it is not enough for the historian to say simply that what Brown has done is itself a historical phenomenon and could not have happened in an earlier period of history, though that may be true. For if Brown's work tells us something about the contemporary religious situation, as I think it does, that situation provides the living context for historical work and thought. History in that context must be different from what it was in the world of comfortable divisions of mankind into followers of the several great religions, the primitives, and the unbelievers. There is something profoundly antihistorical in Brown's work, though he relies enormously on historical scholarship and his own training as a classicist is evident on every page, and that is his insistence on the absolute contemporaneity of every statement, whether by an Old Testament prophet, the Buddha, a primitive shaman, or a modern psychotic. That is part of the power of his vision, that nothing is deprived of its immediacy by any temporal or historical hierarchy. Obviously this does not do away with history, but it places the whole problem of the writing and teaching of history, especially history of religion, in a new light. In a way the work of Mircea Eliade and his followers has been doing something quite similar, but the full implications of their work have been somewhat muted by the relatively exotic material to which they have largely confined themselves: primitive and non-Western religions.

The implication of what Brown has done for the social scientific study of religion is, if anything, even more radical. What this enormously well-educated "secular" intellectual is telling us is that Christianity and other religions are talking about the same realities that contemporary social science is talking about, often more adequately and more effectively. Religion is obviously not, for Brown, what it is for one social scientist who recently termed it the "belief in non-existent beings," but rather it is a symbolic form for dealing with reality. Brown is quite happy to flatten all the methodological barriers that have been used to erect a wall of separation between social science and theology. Insofar as both are basically talking about the human situation there must be parallels between them, points of translation where one can illuminate and criticize the other. Here Brown is implicitly pointing out the dogmatic presuppositions of social science, our bland assumption that the way we view the world is the way it actually is and that all other ways of looking at it are derived from ignorance or error. But I am less interested in emphasizing the critical implications of Brown's view than the liberating ones. If the resources of the world's religious thought could be made vitally available to social science, what rich possibilities there would be.

It is in the nature of the book that the systematic implications of its insights are not developed; indeed, any attempt to extract sentences from here and there to make a continuous argument will only end in contradiction. To develop any of the innumerable hints and beginnings it is necessary rather quickly to leave the book behind, as I have done frequently even in these few pages. From many points of view Herbert Fingarette's brilliant book, *The Self in Transformation,* is a far more logically developed statement of a parallel position, especially in that it too works simultaneously with the languages of social science, poetry, and Eastern and Western religion. But while Fingarette's book is offered as an "existential gesture" (p. 9), as "studies *in* transformation and not about transformation" (p. 2), it must be said that Brown's book goes considerably further in realizing its goal. Since both deal with the most central issue in the understanding of human culture, the relation between the conscious and the unconscious, we could perhaps borrow from D. T. Suzuki, and call Fingarette "consciously unconscious," while Brown is "unconsciously conscious."

For not only does Brown break down the boundaries between the great religions, between historical periods, and between theology and social science, he breaks down the boundaries between emotion and intellect, between poetry and analysis. The image of breaking the boundaries (which is Brown's) carries implications of chaos, and there is chaos in the book, and of madness, and Brown is quite deliberately mad. But it is the chaos and madness of Blake and Yeats, who recur so frequently on his pages, and who are two of the most thoughtful poets who ever wrote English. Indeed, what Brown is telling us is that the fragmentation of our culture is unnecessary, that the real madmen are those who think Yeats should be read only by professors of English but never by professors of sociology, or if by the latter only for relaxation, not to have their fundamental assumptions set on end.

For after all, both thinking and feeling are bodily functions, and can be reunited in our bodies just as our bodies can be reunited in the one body of man. Symbolism is the link between conscious and unconscious, it is the way out of all dividing literalisms; it is the road to resurrection and reunion: "The antinomy between mind and body, word and deed, speech and silence, overcome. Everything is only a metaphor; there is only poetry" (p. 266).

What a strange time in history to come across a book so overflowing with life. While displaying subtle analysis and vast learning, this book is, and this is what is so strange, the living word. Instead of the prophetic horror that seems to have gripped so many of our most sensitive minds, we find here a mood beyond horror (though knowing with Yeats that "Nothing can be sole or whole/That has not been rent" [p. 184]), not only a glimpse of fulfillment but participation in it. With this book we are already coming out of the wilderness and beginning to enter into our inheritance. The last times are at hand; the very alarms and catastrophes prove it. But the table is laid and the poor have sat down to the feast. Here is food indeed and drink indeed.

A strange book has required a strange book review. Among many possible interpretations of Brown, this is only one. Least of all am I trying to argue that I have understood the "real" Brown. He would be the first to point out the illusion of any such claim. But I am convinced that *Love's Body* represents a major contribution to the reintegration of our differentiated and fragmented culture, where the religious has been alienated from the secular and the poetic from the scientific. Even more it gives us hints and clues to the reunification of our lives.

15 Between Religion and Social Science

I

IN THIS ESSAY, let me talk about the religious implications of social science, a phrase that contains a certain amount of deliberate ambiguity. It suggests that social science not only has implications for religion, but that it has religious implications or aspects within itself. I start with the assumption that the relation between religion and social science is complex and in some ways organic. This is in conscious contrast to one view of secularization, the view that there is only a mechanical relation between science and religion, namely, the more of the one the less of the other, and that with the rise of science in the modern world religion has been steadily declining. This notion of secularization is far from a simple empirical generalization. It is part of a theory of modern society, a theory that can almost be called a myth because it functions to create an emotionally coherent picture of reality. It is in this sense religious, not scientific at all. This theory or myth is that of the Enlightenment, which views science as the bringer of light relative to which religion and other dark things will vanish away. The story I want to tell is that of another theory that also has its mythic dimensions, and that also has emerged out of social science itself, but that has a different conception of the human spirit, one in which

This chapter consists of two papers, one given at the University of California at Los Angeles in April 1969 in connection with the celebration of their fiftieth anniversary, the other delivered to a joint session of the American Academy of Religion and the Society for the Scientific Study of Religion in Cambridge, Massachusetts, in October 1969. They are brought together here because they deal with much the same material in somewhat different ways. They are like two photographs of the same scene from somewhat different angles. I think the resulting stereoscopic vision is more interesting than would be the result of trying to collapse them into a single essay. They clearly state the reasons for my belief in the intimate connection between religion and social science.

religion has an integral place in a new conception of the unity of human consciousness.

The Enlightenment theory of secularization and of the relation of religion and science is itself only understandable as a reaction to a particular religious tradition, one with a strong cognitive bias and a stress on orthodox belief. Had the Enlightenment occurred first in a culture dominated by Zen Buddhism, for example, the outcome would have been very different, for Zen never set a date for the creation of the world, argued for the literal inspiration of any scripture, or based any claim on the alleged occurrence of miracles. But the Christian faith in the eighteenth and nineteenth centuries contained a weighty baggage of cognitive assertions about nature and history that could be either disproved or rendered improbable by a critical science. There were many, of course, who argued for the "reasonableness of Christianity" even as early as the eighteenth century. But they tended to place inordinate hope in the gaps in existing scientific knowledge, which it was believed only religious truths could fill. When these gaps were closed by science itself it was a terrible blow. No blow was greater than Darwin's theory of natural selection, which provided the first scientific theory of the origin of species. Before that no one knew how species originated, so a theory of special creation by God was at least a defensible position.

Perhaps even more serious for the cognitive claims of religion than the challenge of the natural sciences was the criticism of the budding social sciences, which tended to explain religious beliefs in terms of ignorance and error or as deliberate falsehoods designed to keep the lower classes resigned to their miserable social conditions. Examples would be the anthropological theory that belief in spirits arose from primitive man's attribution of external reality to the figures who appear in dreams or the Marxian notion of religion as the opium of the people. By the late nineteenth century it seemed obvious to many that religion was on its way out and was soon to be replaced entirely by science. Theologians had never been so defensive. But at just this moment certain dramatic gaps in the Enlightenment view of man began to develop in the social sciences themselves, gaps which, potentially at least, put the whole question of religion in a new light.

Perhaps the most dramatic example was Freud's discovery of the unconscious. In his great book, *The Interpretation of Dreams,* Freud for the first time put the unconscious and its modes of operation under scientific scrutiny. In one sense, of course, this was the culmination of the Enlightenment. The unconscious itself was finally subject to conscious investigation. But in another sense Freud was the gravedigger of the Enlightenment, the man who disclosed that beneath the frail conscious ego are the enormous nonrational forces of the unconscious. By the very nature of the case the unconscious proved refractory to rational analysis. Freud tried a number of formulations during the course of his productive life and never claimed to have fully plumbed those depths. Those who prefer to think of the world in neat conceptual packages resisted the concept of the unconscious from the beginning, and there are some who still hold out against it. But the discovery of the unconscious remains the single most important contribution of psychoanalysis to modern thought.

At about the same time that Freud was working out his theories of personality, Emile Durkheim was trying to understand the fundamental nature of society. In his later years he came to view society as a set of collective representations, common symbols, existing in the minds of its members. When, in his last major book, *The Elementary Forms of the Religious Life,* he tried to face the problem of where the collective representations come from and how they get into people's heads, he developed the idea of collective effervescence. Collective effervescence was Durkheim's term for the kind of group frenzy that seemed to occur in some of the rituals of the Australian Aborigines, but he also found it in such mass outbursts as the French Revolution. It was in these conditions of intense group activity, he thought, that collective representations are impressed on the minds of group members, and, as in the case of the French Revolution, new collective representations are born. While the notion of collective effervescence was by no means as influential as Freud's idea of the unconscious, it was quite important to Durkheim, providing a critical element in his theory of society. Perhaps it has been a mistake to overlook it. It is a concept much like that of the unconscious—it could almost be called a social unconscious—and it, too, serves to point to depths within human action that are not fully understood but do not fit into the convenient patterns of Enlightenment thought, focusing around the twin ideas of interest maximization and cognitive accuracy.

The third term is very familiar though in an increasingly debased form. That is Max Weber's notion of charisma, developed contemporaneously with Freud's and Durkheim's ideas. Charisma is a concept central not only to Weber's sociology of religion but to his sociology of authority, for charismatic authority, along with rational-legal and traditional, is one of the three types of authority that lie at the basis of any social order. Unlike the present vulgarized usage of the term, where it has come close to being a mere synonym for popularity, charisma for Weber denoted some quality of the extraordinary, as its ancient religious usage in the sense of a divine gift or grace would imply. Charisma was especially important for Weber in that it was one of the most important ways in which something new could enter the historical process. The charismatic leader or prophet, on the sheer basis of his own extraordinary gift or divine calling, could introduce fundamentally new normative demands that would otherwise have small chance of acceptance. Of course, Weber was not using the term in its literal religious meaning. He left undetermined the exact mechanism by which charisma operates either in the prophet or on his followers. In this respect as well as in others charisma is a concept similar to those of Freud and Durkheim already discussed.

To some extent what I have said parallels the famous argument of Talcott Parsons in *The Structure of Social Action* that the great generation of social scientists at the turn of the century, in coming to deal with the phenomenon of religion, had to take into account nonrational factors that did not fit previous patterns of social explanation. All three of these writers were preoccupied with religion—an interesting fact in itself—and all three developed theories of religion. Especially important is the presence in their explanatory conceptual apparatus of central terms that do not so much explain anything as point to dark recesses where powerful but poorly understood forces and processes seem to be affecting human action.

What I am suggesting is that the fact that these three great nonbelievers, the most seminal minds in modern social science, each in his own way ran up against nonrational, noncognitive factors of central importance to the understanding of human action, but which did not yield readily to any available conceptual resources, is in itself a fact of great significance for religion in the twentieth century. Convinced of the invalidity of traditional religion, each rediscovered the power of the religious consciousness. What could perhaps be suggested on the basis of the work of these men is that when Western religion chose to make its stand purely on the ground of cognitive adequacy, it was forgetting the nature of the reality with which religion has to deal and the kind of symbols religion uses. Western religion in this context refers mainly to its theological defenders, not to the evangelists and preachers who addressed themselves to the anxieties, hopes, fears, and emotions of their hearers. Even among the theologians there were men like Friedrich Schleiermacher, who pointed out that religion is not primarily cognitive.

It is unfortunate but not uncommon that the insights of the masters are not readily appropriated by the followers. In this case the great breakthrough documented by Talcott Parsons in *The Structure of Social Action* has by no means entirely stuck. Much of social science has relapsed into the positivist utilitarian idiom in which only "hard and realistic" assumptions about human nature are allowed. In this idiom, human action is likened to a game where every player is trying to maximize his self-interest or is concerned only with the *quid pro quo* in an exchange network, and where there is no place for the murky concepts to which Freud, Durkheim, and Weber were driven. Religion for those of this persuasion could hardly be less important, or if its survival is recognized, it is explained away as a response to some sort of deprivation. It must be admitted that such views are widespread in social science today. They are convenient, for they fit the governing myth in which the world is seen as a highly complex machine entirely subject to rational calculation. Such a myth, alas, exists not only among social scientists but among those close to the buttons that could touch off nuclear war—men who deal with nuclear strategy simply as an extension of game theory.

A different view, both of social science and religion, has certainly not died out in social science. Some of the systems theorists such as Parsons and Karl Deutsch have conceived of human action as multilayered and open. Deutsch, for example, has spoken of the propensity for all highly complex systems to break down, and has borrowed the theological term "grace" to designate the indispensable but unpredictable situational conditions that seem to be necessary in order for any complex system to function at all.[1] Parsons in his discussion of symbol systems has argued that the ultimate nature of reality is not subject to empirical specification, though any cultural system must have some way of symbolizing it.[2] What he calls "constitutive symbols" are not cognitive in the sense of scientific statements, though they provide the terms in which reality is coherent. He also speaks of expressive and moral symbol systems as partly autonomous. The point is not that these various types of symbol systems are entirely independent from each other, for there must certainly be some integration between them in any functioning culture, but that no one of them has a privileged position. Constitutive, expressive, and moral symbol systems for Parsons can never simply be deduced from cognitive symbol systems. This means that science can never wholly take over the job of making sense of the world. And Parsons has long insisted that part of the reality that man needs to make sense of is nonempirical, simply unavailable to any of the resources of science. In this way Parsons has kept alive the openness to the mystery of being, which the earlier great generation of social scientists had somewhat grudgingly come to recognize.

No one in that earlier generation of social scientists had a greater sense of the openness and multiplicity of reality than William James. Building partly on James, the Austrian-American social philosopher Alfred Schutz developed the idea of multiple realities,[3] which has been recently expounded by Peter Berger and Thomas Luckmann.[4] Basic to Schutz's idea is that reality is never simply given, it is constructed. The apprehension of reality is always an active process involving subject and object. Multiple realities arise because of the variety of modes of consciousness and schemas of interpretation that link the two. Schutz pointed out that besides the world of everyday life, which is the social world par excellence, there is the world of dreams, the world of art, the world of science, the world of religion. By showing that these worlds are partially autonomous and irreducible one to the other Schutz gave another powerful argument for the openness and multiplicity of the human spirit.

A similar point has been made by those who have criticized the correspondence theory of language. For certain purposes it may be convenient to imagine language as a passive reflection of some alleged objective reality. Strict correspondence between words and things may be highly desirable. But such strict correspondence, relative at best, can be maintained only under the operation of certain rigorous standards that are highly unlike the normal use of language. As Wittgenstein said, "Uttering a word is like striking a note on the keyboard of the imagination."[5] Language exists not simply to mirror passively some given world of objects. Imaginative language creates new meanings, defines new worlds. Herbert Fingarette, a philosopher influenced by Wittgenstein and Freud, argues that in psychoanalysis the unconscious is not simply uncovered, revealed in its previously hidden reality. Rather, a new imaginative interpretation of the patient's life is worked out that opens possibilities previously closed.

That which was unconscious is transformed, not simply revealed through being symbolized.[6] As Norman O. Brown has pointed out, the symbol does not stand for the hidden reality but is the living link that joins the hidden and the revealed.[7] In general, this understanding of language, which appreciates its imaginative function as not decorative but fundamental, is closer to that of the poets than of the physicists, thought it must be added parenthetically that the physicists have often been more aware than their social scientific imitators that their language, too, is in large part imaginative. When William Butler Yeats said,

And I declare my faith:
I mock Plotinus' thought
And cry in Plato's teeth,
Death and life were not
Till man made up the whole,
Made lock, stock and barrel
Out of his bitter soul,
Aye, sun and moon and star, all,
And further add to that
That, being dead, we rise,
Dream and so create
Translunar paradise.[8]

we can understand it not as a flight of fancy but as a profound insight into human reality.

Let us return to the central issue of the relation between social science and religion. It was entirely necessary during the course of modern Western history for science in general and social science in particular to differentiate themselves from theology. The cognitive or pseudocognitive bias of Western religion made this process extremely painful, for some centuries close to warfare between science and religion. Partly because of the bitterness of the struggle some scientists and social scientists took on the characteristics of their most retrogressive opponents; hence we can speak of the rise of a literalist, fundamentalist science in opposition to a literalist, fundamentalist religion. It was protagonists of this sort who saw the struggle as a battle to the death, which only one side could win.

In a few scattered examples I have tried to show how the development of social science itself, especially since the turn of the century, has come to a new appreciation of the importance of precisely those aspects of human existence with which science cannot adequately deal and that have classically been within the realm of religion. We thus have the resources for carrying through a nonantagonistic differentiation, leaving behind the long and bitter controversy between religion and science. It is true that in recent decades the struggle has not been intense, but this has been mainly because of a tacit agreement between science and religion to ignore each other. Differentiation without any new integration however can be as destructive as open warfare; it can lead to the fragmentation and anomie that our universities presently exemplify. It is not enough simply to speak of the autonomy of various spheres when the meaningfulness of our entire intellectual endeavor is in question. It is my feeling that the resources for a new kind of integration actually exist and that such a new integration would contribute much to the reunification and reinvigoration of our culture by returning to the idea of truth not only rigor but vitality and comprehensiveness. In this way the desiccation of our culture, which is what secularization has often meant, might begin to be reversed.

When I speak of integration I do not mean some kind of fantastic syncretism of science and religion. They have different purposes, different limitations, different modes of action. But they are both part, and I would argue a necessary part, of every culture and every person. They need to exist in some vital and healthy whole in which each is integral. This means not simply a tacit agreement to ignore each other but open interchange between them with all the possibilities of mutual growth and transformation that that entails.

It seems to me that if religion could overcome its misplaced defensiveness and pull down the barricades it has erected on the wrong streets, it could make a major contribution to our present cultural crisis. For religion is not really a kind of pseudogeology or pseudohistory but an imaginative statement about the truth of the totality of human experience. So-called postreligious man, the cool, self-confident secular man that even some theologians have recently celebrated, is trapped in a literal and circumscribed reality that is classically described in religious terms as the world of death and sin, the fallen world, the world of illusion. Postreligious man is trapped in hell. The world of everday reality is a socially and personally constructed world. If one confuses that world with reality itself one then becomes trapped in one's own delusions, one projects one's wishes and fears onto others and one acts out one's own madness all the while believing one is a clearheaded realist. Christianity, Buddhism, and other religions have long known about such delusions. They are a kind of demonic possession, for the man who believes he is most in control of his world is just the one most in the power of demons.

In order to break through the literal univocal interpretation of reality that our pseudoscientific secular culture espouses, it is necessary for religion to communicate nonordinary reality that breaks into ordinary reality and exposes its pretensions. When ordinary reality turns into a nightmare, as it increasingly has in modern society, only some transcendental perspective offers any hope. It is of course impossible to prove Christianity or any religion, but it is impossible to prove cognitively or scientifically any ultimate perspective on human life, including Marxism, rationalism, or any kind of scientism. The adequacy of any ultimate perspective is its ability to transform human experience so that it yields life instead of death. Our present fragmented and disorganized culture does not rank high on that criterion.

It is not my main purpose to deliver a Jeremiad for I think there is much to be hopeful about. I feel that there are greater resources now for healing the split between the imaginative and the cognitive, the intellectual and the emotional, and the scientific and the religious aspects of our culture and our consciousness than there have been for centuries. Social science is beginning, faintly and crudely, to be able to cope with the richness of reality as religion has seen it. Religious thinkers like Paul Tillich and Martin Buber have seen the importance of these gropings and have helped to relate the theological enterprise to them. From my own knowledge of the major American divinity schools I would say there has never been a more open interest in the social sciences, not merely as tools for pastoral counseling or the organization of inner-city parishes, but for suggestions about the theological enterprise itself. This situation has become possible only because both sides have seen that we can translate, painfully and tentatively, between different realms of reality without reducing the language of one to the language of the other. In particular some social scientists have come to feel that there are profound depths in the religious symbols that we have scarcely begun to fathom and that we have much to learn from any exchange. While remaining committed to Enlightenment rationalism as the foundation of scientific work and accepting its canons with respect to our research, we nevertheless know that this is only one road to reality. It stands in tension with and under the judgment of other modes of consciousness. And finally we know that the great symbols that justify science itself rest on unprovable assumptions sustained at the deepest levels of our consciousness.

My conclusion, then, runs about as contrary to so-called secularization theory as is humanly possible. It is my feeling that religion, instead of becoming increasingly peripheral and vestigial, is again moving into the center of our cultural preoccupations. This is happening both for purely intellectual reasons having to do with the reemergence of the religious issue in the sciences of man and for practical historical reasons having to do with the increasing disillusionment with a world built on utilitarianism and science alone. Religion was the traditional mode by which men interpreted their world to themselves. Increasingly modern man has turned to social science for this interpretation. As social science has attempted more and more to grasp the totality of man it has recognized many of the preoccupations of traditional religion. As traditional religion has sought to relate to the contemporary world it has leaned more and more on social scientific contributions to the understanding of man.

It seems to me that in the fruitful interchange between social science and religion we may be seeing the beginnings of the reintegration of our culture, a new possibility of the unity of consciousness. If so, it will not be on the basis of any new orthodoxy, either religious or scientific. Such a new integration will be based on the rejection of all univocal understandings of reality, of all identifications of one conception of reality with reality itself. It will recognize the multiplicity of the human spirit, and the necessity to translate constantly between different scientific and imaginative vocabularies. It will recognize the human proclivity to fall comfortably into some single literal interpretation of the world and therefore the necessity to be continuously open to rebirth in a new heaven and a new earth. It will recognize that in both scientific and religious culture all we have finally are symbols, but that there is an enormous difference between the dead letter and the living word.

II

There is probably nothing more important than intellectual history to help us understand how our culture has become so fragmented and dissociated that we find it almost impossible to communicate the integrated meaning our young people so passionately require of us. Aware of my lack of competence in intellectual history, I must nonetheless venture into it in order to deal with one central aspect of this fragmentation, namely, the split between theological and scientific (and here I mean mainly social scientific) language about Christianity or, more generally, the split between religious man and scientific man in the West.

Without going back before the seventeenth century, one can perhaps say that from that time almost to the present the dominant theological defense of Christianity has been what may be called "historical realism." The roots of this historical realism can be traced back to biblical historicism, Greek rationalism, and the new awareness of scientific method emerging in the seventeenth century. The figural and symbolic interpretation of Scripture that was characteristic of medieval thought was almost eliminated by Reformation and counter-Reformation theology. Modern consciousness required clear and distinct ideas, definite unambiguous relationships, and a conception of the past "as it actually was." The proponents of "reasonable Christianity" worked out a theology that seemed to fit these requirements. It is true that some of the most significant theological minds —such as Blaise Pascal, Jonathan Edwards, Friedrich Schleiermacher, and Kierkegaard—don't quite fit this formulation. Nevertheless for broad strata of educated laymen, and above all for the secular intellectuals, it was this understanding of Christianity that was decisive. Lest anyone think this kind of Christian thought is dead let him pause for a moment to consider the recent popularity of apologists who have argued that "Christ must have been who he said he was or he was the greatest fraud in history."

There have always been those willing to pick up the gauntlet with that kind of argument. Particularly in the eighteenth century many secular intellectuals argued that Christ, or if not Christ certainly the priests, were indeed frauds. Meeting Christianity on the ground of historical realism they rejected it. When faced with the inevitable question of how something clearly fraudulent and indeed absurd could have been so powerful in human history, they answered that religion was propagated for the sake of political despotism, maintained by an unholy alliance of priestcraft and political despotism. This argument was a species of "consequential reductionism," the explanation of religion in terms of its functional consequences, which in cruder or subtler form has been a standard piece of intellectual equipment in the modern secular intellectuals' understanding of religion ever since.

The nineteenth century began with a partial reaction against the abstract rationalism of the Enlightenment and saw a growing awareness of the complex role of religion in the development of human consciousness. Yet at the same time the certainty grew among the secular intellectuals that Christianity, still defended largely by the old arguments and the old formulas, and with it religion generally, could not be taken seriously in its own terms. There grew up alongside of the continuing use of consequential reductionism several varieties of what I would call "symbolic reductionism." From this point of view religion is not entirely fraudulent. It contains a certain truth. But it is necessary for the modern intellectual to discover what that truth is that is hidden in the fantastic myths and rituals of religion. Much of nineteenth-century social science developed out of the search for the kernel of truth hidden in the falsity of religion.

One of the great intellectual strategies of the symbolic reductionists was to treat religion as a phase in the history of science. Primitive man, unable to understand the great natural phenomena of night and day, summer and winter, storm and drought, developed the fantastic hypotheses of religion to account for them. This kind of evolutionary rationalism has been enormously pervasive and has influenced religious thought as well as secular. How convenient for the Sunday school teacher to be able to explain the strange dietary rules of the ancient Hebrews in terms of hygiene—an intuitive awareness that shellfish and pork easily spoil under the warm climatic conditions of the Middle East! Another version of evolutionary rationalism that the nineteenth century developed with vast persuasiveness was the conception of religion as a stage in the development of human morality. The hidden truth of religion was the gradually growing perception of man's ethical responsibilities. The monotheistic God of the Bible could then be considered as the expression of a high ideal of man's ethical action.

For those perplexed that religion should continue to survive even in scientifically and ethically enlightened times, more immediate, more existential forms of symbolic reductionism were developed. Following Ludwig Feuerbach's treatment of religion as the projection of human nature, Marx developed his famous conception of religion as the opium of the people. This is usually treated as a form of consequential reductionism, which it perhaps is, but if we look at the *locus classicus* we can see that it is even more an existential version of symbolic reductionism. In his introduction to the "Critique of Hegel's Philosophy of Right," Marx wrote: "*Religious* suffering is at the same time an *expression* of real suffering and a *protest* against real suffering. Religion is the sigh of the oppressed creature, the heart of a heartless world, and the soul of soulless conditions. It is the *opium* of the people."[9]

From the early decades of the twentieth century symbolic reductionist theories of religion gained new subtlety and new complexity. Freud and Durkheim developed comprehensive formulas for the translation of religious symbols into their real meanings. Freud, first in *Totem and Taboo,* and then more starkly in *The Future of an Illusion,* disclosed that the real meaning of religion is to be found in the Oedipus complex that it symbolically expresses. The biblical God stands for the primordial father toward whom the sons feel both rebellious and guilty. Christ sums up a whole set of conflicting Oedipal wishes: the wish to kill the father, the wish to be killed for one's guilty wishes, and the wish to be raised to the right hand of the father. Finally, for Freud, the psychologically courageous man will discard the religious symbols that cloak his neurosis and face his inner problems directly.

For Durkheim the reality behind the symbol was not the Oedipus complex but society, and the morality that expresses it. In one of his most important essays "Individualism and the Intellectuals,"[10] he attempts to describe the religion and morality appropriate to his own society. He finds this in a religion of humanity and a morality of ethical individualism. How does he treat Christianity? "It is a singular error," he says, "to present individualist morality as the antagonist of Christian morality; on the contrary it is derived from it." In contrast to the religion of the ancient city-state, he says, Christianity moved the center of the moral life from outside to within the individual, who becomes the sovereign judge of his conduct without having to render account to anyone but himself and God. But, he says, today this morality does not need to be disguised under symbols or dissimulated with the aid of metaphors. A developed individualism, the appropriate morality of modern society, does not need the symbolic clothing of Christianity.[11]

Unlike Marx, Freud, and Durkheim, Max Weber made no claim to have the key to the reality that lies behind the façade of religious symbolization. He treated religions as systems of meaning to be understood in their own terms from the point of view of those who believe in them, even though in the observer they strike no personal response. In this attitude he was at one with a whole tradition of German cultural historians and phenomenologists. For all the sensitivity with which he treats Calvinism, for example, it is the consequences for the actions of the believers that interest him, not the beliefs themselves. Without ever quite taking the position of consequential reductionism, Weber still manages to convey the feeling that the scientific observer cannot finally take seriously the beliefs he is studying even though he must take seriously the fact that beliefs have profound social consequences.

For the moment I am not trying to refute any of these theories of religion. They all have a great deal of truth in them as far as they go. But it is notable that the best minds in social science by the third decade of the twentieth century were deeply alienated from the Western religious tradition. None of them were believers in the ordinary sense of that word. All of them believed themselves to be in possession of a truth superior to that of religion. But since none of them except very hesitantly and partially wanted to fill the role that religion had previously played, they contributed to the deep split in our culture between religion and science, a break just at that highest level of meaning where integation is of the greatest importance.

Meanwhile, back at the seminary, things went on much as usual. The same old books were picked up, thumbed through, and put down again. The contemporary proponents of the historical realist position cut and trimmed what no longer seemed tenable and hoped for the best. A Karl Barth had the courage to give vivid expression to the grand themes of biblical and Reformation theology as though nothing had happened intellectually in the nineteenth and twentieth centuries, at least nothing that could not be refuted with the magnificent rhetoric of divine initiative and revelation. A few—one thinks of Martin Buber and Paul Tillich—saw the problem and tried to heal the split. In their more ecstatic moments it is even possible to say that they did heal the split. But neither was quite able to come up with a theoretical formulation that would spell out their ecstatic insights.

It is my contention that implicit in the work of the great symbolic reductionists was another possible position with entirely different implications for the place of religion in our culture, a position I will call "symbolic realism" and will spend the rest of this essay trying to describe. Not only the great social scientists but many philosophical, literary, linguistic, and religious thinkers have contributed to this position, which has been gestating for a long time and has become increasingly explicit in the last twenty years.

Both consequential reductionism and symbolic reductionism are expressions of an objective cognitive bias that has dominated Western thought ever since the discovery of scientific method in the seventeenth cenutry. This position has held that the only valid knowledge is in the form af falsifiable scientific hypotheses. The task then with respect to religion has been to discover the falsifiable propositions hidden within it, to discard the unverifiable assertions and those clearly false, and, even with respect to the ones that seem valid, to abandon the symbolic and metaphorical disguise in which they are cloaked. Both Durkheim and Freud, who are worth considering for a moment in this connection, ardently held to this conception of knowledge. Yet the work of both contains deep inner contradictions precisely with respect to this point.

Durkheim came to see that the most fundamental cultural forms, the collective representations, are not the product of the isolated reflective intelligence but are born out of the intense atmosphere of collective effervescence. Collective representations are based first of all on the sentiment of respect that they exact from individuals, and it is only through their discipline that rational thought becomes possible. Rational inquiry, then, rests on a necessary substratum of sentiments and representations that have neither the form nor the function of scientific hypotheses. Nor did Durkheim believe that the element of the sacred, which is what he called the symbolic expression of the collective vitality at the basis of society and culture, could ever be outgrown. It would always be an essential feature of social life, and the great terms which moved him and which he felt were so essential to modern society—individuality, reason, truth, morality, and society itself—were, as he knew, symbols, collective representations. In fact, he came to see that society itself is a symbolic reality. In his own terms, finally, symbolic reductionism comes to be self-contradictory and self-destructive. It is the reality of symbols that his life work goes to prove.

Freud's greatest discovery was the existence and nature of the unconscious. In his first and in many ways most fundamental major work, *The Interpretation of Dreams,* he showed that dreams are the royal road to the unconscious. Only through dreamlike symbolism can the primary process of the unconscious express itself. Although the rational understanding that he called secondary process can gradually increase its effective control, Freud never thought it could replace the unconscious. Indeed, he emphasized the relative weakness and fragility of rational processes. And in his own work he again and again abandoned the form of scientific hypothesis for the language of myth, image, and symbol, much to the dismay of subsequent academic psychologists. He named his most important psychological complex after a Greek myth. In his late years he constructed his own myth, the myth of the struggle of Eros and the death-instinct, in order to express his deepest intuitions. The unmasker of all symbols finally if implicitly admitted the necessity and reality of symbols themselves.

In recent years the knowledge that noncognitive and nonscientific symbols are constitutive of human personality and society, are real in the fullest sense of the word, has deepened and consolidated. Rather than the norm of scientific objectivity invading all spheres of human experience, the role of noncognitive factors in science itself have become increasingly recognized. As the philosopher of science Michael Polanyi says, ". . . into every act of knowing there enters a passionate contribution of the person knowing. . . . This coefficient is no mere imperfection but a vital component of his knowledge."[12] What this signals is a shift away from the mechanical model of early natural science, in which reality was seen as residing in the object, the function of the observer was simply to find out the laws in accordance with which the object behaves, and "subjective" was synonymous with "unreal," "untrue," and "fallacious." For this mechanical model there has increasingly been substituted the interactionist model of social science, or what Talcott Parsons calls "action theory." Here reality is seen to reside not just in the object but in the subject, and particularly in the relation between subject and object. The canons of empirical science apply primarily to symbols that attempt to express the nature of objects, but there are nonobjective symbols that express the feelings, values, and hopes of subjects, or that organize and regulate the flow of interaction between subjects and objects, or that attempt to sum up the whole subject-object complex or even point to the context or ground of that whole. These symbols, too, express reality and are not reducible to empirical propositions. This is the position of symbolic realism.

If we define religion as that symbol system that serves to evoke what Herbert Richardson calls the "felt-whole,"[13] that is, the totality that includes subject and object and provides the context in which life and action finally have meaning, then I am prepared to claim that as Durkheim said of society, religion is a reality *sui generis.* To put it bluntly, religion is true. This is not to say that every religious symbol is equally valid any more than every scientific theory is equally valid. But it does mean that since religious symbolization and religious experience are inherent in the structure of human existence, all reductionism must be abandoned. Symbolic realism is the only adequate basis for the social scientific study of religion. When I say religion is a reality *sui generis* I am certainly not supporting the claims of the historical realist theologians, who are still working with a cognitive conception of religious belief that makes it parallel to objectivist scientific description. But if the theologian comes to his subject with the assumptions of symbolic realism, as many seem to be doing, then we are in a situation where for the first time in centuries theologian and secular intellectual can speak the same language. Their tasks are different but their conceptual framework is shared. What this can mean for the reintegration of our fragmented culture is almost beyond calculation.

But if a new integration is incipient, fragmentation still describes the present reality. Concentrating so heavily on the mastery of objects, we have too long neglected what Anais Nin calls the "Cities of the Interior,"[14] and everywhere these neglected cities are in revolt. We have concentrated too much on what Polanyi calls explicit knowledge and too little on what he calls implicit knowing, and we have forgotten that the implicit knowing is the more fundamental, for all explicit knowledge depends on its unconscious assumptions.[15] As Yeats says,

> Whatever flames upon the night
> Man's own resinous heart has fed.[16]

We see the flames but we have forgotten the heart and its reasons that reason knows not of. The price of this neglect of the interior life (and I use interior not only to refer to the individual; there is a collective interior that contains vast forces) is the reification of the superficial, an entrapment in the world of existing objects and structures.

But the life of the interior, though blocked, is never destroyed. When thwarted and repressed the interior life takes its revenge in the form of demonic possession. Just those who feel they are most completely rational and pragmatic, and most fully objective in their assessment of reality, are most in the power of deep unconscious fantasies. Whole nations in this century have blindly acted out dark myths of destruction all the while imagining their actions dictated by external necessity. In our own country both the National Security Council and the Students for a Democratic Society (SDS) claim to be acting in accordance with the iron laws of politics at the same time that they seem trapped dreamlike in their own unconscious scenarios. All of this is the price we have paid for relegating art to the periphery of life, denying the central integrating role of myth and ritual, and letting our morality be dictated by our politics. For these reasons the issues of concern here are not academic, are not, to use a word that I have come to loathe in recent months, irrelevant. The future of our society, perhaps of life on this planet, depends on how we face them.

Perhaps the first fruit of symbolic realism, of taking seriously noncognitive symbols and the realms of experience they express, is to introduce a note of skepticism about all talk of reality. "Reality is never as real as we think."[17] Since for human beings reality is never simply "out there," but always also involves an "in here" and some way in which the two are related, it is almost certain that anything "out there" will have many meanings. Even a natural scientist selects those aspects of the external world for study that have an inner meaning to him, that reflect some often hidden inner conflict. But this is true of all of us. We must develop multiple schemas of interpretation with respect not only to others but ourselves. We must learn to keep the channels of communication open between the various levels of consciousness. We must realize with Alfred Schutz that there are multiple realities[18] and that human growth requires the ability to move easily between them and will be blocked by setting up one as a despot to tyrannize over the others. Perhaps this is partly what is meant by what today is called "multimedia communication," but it is even more important to remember that any one medium or any one symbol has many meanings and many contexts of interpretation.

Let me conclude by applying these general remarks to the field of religion and to the problems that face those of us who think about religion today. If art and literature primarily express the realm of inner meaning and are free to explore even the most aberrant and idiosyncratic wishes, hopes, and anxieties, religion is always concerned with the link between subject and object, with the whole that contains them and forms their ground. Though religion is not primarily subjective it is not objective either. It symbolizes unities in which we participate, which we know, in Polanyi's words, not by observing but by dwelling in them.[19] While neither the churches nor our secular culture seem to be doing a terribly good job of providing the symbols that evoke the wholeness of life and give meaning to our participation in it, we must nonetheless look to whatever in our own culture or in any culture has played this role.

If we think especially of contemporary Christianity there are a number of theologians whose work seems relevant; such names as Wilfred Smith, Richard Neibuhr, Gordon Kaufmann, and Herbert Richardson come to mind. But for me Paul Tillich is still the great theologian of the century, perhaps because it was through his work that Christian symbols first began to live again for me after my adolescent loss of faith. Certainly no one had a clearer sense of the fatal consequences of objectivism in religion. When Tillich objected to such phrases as "God exists" or "God is a Being" or "the Supreme Being," it was because he felt they made God into an object, something finite, a being alongside other beings. His own conception of God was far more transcendent than the neofundamentalists ever realized. And yet even Tillich succumbed perhaps too much to the mania for interpretation, for discovering the rational core beneath the symbol, and the metaphysical structure in which he restated the fundamental Christian truths is after all not very persuasive. As one more schema of interpretation alongside others it certainly has its uses, but when he says that the statement "God is being-itself" is not symbolic he seems to be engaging in a kind of metaphysical reductionism.[20] Perhaps his greatest contribution and the line of work that is still worth pursuing today was his restless quest for the "dimension of depth" in all human social and cultural forms. This was his great contribution to breaking out of the institutional ghetto and seeing once more, as Augustine did, the figure of Christ in the whole world.

Two secular intellectuals have made major contributions in recent years to the position I am trying to set forth: Herbert Fingarette in *The Self in Transformation*[21] and Norman O. Brown in *Love's Body*.[22] Both of them oppose any kind of symbolic reductionism; both of them know that reality is inner as well as outer and that the symbol is not decoration but our only way of apprehending the real.

They both have much to teach us about the multiplicity of vision—poetic, Buddhist, primitive, as well as Christian—which has become a possibility and, indeed, a necessity in the modern world. The work of these men is the most vivid illustration I know of the rapprochement between the language of religion and the language of the scientific analysis of religion.

As a sociologist I am by no means prepared to abandon the work of the great consequential and symbolic reductionists. They have pointed out valid implications of religious life that were not previously understood. But I am prepared to reject their assumption that they spoke from a higher level of truth than the religious systems they studied. I would point out instead their own implicit religious positions. Most of all I am not prepared to accept the implication that the religious issue is dead and that religious symbols have nothing directly to say to us.

Superficially the phenomenological school seems preferable on this score since it insists on describing religious symbols as closely as possible in the terms of those who hold them. But here there is the temptation to treat religious systems as embalmed specimens that could not possibly speak directly to those outside the charmed circle of believers.

I believe that those of us who study religion must have a kind of double vision; at the same time that we try to study religious systems as objects we need also to apprehend them as ourselves religious subjects. Neither evolutionist nor historical relativist nor theological triumphalist positions should allow us to deny that religion is one, I don't mean to say that all religions are saying the same thing in doctrinal or ethical terms; obviously they are not. But religion is one for the same reason that science is one—though in different ways—because man is one. No expression of man's attempt to grasp the meaning and unity of his existence, not even a myth of a primitive Australian, is without meaning and value to me. Perhaps this assertion will seem less radical to many young people today, for example to the young anthropologist Carlos Casteneva who apprenticed himself to a Yaqui shaman, than it does to those trained in my generation. I am not advocating the abandonment of the canons of scientific objectivity or value neutrality, those austere disciplines that will always have their place in scientific work. But those canons were never meant to be ends in themselves, certainly not by Weber, who was passionately committed to ethical and political concerns.

They are methodological strictures. They neither relieve us of the obligation to study our subject as whole persons, which means in part as religious persons, nor do they relieve us of the burden of communicating to our students the meaning and value of religion along with its analysis. If this seems to confuse the role of theologian and scientist, of teaching religion and teaching about religion, then so be it.[23] The radical split between knowledge and commitment that exists in our culture and in our universities is not ultimately tenable. Differentiation has gone about as far as it can go. It is time for a new integration.

NOTES

1 Karl W. Deutsch, *The Nerves of Government* (Glencoe, Ill.: Free Press, 1963), pp. 217, 236–240.

2 Talcott Parsons, Introduction to Part IV, "Culture and the Social System," in Talcott Parsons *et al.*, eds., *Theories of Society* (Glencoe, Ill.: Free Press, 1961).

3 Alfred Schutz, *Collected Papers,* vol. 1 (The Hague: Nijhoff, 1962), pp. 209–59.

4 Peter L. Berger and Thomas Luckmann, *The Social Construction of Reality* (New York: Doubleday & Co., 1966).

5 Ludwig Wittgenstein, *Philosophical Investigations* (New York: Macmillan Co., 1968), p. 4.

6 Herbert Fingarette, *The Self in Transformation* (New York: Harper & Row, Harper Torchbooks, 1965), pt. 1.

7 Norman O. Brown, *Love's Body* (New York: Random House, Vintage Books, 1968), pp. 216–17, 257–58, and elsewhere.

8 William Butler Yeats, *The Variorum Edition of the Poems* (New York: Macmillan Co., 1968), pp. 414–15.

9 Karl Marx, *Early Writings* (New York: McGraw–Hill, 1964), pp. 43–44.

10 Emile Durkheim, "L'Individualisme et les intellectuels," *Revue Bleue,* 4e ser. 10 (1898): 7–13.

11 *Ibid.,* p. 11.

12 Michael Polanyi, *Personal Knowledge* (New York: Harper & Row, Harper Torchbooks, 1964), p. xiv.

13 Herbert W. Richardson, *Toward an American Theology* (New York: Harper & Row, 1967), chap. 3, esp. p. 64.

14 The title of her multivolume "continuous novel."

15 Polanyi, *op. cit.,* p. x.

16 Yeats, *op. cit.,* p. 438.

17 Daniel Stern, in Anais Nin, *The Novel of the Future* (New York: Macmillan Co., 1968), p. 200.

18 Schutz, *op. cit.*

19 Polanyi, *op. cit.*

20 Paul Tillich, *Systematic Theology,* vol. 1 (Chicago: Univ. of Chicago Press, 1951), p. 238.

21 Fingarette, *op. cit.*

22 Brown, *op. cit.*

23 Randall Huntsberry, of the Department of Religion, Wesleyan University, has recently discussed the untenability of the distinction between teaching religion and teaching about religion in an unpublished paper, "Secular Education and Its Religion."

Appendix: The Systematic Study of Religion

THIS ESSAY is a series of tentative notes on several of the problems involved in the systematic study of religion. They are arranged under a set of categories that it is hoped are exhaustive at this level of analysis. The first three categories—religious symbol systems, religious action, and religious institutions—may be considered to exhaust the structural analysis of religion. Three more categories—religion and socialization, religion and social differentiation, and religious pathology—have been added to cover the analysis of religious process. The same set of reference points is used for the description of structure and process, leading to the possibility that in the relatively near future the first three categories will be sufficient for the analysis of both. Largely due to the direction of previous work, the comments will be extensive under some categories while others will be little more than indications for future work.

Religious Symbol Systems

Before making a few remarks on the content of religious symbolism, it might be well to comment briefly on religious symbolism in relation to symbolism in general. Symbols are cultural objects that serve to give meaning to acts or objects by classifying them in categories that include other acts or objects. They provide a context of meaning for discrete acts and objects. Meaning in this sense is

This essay was written in the spring of 1955 but has never been published. It was an effort to think through the main theoretical problems in the scientific study of religion at a point when I was still caught in the unfolding of the Parsonian theoretical scheme. While portions of the paper will be esoteric to all but the most devoted students of Parsons' work, much of it is easily accessible and, I think, still of some interest. Needless to say, though I have moved away from heavy use of explicitly Parsonian vocabulary and have shifted some of the emphases that can be discerned in this paper, I consider my subsequent work more a development than a repudiation of Parsonian theory.

location in a context, in a larger interrelated framework defined by values or norms of a more general order than the specific act or object. Human action is almost by definition symbolic action, which is another way of saying that it always involves culture. One prerequisite to the functioning of any action system is that action must have meaning. When action approaches meaninglessness the organization of the system of action, whether personality or social system, is seriously threatened. A simple example is what happens when men are ordered to dig a ditch and refill it at once. Fatigue is manifested much earlier than it would be in a situation where a comparable amount of physical energy is spent on a meaningful task. It may be taken as a sign of the malaise and disorganization that result from meaningless action. The action is meaningless because there is no superordinate context, no overall design of which this action is a part. If one feels a moral obligation to vote, it is not because voting is a virtue in itself, but because it is seen as an important element in a superordinate system called democracy.

There tends to be a vested interest in the maintenance of the stability of these superordinate meaning systems, for only if such systems are postulated are many concrete actions worth doing. If the larger context is deprived of validity, the specific activity is strictly meaningless. In sufficiently important circumstances the emotional investment in the maintenance of such superordinate systems is extremely great and may take the form of irrational attachment and hostile reaction to any threat. When this occurs one is apt to say that the superordinate system has become in some sense "sacred." For certain persons or groups, symbol systems in the area of politics or kinship may be in this sense "sacred" without any direct relation to what is ordinarily thought of as religion, although this term, too, is used in a broad sense when we say, "Politics is his religion," or "He is religious about his golf."

Apparently "just do it" as a legitimizing principle can only exist in narrowly specified limits and cannot be a major mode in any society. This is because of the nature of symbolism. A world made up of completely discrete, atomistic, and unintegrated moral requirements would be incompatible with an organized personality. It would be "culturally psychotic," and could not be lived in by normal human beings. Thus norms for action in all spheres of social life tend to be related to superordinate symbol systems that give them meaning. These in turn tend to be related to still higher order symbols from which they derive meaning, and so on, in a hierarchy that empirically includes a great number of steps. It is possible that sacredness, in the sense used above, can be an attribute of any level of this hierarchy, but it usually occurs only in the higher, more generalized levels.

In any specific instance it is likely that not two but three levels are involved. First there is the level of the concrete action in question; second there is the level of the norms that give meaning to a range of action of which the action in question is an instance; and third there is the symbol system that gives meaning and coherence to the norms themselves. Often the primary commitment in such a three-stage system is to the middle level. Specific activities covered by the norm can be changed easily and rapidly as long as they do not infringe upon the norm. On the other hand the third level, the level above the norm, is subject to rationalization. If the most binding commitment is to the norm, the superordinate level, the "reasons why" the norm is valid, may actually be varied without too great disorganization. If one "reason why" has become discredited, another with more apparent validity may be easily substituted. Under certain conditions, however, especially when the norm itself is seriously threatened, there may be a tendency to shift the locus of commitment upward. In this case the "reasons why" may be adhered to even at the cost of changing the institutionalized norms. This is one of the factors that gives such "reasons why" a strategic role in social change.

The religious factor proper enters at that moment when the existential referent of the superordinate symbol system is nonempirical. In fact there may be a gradual shading off. The "reason why" phrased as "for the family," does not seem far from "for the ancestors," but by this definition the former is secular and the latter religious.

For most people in most periods a relatively stable balance is struck between the quest for meaning and the preoccupation with the concerns of everyday. Certain relatively high level superordinate symbol systems are accepted as, for working purposes, conclusive, and there is no interest in pushing on to more general levels of meaning. For certain kinds of personalities in all periods, and for a great many personalities in periods when values and beliefs formerly accepted are called into serious question, there may be strong motivation to discover more general levels of meaning. Especially if socially accepted standards and expectations of personal gratification and moral behavior are seriously abrogated by actual conditions, there will be an attempt to find the meaning of what has happened by reference to some supersocial, nonempirical symbol system, namely religion.

A point of great importance about a religious symbol system is that the symbolization of its existential referent cannot be derived from its inherent qualities, since it is nonempirical, but must be *projected* on the basis of some aspect or aspects of empirical reality. The key aspects usually projected are the structure of the macroscopic society and a stage or stages of the socialization process. However the logic of the quest for meaning tends to continue in the religious sphere. Relatively specific religious symbols tend to be subsumed, under certain conditions, under more generalized symbols. At a certain point the quest for meaning tends to push the boundary of the empirical itself. It refuses all projections as having any ultimate validity; it denies that the religious object has the quality of "existence" that would make it one more finite object, and questions whether one can speak of a religious object at all. With Paul Tillich the point is reached where "We cannot speak adequately of the 'object of religion' without simultaneously removing its character as an object. That which is ultimate gives itself only to the attitude of ultimate concern."

Nevertheless, Tillich would agree that in speaking of that which is always transcending the boundary, even though it is never transcendental, intermediate symbolism must be used. Every religion must use symbolism, even when, like Zen Buddhism, it is only to break the symbolism. It is the principal task of the study of religious symbolism to determine the axes along which such symbols are organized, and thus to arrive at a typology of religious symbols.

It is impossible at the present time for me to present more than a few suggestions in this important area. Ruth Benedict's classification may be taken as a useful starting point.[1] She divides the supernatural into two categories: 1) Mana, supernatural power as an attribute of objects, and 2) Animism, supernatural power as will and intention. This would seem clearly to be in pattern-variable terms the distinction between quality and performance, though it seems also to involve a distinction between a "physical" object and a "social" object. The first kind of power can be manipulated by men through the employment of the right mechanistic techniques.

It is an attribute of both men and things, both "have" mana. The second kind of power is seen as embodied in certain kinds of supernatural "actors" who can be controlled through *interaction,* through personal relations. Clearly there are cases in which the two attributes are not entirely differentiated. The Navaho and Zuni, for example, view their "deities" almost as manifestations of objective power rather than as highly individualized personalities. They are to be controlled perhaps more by mechanistic actions than through personal relations, though both aspects are present.

This distinction is crosscut by another, the universalism-particularism distinction, to produce still further types. The combination of universalism and performance results in a deity who is characterized by will and intention, and whose concern with the world is based on absolutely universalistic principles. This is the God of justice, the upholder of moral standards, the God who is no respecter of persons. This is the central deity in the three Judaic religions, but within Christianity more characteristic of ascetic Protestantism than of Catholicism.

The combination of particularism and performance results in a deity who is characterized by will and intention, but who has a particularistic concern for people in the world. This is the God of love, the Christ who died for *me,* the God who cares about persons as individuals. Hero and savior gods of a wide variety of types belong in this category, and the theme of the deity who is also human is especially common here. We may consider both these types as differentiations out of a more generalized animism.

Similarly two further types seem to differentiate out from the generalized idea of mana. First, the combination of universalism and quality results in the notion of Natural Law. The Stoic concept of Fate is a supernatural entity of this type. Divine power is conceived entirely in terms of objective universalistic laws, and can be manipulated if at all only by conformity to those laws. This symbolization of the divine clearly is closely related to the scientific view of the world, differing from it mainly in that it involves the quality of commitment on the part of men, and is seen as a moral principle rather than merely in cognitive terms.

Finally the combination of particularism and quality results in a concept of a ground of being that somehow unites man and the universe. Examples are the Chinese *Tao* and the Buddhist nirvana, but this is the main conception of the divine of intellectual mystics of all traditions. The central idea may perhaps be summed up in the words of one of the great mystics of Islam: I am reality.

So far religious symbols have been discussed only in terms of the abstract categories of the pattern variables, which define the basic kinds of symbols in all spheres. Another method of approach, which would supplement the present one, is that based on the socialization process. Here we would discuss the relation of deities of the above types to stages in the socialization process, together with further refinements resulting from projections from family roles, for example, father deities, mother deities, and child deities. In addition, the relation of the macroscopic social system to religious symbolism would have to be discussed. Projection of individual deities based on social roles, as for example God as king, warrior gods, artisan gods, and so on, is one aspect of this problem. The other is the projection of relationships between deities in the supernatural world that may be based on projections of the earthly social system. It is not possible to pursue these problems further here.

Though the symbolization of the divine is perhaps the heart of the problem, the study of religious symbolism must also deal with symbols at several less general levels. Especially important are the symbols involved in sacraments, in ritual acts and objects. The task of isolating the crucial levels of religious symbolism and of classifying the major types at each level is an enormous one, but one that should prove extremely fruitful.

Religious Action

The religious action system I take to be the pattern-maintenance (or L) subsystem of the pattern-maintenance subsystem of the total social system. That it belongs primarily in the L subsystem seems fairly clear, and that it focuses on LL is also clear, especially in respect to consideration of the external boundaries of LL. It is, however, somewhat dangerous to carry the analysis of the LL subsystem as far as I have before the rest of L has been carefully analyzed. Other elements besides religion may be found to belong in LL and religion may not be confined to LL. On the basis of an admittedly incomplete understanding of the total L subsystem, however, it seems best to treat the LL subsystem and the system of religious action as the same in this very tentative analysis. The terminology has been changed considerably from the mimeographed version of the motivational system as of January 1955, but I think that very often the changes are merely specifications.

We may start with a consideration of the external boundaries of LL. The input from the cultural system is ultimate meaning. Meaning implies a cultural element, but the exact status of the cultural system in this context is not entirely clear. It is almost to be considered in an existential projection, as the Logos. The input from the system imperatives is ultimate power, which includes both ultimate potentialities and ultimate frustrations. Here we are on the religious boundary line; we are dealing with the problems of being and meaning. It is this above all that leads one to think LL will be primarily the locus of religious action.

The output to the cultural system is the specification of norms through the processes of projection, rationalization, and generalization. The output to the system imperatives is value-commitment to certain potentialities in spite of certain frustrations.

Our analysis of the internal structure of the religious action system starts with a consideration of its goal aspect. The goal-attainment aspect seems to be the establishment of some sort of relation with the superordinate system that lies over the boundary of LL by means of religious action such that the pattern is maintained and tension managed. This seems to define what is usually meant by "worship." The boundary of this subsystem is with the goal subsystem of LA, a subsystem that has to do with the acceptance of common values in the personality, with superego functions. The output of LLg to LAg, then, is the symbolic expression of common values, and the return input is commitment.

The adaptive problem of the religious action system may be seen as how to relate commitment to religious values to life in the world. The solution of this problem is religious ethical action. The boundary of this subsystem is with the adaptive subsystem of LI. LI in general is the area of social responsibility, the balance of public and private responsibility, and it has an input-output relation with the polity. It has, however, been the least studied of all the subsystems of L and so we must be rather tentative in treating this boundary. The output of LLa to LIa is taken to be moral judgment; that is, the religious ethical action system judges all spheres of social commitment, justifies some, and condemns others. The return input is acceptance of superordinate (religious) norms.

I have called the pattern-maintenance subsystem of L "faith."

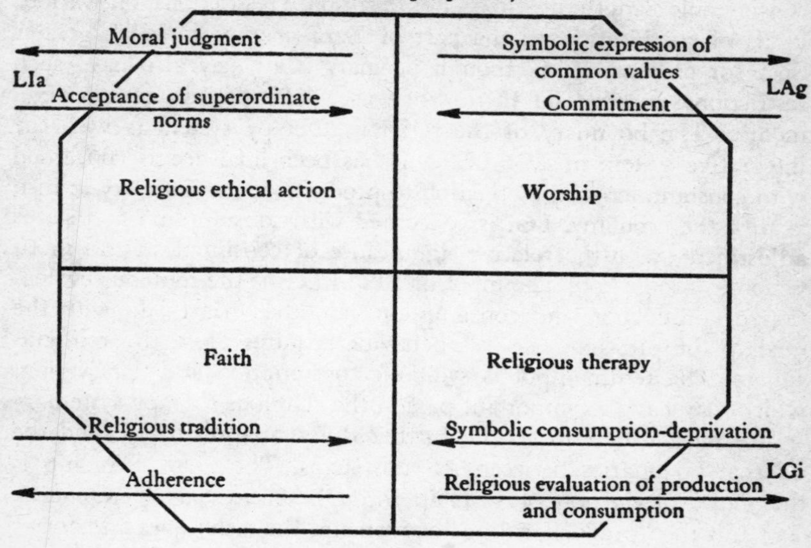

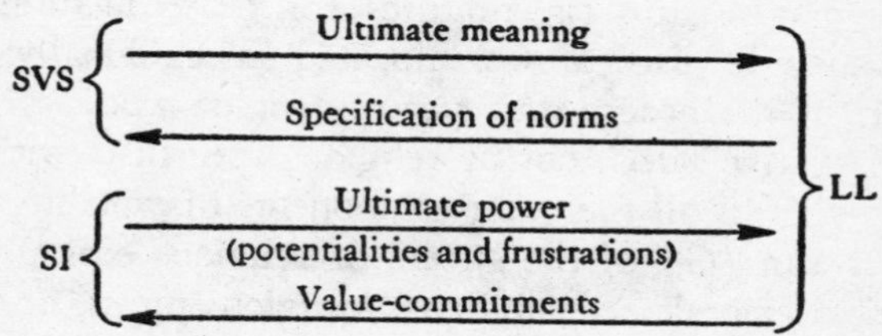

This implies commitment to a belief system. The input is religious tradition and the output is adherence.

The integrative problem seems to be how to maintain a coherent system of worship, religious ethical action, and faith for a variety of people who may be in different life situations and under different strains. I have called this the religious therapy system. This system regulates performance and regression relative to the whole functioning of the religious system. It is particularly oriented, as all therapy is, to the gratification-deprivation balance. Not only will demands that affect this balance shift during the course of therapeutic ritual for the same person or persons, but there may be differential demands made on different persons or groups that persist over a considerable length of time. For example, restrictions on various kinds of gratification on the part of Zuni priests are much greater than for ordinary Zuni, though ordinary Zuni may also have such restrictions imposed on them when they take part in certain ceremonies. The boundary of the religious therapy system is with the integrative system of LG. LG as it has been analyzed is concerned with consumption and motivation to production; its boundary in turn is with the economy. LGi is concerned with consumption and status adjustment, with the relative significance of consumption and motivation to production. The input of LLi to LGi is the religious evaluation of production and consumption, and thus has to do with the quantity of prestige that this behavior acquires from the religious sphere. The return input is symbolic consumption and deprivation, which may have an important part in the religious therapy system.

We must turn now to the further differentiation of LL and the internal boundaries between its subsystems. The G of Worship is the actual production of worship through services and ceremonies. The L is the "production line" or worship, the techniques and forms available for use, which may be called liturgy. The A is the regulation of facilities and conditions of worship, since worship always requires time and usually expenditures for other facilities, maintenance of a suitable place of worship, and so on. Finally, the I is the regulation of the order, aim, and content of worship. This involves the "executive" decisions of religious specialists with respect to the coordination of all the other components of worship.

The goal or aim (G) of the system of religious ethical action is the attainment of moral acceptability in religious terms, or, to use a traditional Christian term, justification. The adaptive aspect is the actual performance of religious duties toward this end. The religious ethic provides the fundamental norms and commitments for ethical action (L). Finally the I aspect is the regulation and specification of ethical action. This may involve the consultation of "moral experts" for help and guidance.

The G of Faith is the affirmation of faith. The A is affirmation in spite of all contingency, discrepancy, and evil. The L is the actual system of beliefs, which in more sophisticated religions becomes systematized as theology. Finally, the I is the regulation of belief commitments in conformity with the rest of the Faith system.

The goal of the religious therapy system is the return of the recipient to some condition of religious "health" by means of curative, saving techniques. In Christian terms this is salvation. The adaptive problem here is to determine the causes of the disturbance and the most favorable techniques of cure. This would seem to be the locus of the arts of divination and diagnostics from the religious point of view. The pattern-maintenance subsystem provides the basic theory of "disease" or alienation and of how this may be overcome, and the integrative subsystem regulates the whole of the therapeutic process. This is the locus of the role of shamans, medicine men, and of religious curing at all levels of religious sophistication.

The boundary exchanges do not require extended comment. They are virtually self-explanatory and illustrate the fact that each of the four subsystems is closely bound up with the functioning of the other three. The ethical action system provides facilities to the worship system through such things as tithes, contribution of labor, and so on. The worship system provides sacraments and symbols that play an important part in the therapy system. The therapy system provides a specification of kinds of evil and their cures that aids the affirmation of faith in spite of evil. The faith system provides the justifying power of faith to the ethical action system, which alone cannot guarantee moral acceptability. The religious ethical system provides certain ethical acts that may contribute to the therapy system as acts of penance, and so on.

Some religions stress certain of the subsystems at the expense of others. Early Calvinism stressed faith and ethical action more than worship or therapy, whereas certain primitive religions have elaborate worship and therapy systems but relatively rudimentary concern with faith and ethical action. Liberal Protestantism has shown concern with ethical action and worship and paid less attention to faith and therapy, whereas certain extreme mystics have stayed within the therapy system and shown little concern with the rest of the religious life. This relates undoubtedly to various value commitments and various conceptions of the divine. A complete typology of religion would have to take all these factors into consideration.

I have already described the external boundaries of the religious action system but it might be well to comment a little further on

LL

RELIGIOUS ETHICAL ACTION

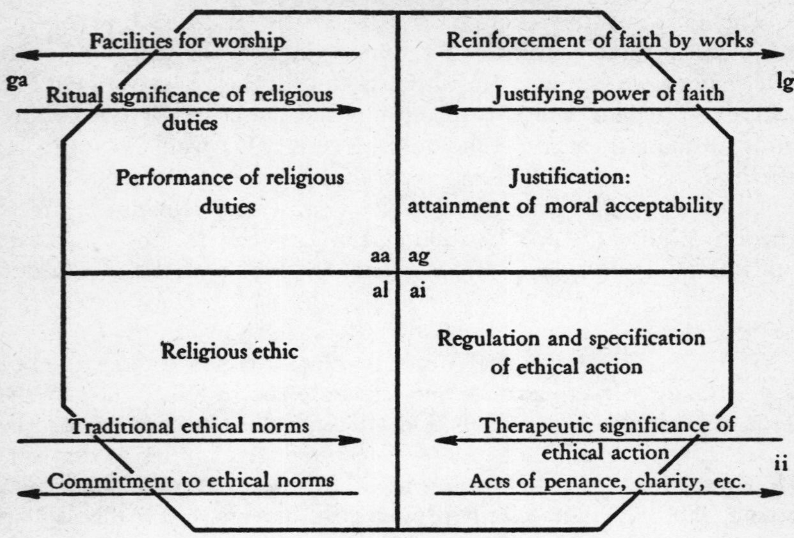

FAITH

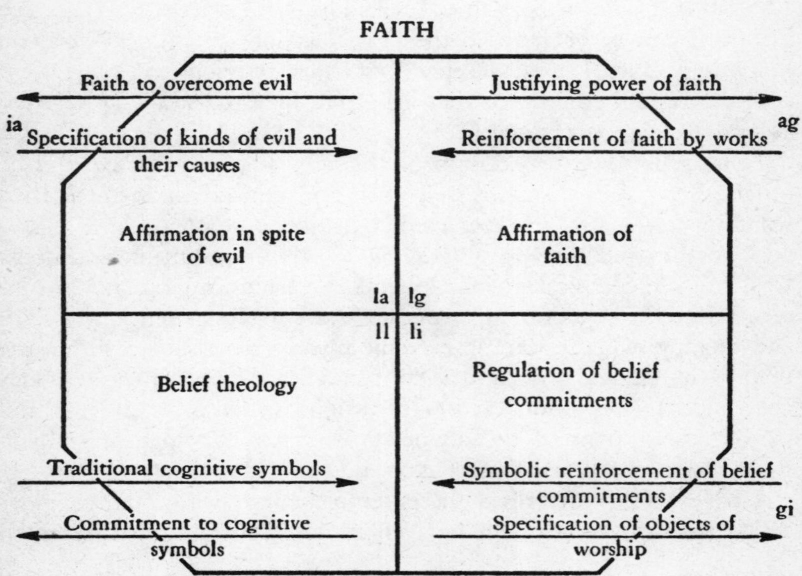

LL

WORSHIP

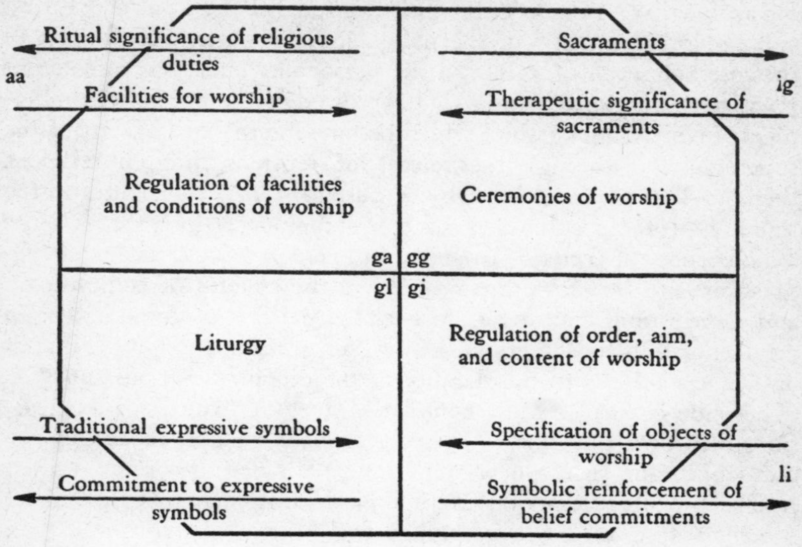

RELIGIOUS THERAPY

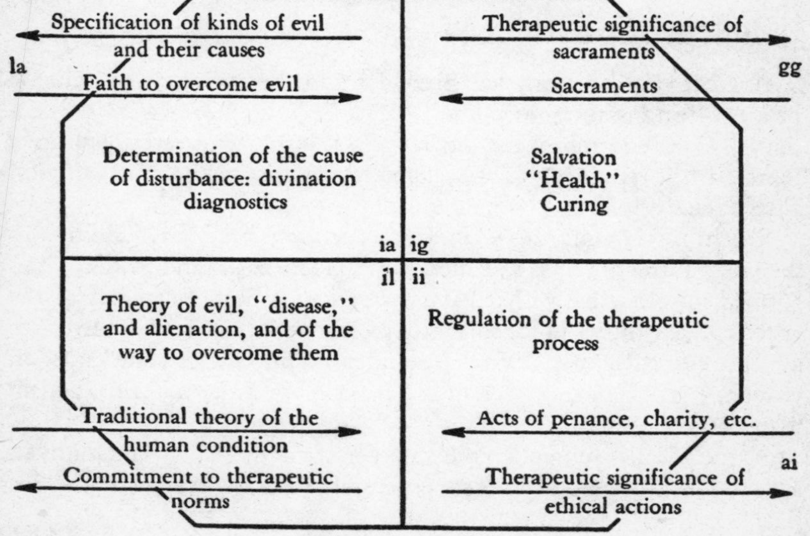

them. In a stable situation religion contributes to the maintenance of social responsibility (LI) by providing ultimate justification for institutionalized values. This in turn, through the output of LI, contributes to the stability of the polity. Religious action contributes to the internalization of values in the personality, and thus to commitment to institutional patterns (LA) through the symbolic commitments involved in worship, which become internalized as part of the superego, and through the release of tensions through religious therapy. This in turn, through the output of LA, contributes to the stability of the institutional system. Religious action, through the maintenance of certain balances of performance relative to regression, and by providing meaning in the spheres of consumption and deprivation, contributes to a stable balance of commitment to production and consumption (LG). This in turn, through the output of LG, contributes to the stability of the economy. Serious shifts on either side of any of these boundaries, however, can have repercussions all down the line. If these are serious enough to destroy the old equilibrium then a new one must be attained; this process often results in at least temporary pathological phenomena. These general problems of change and pathology will be returned to in the final three sections, which are devoted to process, but the basis for the discussion of these problems has already been laid in the preceding structural analysis.

Religious Institutions

A great deal of work has been done in the sociology of religion proper—for instance, Joachim Wach's *Sociology of Religion* is essentially an enormous list of religious institutions arranged in a loose ad hoc typology[2]—but systematic analysis is still in its infancy. I have relatively little to contribute on this point.

Wach is certainly right in distinguishing between collectivities that are formed on a specifically religious basis and collectivities formed on other bases that have a religious aspect. Examples of the latter may be found in kinship groups, where a lineage may also have an ancestor cult; in political groupings, as in city or state cults; in economic groupings, as in guilds that worship a patron saint; and in many other instances.

A specifically religious collectivity is one in which commitment to some conception of the supernatural, to what lies over the LL boundary, has been taken as the basis for solidarity. A very crude and preliminary typology may be derived from a consideration of the kinds of collectivity emerging from commitment to the types of the supernatural distinguished in the first section of this essay. Commitment to a God of the universalistic-achievement type, the "God of justice," involves primarily a declaration of allegiance and obedience. This involves the acceptance of the absolute power of this God and a commitment to obey his commandments. The classic case is surely Islam, where the fundamental criterion of membership in the religious collectivity is an acceptance of the declaration "There is no god but God, and Muhammad is his prophet," and though this is sufficient to be in some sense a Muslim, the good Muslim is one who also conforms meticulously to Muslim law, which contains divine commandments.

Commitment to a God of the particularistic-achievement type, the God of love, involves primarily the acceptance of the God as one's benefactor and savior and participation in those ordinances that the God has instituted for one's benefit or salvation. The Greek mystery cults present the type case of this kind of commitment, and the collectivity is formed of those who have partaken of the mysteries that bestow regeneration. It is interesting that Christianity, which has religious symbolism of both types in God the Father and Christ, uses both these kinds of commitment as the basis of religious solidarity. A consideration of the different groups within Christianity would show wide differences in emphasis, but almost all groups would contain both aspects.

While both of the above types of commitment are capable of supporting strong solidarities because they involve the necessity of ethical or ritual action in common, the remaining two types develop much less cohesive collectivities on the whole. Commitment to a universalistic-quality symbolization of the supernatural, to a divine order, does not involve any necessity for collective action. Where collectivities have grown up in connection with a religion of this kind—most notably the philosophic faiths of antiquity, whether Platonic, Stoic, or Epicurean—the basis of solidarity has usually been that of teacher and pupil, of the "school." The school is important because it retains the correct knowledge of the Truth, but once the Truth is learned the basis for extended solidarity crumbles. Such groups tend to break up into as many collectivities as there are outstanding teachers.

Commitment to a particularistic-quality symbolization of the supernatural, to a Ground of Being in which one can lose one's self, is somewhat similar to the last type. Here again the relation of master and pupil is primary and the importance of the group is largely in terms of its containing the correct esoteric tradition and mystical techniques. Collectivities formed on this basis may, however, be more extensive geographically and more lasting in time than those of the last type for several reasons. The relation of master and pupil may be considerably more intense where the aim is not to impart knowledge but the experience of enlightenment. This relation will be close to that of the transference relation in psychotherapy. Furthermore the quest for mystical union is often aided by certain group exercises and by physical segregation for varying lengths of time. For these reasons collectivities whose aim is primarily mystical, as for example the Sufi Brotherhoods in Islam, and certain Buddhist sects in the Far East, may have fairly extensive organizations in space and time, though they do show the tendency to form suborders and subsects composed of the followers of especially outstanding teachers. In this they are similar to the last type. It is interesting to note that one major world religion, Buddhism, began its career on essentially this type of commitment, to a concept of the supernatural of the particularism-quality type. The symbolism, however, soon developed in the direction of the particularism-achievement type, especially in the more popular branches, and commitment to both these types is important to this day. It is interesting that Buddhism has on the whole been free throughout its long history of the fanatical kind of commitment that seems peculiarly associated with symbolism of the universalistic-achievement kind, and that has plagued all three of the Judaic religions.

Much more refined classifications of religious collectivities can undoubtedly be made when more work is devoted to this field.

Religion and the Socialization Process

With this category we enter the province of what is ordinarily called the psychology of religion. A few general remarks might be useful concerning the relation of personality and social system, a problem peculiarly perplexing in the study of religion.

In the scheme of analysis that is being used here, the same basic paradigm is used to analyze both personality and social system. We should therefore expect analogies in structure, and work at either of these levels should prove suggestive for work on the other. Actually, since both personality and social system are, in the technical sense, action systems, the analogies between them should be closer than those of either of them to the biological organism, fruitful though the latter have been.

However, personality and social system are not merely systems at different levels; they interpenetrate. They share the same "parts." Therefore in discussing social system we must also discuss personality and vice versa. It is therefore important to keep clear in any discussion of the two systems what is an analogue to personality on the social system level and what is a personality problem for the social system.

Religion is an area where this problem of the relation of personality and social system is particularly acute. As we have seen, it is to be located primarily in the pattern-maintenance tension-management (L) subsystem of society, which is that aspect of the social system most closely concerned with personality and motivation. That religion is an aspect of social life closely related to problems of personality is something that students of religion have known for a long time, for they have seen that it is bound up with the deepest levels of personality, with its integration and its pathology. It is my task here to follow out the implications of that fact in somewhat more detail.

The primary functions of the family, especially the nuclear family, also belong in the L subsystem. These are fundamentally the same as those of religion: pattern maintenance and tension management, especially for our purposes in the process of socialization. The contexts in which they carry out these functions are in the main different, but they overlap, and their symbolic connection is even closer than their actual connection. The analogies and interrelations between family and religion will be the primary theme of this discussion.

The family is concerned with the management of personality tensions that have their origin in needs with an organic substratum. Its orientation is primarily to the "normal" needs of personality and organism. Religion is concerned with the management of personality tensions arising from the "condition of man," from the ultimate frustrations of the human situation. Since, however, most men do not undertake an ontological analysis of the human situation, the symbolism they use in understanding these ultimate frustrations is closely derived from situations of frustration within the family, and especially the acute frustrations of childhood.

Frustration, as we know, creates the kinds of strain that can lead to deviance. Social control mechanisms come into play when the frustrations are severe and the danger of deviance is great. Social control mechanisms called into play in situations of deep personality frustration are largely confined to the family in childhood. With respect to adults, however, such frustration cannot be dealt with solely in the family. This is because it is the agents of social control themselves who are affected, and there is no superordinate level within the family to deal with the problem. One of the primary functions of religion is to deal with frustration in this sort of a situation. Professor Talcott Parsons' analysis of the funeral ritual as a mechanism of social control serves as a type case in this area. Similarly, the anxiety built up through a sense of guilt may be relieved through a sacrament of penance involving confession.

Other ritual responses to relatively specific kinds of frustrations and anxieties could be enumerated. What is most interesting is certain general properties of these ritual situations. They all involve a reference greater than the family. They are concerned with tensions that tend to be too much for the family to handle. All of these situations involve a controlled regression; one is allowed within limits to act out feelings ordinarily repressed. The religious specialists act so as to keep this acting-out within limits, and they use their relation to the superordinate religious system to maintain these limits. It is important that the person undergoing frustration is in some degree allowed to take a more dependent role with respect to the religious specialist and the superordinate religious entity than he could in ordinary everyday relationships. This is part of the "therapy" of the ritual. It should be remembered that the symbolism of the situation is very often drawn from the family and childhood situations.

We may speak of a generalized state of frustration and anxiety without reference to the specific frustrations handled by specific rituals. In religious terms this is called a state of alienation. All religions, I believe, must deal with the problem of alienation in this general sense to some degree. It is central, however, to the salvation religions that have dominated the major civilizations of the world.

Salvation may be seen as an attempt to solve the generalized problem of frustration ultimately. It is interesting that the major modes of solving the problem of alienation seem to be based symbolically on different stages of the socialization process. Mysticism, which seeks the dissolution of the distinction between subject and object, may be seen as an attempt to reestablish the stage of primary identification before mother and child have become differentiated into two systems. Devotionalism, which seeks a perfect love relationship with a parent deity without the dissolution of the self, may be seen as attempting to reestablish the stage of love-dependency before the mother-child relation has been disturbed by any conflicting outside claims. Salvation through faith and obedience would seem to relate to the Oedipal crisis. It seeks to attain salvation by renouncing all ambitions of one's own and casting oneself on the mercy of the good father.

This discussion has tried to bring out that in its tension-management aspect, religion is closely related symbolically to the family, and that it allows in carefully controlled contexts regression to earlier levels of personality adjustment for therapeutic purposes. If the religious therapy system is functioning well this regression is only temporary and fortifies the personality for behavior on the mature level. Regression in this sense is not the same as pathological regression in which the higher stages of personality organization are abandoned, though that the two can be associated is indicated by many instances from the history of religion. It is this therapeutic role of religion which supplies one of the bases for Parsons' assertion that religion is in a sense the id of the social system.

Another basis for that assertion can be only briefly sketched here and belongs logically in the next section. Religion is not concerned only with individual tension-management, which is relatively random with respect to the state of the social system. Religion is also concerned with situations in which conditions in the society cause a general rise in tension. Rituals in these situations are performed not for individuals but for society as a whole. Regressive elements are not lacking in such ritual any more than in rituals performed for individuals, and they tend to take the form of looking back to a "better day." Some earlier more peaceful or more heroic period will be symbolically called to mind and may have a central place in the symbolism. The desire to return to a less differentiated social system when "life was simpler" may be a close analogy to the desire to return to earlier and simpler stages of personality development. To the extent that religion contains the residue of these earlier social stages and manipulates their expressive meaning in the present, it may be said to have id functions for the social system.

We have sketched above some of the tension-management or id functions of religion, and will now turn to some of its socialization or superego functions. Here again it will be helpful to see the close relation between the functions of the family and the functions of religion.

At every transition in the socialization process three system levels are involved. One is the system in which the child is currently functioning, say the mother-child love-dependency system. Second is the system into which the child is moving, in this case the nuclear family. Third is the system superordinate to the second system, in this case the total society, specifically symbolized by the father's involvement in the occupational system. The key role of the father in this transition is precisely dependent on his role in the superordinate system. He represents not only the values of the new system but also transcendent powers and values beyond that system. The morality of the nuclear family is accepted in part because the parents, especially the father, are seen as controlling knowledge and power, which seem from the child's point of view to be of ultimate magnitude. It is the internalization of such an image of the father that is the focus of the superego in the personality, and is indeed identical with the primitive superego.

As Freud has pointed out, by adolescence the child's experience in the world has sadly punctured his image of the ultimate power and knowledge of the parents. The parents then do not have the leverage to accomplish the final stage of the socialization process. Here again we have a transition: the child at the nuclear family level, about to move into full adult participation in the social system. What is the third level, superordinate to the social system? I would contend that the superordinate religious system provides that level. This seems to give a special significance to the very widespread rite of religious initiation at adolescence, in our own recent past the conversion experience that was a normal part of late adolescence in the Protestant sects. This correlates with a broader symbolic restructuring of the superego, including values and ideals of a wider meaning than the earlier internalized father image. Of course the symbolic content of the initiation or conversion in late adolescence may include projected images of the father or other familial figures and situations, but it always includes imagery which is suprafamilial in reference. Whatever the specific content of this superordinate religious system, it must provide some basis of ultimacy in terms of which the values of the society are legitimized. This is the input of ultimate meaning into the LL subsystem.

For purposes of convenience, the id and the superego functions of religion have been described separately, but it is clear that they are two sides of the same coin—they are the tension-management and pattern-maintenance aspects of the L subsystem.

This has been but a rapid survey of a field that needs careful and intensive work, especially in codifying the immense amount of material that is already known. It is what might be called the normal psychology of religion. We have arbitrarily relegated the abnormal psychology of religion to the section on religious pathology, though logically it might just as well have been treated here.

Religion and Social Differentiation

This field of the history of religion is the one in which I have least to contribute at the present time, but a few remarks on some of the problems involved may be helpful.

We may use the socialization process as it affects the individual personality as a basic analogue for certain large-scale processes of social change that are of central importance in a theory of religious development.[3]

Under ordinary conditions we may assume that religion will continue to fulfill the functions we described above in the section on the religious action system with relatively high stability. Within certain limits, threats from without or within the social system whose effects reach the religious system may be handled by the normal mechanisms. Certain changes may occur, however, that cannot be handled by those mechanisms. For example, adaptive problems may arise of such a serious nature that newly differentiated economic structures are needed to cope with them. This in turn may necessitate more or less serious changes in the institutional system, and the whole situation may be productive of so many anxieties and strains that the problems of the pattern-maintenance system are sharply increased. If such frustrations continue over time and the old religious techniques seem powerless to handle them, the institutionalization of the religious system itself may be called into question. The output of legitimization from the pattern-maintenance subsystem to the polity may be endangered so that the latter, instead of being able to take the lead in meeting the new situation, finds its position threatened and precarious. This situation is analogous to the one in which a child finds himself when he is required to advance to a new stage of maturity. The old techniques no longer work but he does not yet have a personality sufficiently differentiated to handle the new problems.

As we have seen, the situation is one in which the old religion is seriously weakened. Its ritual system is no longer able to handle the increased level of tension and the adherents are beginning to lose their confidence in the ultimacy of the superordinate system as conceived by the old religion. A situation exists in which religious innovation may play an important part in facilitating the transition to a more differentiated society. The old religion may succeed in differentiating its own institutional system and reinterpreting its basic belief system in order to meet the new situation in the area of pattern-maintenance. This may consist of some sort of reform movement that, under the guise of a return to earlier traditions, may actually develop a new form of the religion more adapted to the new situation. The improved situation in the pattern-maintenance system could then have important repercussions in the other subsystems and improve their chances of success in meeting the new situation. This it would do chiefly by providing a stable superordinate reference that would legitimize the necessary institutional changes and help drain off much of the tension aroused by them. One would expect pathological byproducts even in the most normal of such transitions, and we will return to these in the next section.

There is another possibility in such transitions, however, that is the source of the profound importance of religion in social change. The disturbed situation in which the old religion is no longer able to function adequately may not be able to be met by further differentiations in the belief and institutional systems of the old religion. The situation is one in which it is possible for a prophet or savior to arise who, through a direct encounter with the divine, proposes a radically new religious system and associated value system. This is what may be called charismatic revolution. It is of such great importance because it is one of the two major sources of social change, the other being the process of rationalization and consequent differentiation focusing mainly in the economic sphere.[4]

Charismatic revolution is important because it transcends the social situation that led up to it and cannot be explained in terms of it. The new value systems that emerge from such revolutions may continue to exercise profound influence for millennia, long after the crisis in which they arose has ceased to be significant. This is because basic value systems are highly persistent and capable of a great deal of reinterpretation and specification in new situations without being radically altered. It is clear that a charismatic revolution that may decide in important respects the course of a civilization for thousands of years is a primary datum in the understanding of historical process.

Charismatic revolutions may transcend the situations that gave rise to them in another important respect. They may produce powerful movements that sweep large areas into the new cultural tradition, though these areas may have been affected by the original socially disturbing conditions only slightly if at all. In this process culturally and socially backward areas may be assimilated not only to a new religion but also to a more differentiated social system.

I wish to stress that while charismatic revolutions are undoubtedly instigated by nonreligious social conditions of various sorts, they cannot be wholly explained by them. They have a dynamic of their own that derives from the religious system itself. The specifically religious factors are of the greatest importance and cannot be reduced to the role of reflections of social or economic conditions. Further, the charismatic revolution gives an opportunity to unusual personality types to exercise radical creativity. The opportunity for the direct translation of personal creativity into lasting social and ideological forms is perhaps greater here than at any other point in the social process. Of course no such creation is absolutely *de novo.* It must inevitably be based to some extent on previously existing cultural factors. Charismatic revolution is inherently as amenable to scientific explanation as any other social phenomenon. Its importance lies in the fact that for a brief moment it presents a situation of the highest fluidity in which unrivaled opportunities are present for radical structural changes.

Although here we cannot enter into any detail we may point out one or two broad facts about religious history. Religions may be divided historically into two large categories. First there is primitive religion, which is characteristic of small-scale, nonliterate, largely kinship-organized societies, such as all human societies were up until the third or second millennium B.C. and many societies in the more inaccessible regions of the world still are. Second there are the salvation religions, which are historically characteristic of large-scale, literate societies with political, commercial, and cultural urban centers as foci and peasant bases, such as all the great "civilizations" of the world have been, with the exception only of Western society and its dominions and imitators in the last century or so. The great salvation religions emerged from charismatic revolutions that, as Max Weber noted, have laid down the characteristic features of those civilizations ever since. Actually, primitive and salvation religions are not divided in most cases by a single revolution but by a whole series of differentiations, reformulations, and revolutions of which the emergence of the great world religions is only the last phase. Also, each of the world religions has undergone profound changes since its formulation.

But with these qualifications aside we may still speak of the emergence of these religions as the great watershed in religious history. We seem to be in the midst of social and cultural changes as radical as those that differentiate primitive societies from the great literate civilizations and that a concomitant religious crisis is in evidence. The rise of communism, in a sense the first new "world religion" since the rise of Islam, is a symptom of this. This religious crisis is far from over, and before it is we may expect to see the emergence of new charismatic elements of the greatest importance, but one may not be too far wrong if one predicts that the incorporation of psychoanalytic and sociological insights into the very structure of religious thought may have the greatest importance in the eventual outcome.

Religious Pathology

In this section an analysis of individual and social pathology as they are connected with religion is presented. This subject could have been discussed under the last two headings, but it seemed useful to discuss personal and social pathology in the same section for the light they may shed on each other.

We may begin with a somewhat more extended treatment of the so-called existential anxieties than we have previously given. (This analysis is based on that of Paul Tillich in *The Courage to Be,* with some changes.[5]) These are the anxieties that it is the primary function of religion to handle. They are inherent in the situation of man; no one can avoid them. Each of the four subsystems of the religious action system as analyzed above can be taken as meeting one of these existential anxieties.

Guilt is that anxiety occasioned by the fact that no man can conform perfectly to his own internalized moral standards. The system of religious ethical action provides the means whereby this anxiety can be met by carrying out religious duties and attaining moral acceptability. For certain people, however, the system of religious action instead of alleviating guilt may exacerbate it, leading to intense guilt and self-abasement. For others the system of ethical action may assuage their guilt too much so that they become self-righteous. These would seem to be the pathological outcomes in this sphere.

Loneliness, fear of death, and contingency are the anxieties occasioned by man's finitude. The worship system meets this situation by providing a relation with another who does not suffer from the limitations of finitude and who can take away one's anxiety on this score. Worship provides assurance that "man is not alone." For certain people in some situations, however, worship does not work. Not only do they feel alone in the world but they feel that God has left them, and the anxiety of this sense of utter desertion may be increased by the religious imagery. This is one of the pathological outcomes. The other is the situation where the relation to God becomes so absorbing that it excludes all other relations, leading to complete social isolation.

Suffering, the fact that frustration is absolutely inherent in human life, is met in the religious action system by means of religious therapy. This provides techniques for bringing one through frustrating situations so that suffering will be minimized, and in mystical religions it provides techniques whereby frustration is theoretically rendered impossible, and gratification through union with the divine, the only gratification that is truly imperishable, is assured. For some people religion, instead of meeting suffering, becomes a cause of suffering. Asceticism and self-torture may reach extreme degrees for religious motives, and even suicide may be so motivated. The other pathological outcome is the case of the person who is so wrapped in mystical ecstasies that all other gratifications are abandoned, leading to an extremely limited form of existence.

Meaninglessness is that form of existential anxiety occasioned by the fact that in the last analysis one's most basic value commitments are entirely beyond the realm of proof. They have no certain objective basis. In the religious action system it is the function of faith to meet this anxiety. For some people, however, if religion fails to meet this anxiety it is enormously increased. Religious doubt can concentrate and summarize meaninglessness in an almost overwhelming way. The other pathological outcome is overcommitment, that is, dogmatism that may take such form that it is felt that not only does religious faith meet the problem of religious meaning but it should close all significant problems in the realm of science, technology, and so on, as well.

So far I have been talking about pathology that could apply to individuals within any religious system no matter how normal. If, however, not merely random individuals are showing pathological symptoms but rather the religious system in one or more of its parts has shifted its balance or been impaired in its function so that large numbers of people are being impelled in a pathological direction, then we may begin to speak of the pathology of the system as such. If such a situation has come about, then serious consequences for other systems would follow due to changes in output from the religious system. The main types of religious pathology on the group level are classifiable in terms of these shifts in output.

Endangered commitment to the faith system may lead either to reformulation of the religious symbol system, in limited form or in the form of charismatic revolution, or to overcommitment to the existing system, or to permanent undercommitment (loss of faith). Reformulation may be considered pathological only from the point of view of the old system, but may actually aid in new integrations. Permanent under- and overcommitment must be considered as pathological in a more general sense since they will inevitably interfere with the other subsystems of the religious system, and through them with the rest of society.

Disturbances in the system of religious ethical action may seriously disturb the output of this system to the LI or public responsibility system. It may drastically decrease this output by insisting on the maintenance of certain religious absolutes in spite of system responsibilities. This can result in a withdrawal from the world to a greater or lesser extent, as in the case of some radical Protestant sects. Through the LI system this decrease affects commitment to the polity. Responsibilities of citizenship such as bearing arms and holding office may be renounced. On the other hand, output to the LI system may be drastically increased if the disturbance in the ethical action system leads to the conclusion that the religious ethical norms must be institutionalized as the norms of the world. This will lead to an input into the polity as the religious group seeks to gain power in order to put its plan of the perfect society into effect. This may be called Utopianism.

Disturbances in the worship system may lead to a decrease in the output to the LA or internalization system. Relation to the divine alone is important, and commitment to any derivative norms and values is not required. This is antinomianism. It is very unstable empirically, but if it continued long enough in a group it would decrease the output to the institutional system to the point where any institutionalization at all among the groups affected would be destroyed. Disturbance in the worship system may lead to an increase in output to LA in the case where a great many values and norms are considered sacred and adherence to them takes on ritual significance. This leads to overcommitment to institutional patterns in the LA system and a consequent increase in the output of conformity to the institutional system. This can lead to an extreme ritualization and thus stagnation of social life in general, as for instance, in Tibetan Lamaism.

Disturbances in the therapy system may lead to decreases in the output of evaluation on consumption to the consumption system, that is asceticism. If this is accompanied by a high evaluation on production there may be an increase in the output into the economy, classically the case of the inner-worldly asceticism of the Protestant Ethic. An increase in the value on consumption may lead to unrealistic fantasies of gratification and an interference with realistic adaptation, as in certain nativistic revivals.

The problem of disturbances caused by changes of inputs and outputs is one general to the analytical scheme being used, and I have by no means solved its complexities. Many points in the preceding analysis of pathology need considerable sharpening, and when this is done changes in categories will undoubtedly occur. By way of summary, however, we may note that the classification of religious pathology based on the consequences of shifts in output to the three other major subsystems of the society turns out to be congruent with the principal pathological syndromes of personality as defined by Parsons and Olds.[6] We may place the types side by side.

Disturbances in	*Result in*	*Personality Syndromes*
Religious Therapy System	Nativism* Asceticism*	+ Paranoia – Schizophrenia
Religious Ethical System	+ Utopianism – Withdrawal from the world	+ Mania – Depression
Worship	+ Ritualism – Antinomianism	+ Compulsion neurosis – Psychopathic personality

+ is excessive input, – is insufficient input.

* Because of the duality of production and consumption in LG, what is a plus in one tends to be a minus in the other. Until this problem is clarified it is impossible to say what is excessive and what insufficient input, since these differ with respect to the two components of LG.

This essay into the area of pathology is fraught with difficulty, but the empirical application of the concept of religious pathology is even more difficult. The term can be used relative only to very specific definitions of what is for certain purposes being considered as pathological. It should not be forgotten that "pathological" developments in the sphere of religion have been highly creative as well as highly destructive.

This paper has been largely programmatic and exploratory in nature and its significance lies more in promises than in results. It may be well in concluding to summarize some of those promises.

Carrying the basic paradigm of the social system to the 256-fold level, as was done in the section on religious action, may seem to some to be an extreme overrefinement. On the other hand, the categories put forth there may seem rather crude to the student of comparative religion. The value of the attempt, it seems to me, is that it brings within reach for the first time an articulation between the categories of the general theory of social systems and the categories used by students of religion in the fields of worship, religious ethics, and so on. If such an articulation could be made, a vast amount of material could be codified in terms of the general theory of action and thus be rendered more useful to the study of comparative religion, and to all those who are concerned with the relations of religion and other aspects of society.

A second promise lies in the fact that the same basic variables are used to describe religious symbol systems, religious action, and types of commitment to religious collectivities. Empirical application of these tools should help to establish the kinds of coherence between these elements that is necessary in a functioning religion. To take one example, this approach should allow an entirely new attack on the whole vexed problem of church-sect (ecclesia, denomination, cult, and so on) classification that has taken up so much energy among sociologists of religion.

Finally the use of the same set of variables for the analysis of process, whether it be personality development, social change, or pathology, which are also used in the analysis of structure, should allow not only a closer integration of such fields as the psychology and history of religion with the rest of religious studies, but should contribute to the systematic development of those fields.

Whether the leads put forward in this paper should prove productive or not, the great importance of religion at this historic juncture probably insures that major advances in its scientific understanding will take place in the next few years.

NOTES

1 See Ruth Benedict, in *General Anthropology,* ed. Franz Boas (New York, 1938), esp. pp. 628–32, 634–37.

2 Joachim Wach, *Sociology of Religion* (Chicago: Univ. of Chicago Press, 1951).

3 See Talcott Parsons and Neil Smelser, *Economy and Society* (Glencoe, Ill.: Free Press, 1956), where this kind of treatment of the field of economic history is essayed.

4 *Ibid.,* chap. 5.

5 Paul Tillich, *The Courage To Be* (New Haven: Yale Univ. Press, 1952).

6 Talcott Parsons, James Olds, R. F. Bales *et al., Family, Socialization and Interaction* (Glencoe, Ill.: Free Press, 1955), chap. 5.

Bibliography of Robert N. Bellah

1952

Apache Kinship Systems. Harvard Phi Beta Kappa Prize Essay for 1950. Cambridge: Harvard University Press.

1957

Tokugawa Religion. Glencoe, Ill.: Free Press. (Japanese translation: Nihon Kindaika to Shūkyō Rinri. Tokyo: Miraisha, 1962.)

1958

"The Place of Religion in Human Action." *The Review of Religion* 22:137–54.

"Religious Aspects of Modernization in Turkey and Japan." *The American Journal of Sociology* 64:1–5.

Review of *The Western Apache Clan System: Its Origin and Development,* by Charles R. Kant. *American Anthropologist* 60:586–87.

Review of *Religion, Society and the Individual,* by J. Milton Yinger. *American Anthropologist* 60:382–83.

1959

"Durkheim and History." *American Sociological Review* 24:447–61. (Reprinted in *Emile Durkheim,* edited by Robert A. Nisbet, pp. 153–56. Englewood Cliffs, N.J.: Prentice-Hall, 1965.)

Review of *The Origin of Modern Capitalism and Eastern Asia,* by Norman Jacobs. *American Sociological Review* 24:921–22.

Review of *The Religion of India,* by Max Weber. *American Sociological Review* 24:731–33.

1961

"Religious Tradition and Historical Change." *Transactions of the Institute of Japanese Culture and Classics,* no. 8, pp. 303–11. Kokugakuin University, Tokyo.

"Nihon Kindaika no Ayumi." ("The Path of Japan's Modernization.") *Daihōrin* (Tokyo) 28:26–35.

1962

*"The Religious Situation in the Far East." *Harvard Divinity Bulletin* 26:27–38.

1963

*"Values and Social Change in Modern Japan." *Asian Cultural Studies* (International Christian University, Tokyo) 3:13–56.

*"Reflections on the Protestant Ethic Analogy in Asia." *The Journal of Social Issues* 19:52–60.

*"It Doesn't Go Far Enough." Review of *Honest to God,* by J. A. T. Robinson. *Christianity and Crisis* 23:200–1.

1964

*"Religious Evolution." *American Sociological Review* 29:358–74.

"Research Chronicle: *Tokugawa Religion.*" In *Sociologists at Work,* edited by Philip E. Hammond, pp. 142–60. New York: Basic Books.

1965

"Ienaga Saburo and the Search for Meaning in Modern Japan." In *Changing Japanese Attitudes Toward Modernization,* edited by Marius Jansen, pp. 369–423. Princeton: Princeton University Press.

"Japan's Cultural Identity: Some Reflections on the Work of Watsuji Tetsurō." *Journal of Asian Studies,* 24:573–94.

Editor of *Religion and Progress in Modern Asia,* introduction, epilogue. Glencoe, Ill.: Free Press.

*"Father and Son in Christianity and Confucianism." *The Psychoanalytic Review* 52:236–58.

1966

"Religious Systems." In *The People of Rimroc,* edited by Evon Z. Vogt and Ethel Albert, pp. 227–64. Cambridge: Harvard University Press.

"Words for Paul Tillich." *Harvard Divinity Bulletin* 30:15–16.

"Japanese Religion and World Civilization." *Yomiuri Shimbun* (Tokyo) January.

Review of *The Politics of Modernization,* by David E. Apter. *American Sociological Review* 31:268–69.

1967

*"Civil Religion in America." *Daedalus,* Winter, pp. 1–21.

Review of *The Sociology of Religion,* vols. 1 and 2, by Werner Stark. *Sociological Analysis* 28.

1968

*"Religion, Sociology of." *International Encyclopedia of the Social Sciences.*

Response to commentaries on "Civil Religion in America." In *The Religious Situation: 1968,* edited by Donald R. Cutler, pp. 388–93. Boston: Beacon Press.

*"Meaning and Modernization." *Religious Studies* 4:37–45.

"The Sociology of Religion." In *Knowledge and Society,* edited by Talcott Parsons. Voice of America Forum Lectures.

"The Problems of Violence in Developing Countries." In *Ethical Issues in American Life,* edited by Harold W. Fildey. Report no. 6, Southern Regional Education Board Seminars for Journalists.

"Shinto and Modernization." In *Continuity and Change, Proceedings of the Second International Conference for Shinto Studies.* Kokugakuin University, Tokyo: Institute for Japanese Culture and Classics.

Religion in America, coedited with William G. McLoughlin. Boston: Houghton Mifflin Co.; paperback edition, Boston: Beacon Press.

Review of *The Sociology of Religion,* vol. 3, by Werner Stark. *Sociological Analysis* 29.

Review of *The Religious Situation: 1968,* part 2, edited by Donald R. Cutler. *Journal for the Scientific Study of Religion* 7:290–91.

Review of *Toward an American Theology,* by Herbert W. Richardson. *Harvard Divinity School Bulletin* n.s. 1:18–19.

1969

"Japan, Asia, Religion." *Sociological Inquiry* 39.

*"Transcendence in Contemporary Piety." In *Transcendence,* edited by Herbert W. Richardson and Donald R. Cutler. Boston: Beacon Press.

*"The Dynamics of Worship." In *Multi-Media Worship,* edited by Myron B. Bloy, Jr. New York: Seabury Press.

Preface to *Religion, Order and Law: A Study in Pre-Revolutionary England,* by David Little. New York: Harper Torchbooks.

Forthcoming

"Christian Realism." Guest editorial in *Theology Today.*

*"Christianity and Symbolic Realism." *Journal of the Scientific Study of Religion.* (Part II of Chapter 15 in this volume.)

*"Islamic Tradition and the Problems of Modernization." *International Yearbook of the Sociology of Religion.*

*Review of *Love's Body,* by Norman O. Brown. *History of Religions. Sociological Inquiry.*

*Included in this volume.

Index